Come Help Change THE World

Bill Bright

Come Help Change the World

Published by
New*Life* Publications
A ministry of Campus Crusade for Christ
P.O. Box 620877
Orlando, FL 32862-0877

Edited by Joette Whims.
Design and production by Genesis Publications.

Printed in the United States of America.
Distributed in Canada by Campus Crusade for Christ of Canada, Surrey, B.C.

ISBN 1-56399-132-2

NewLife 2000 in a registered service mark of Campus Crusade for Christ Inc.

Unless otherwise indicated, all Scripture references are taken from the *New International Version*, © 1973, 1978, 1984 by the International Bible Society, Zondervan Bible Publishers, Grand Rapids, Michigan.
Scripture quotations designated TLB are from *The Living Bible*, © 1971 by Tyndale House Publishers, Wheaton, Illinois.
Scripture quotations designated NKJ are from the *New King James* version, © 1979, 1980, 1982 by Thomas Nelson Inc., Publishers, Nashville, Tennessee.

For more information, write:
L.I.F.E. Ministries—P.O. Box 40, Flemington Markets, NSW 2129, Australia
Campus Crusade for Christ of Canada—Box 529, Sumas, WA 98295
Campus Crusade for Christ—Fairgate House, King's Road, Tyseley, Birmingham, B11 2AA, United Kingdom
Lay Institute for Evangelism, Campus Crusade for Christ—P.O. Box 8786, Auckland, 1035, New Zealand
Campus Crusade Asia Ltd.—9 Lock Road #03-03, Paccan Centre, Singapore 108937, Singapore
Great Commission Movement of Nigeria—P.O. Box 500, Jos, Plateau State, Nigeria, West Africa
Campus Crusade for Christ International—P.O. Box 620877, Orlando, FL 32862-0877, USA

NewLife 2000 Movement Profile

NewLife 2000 is the strategy of Campus Crusade for Christ International working in partnership with the Body of Christ to proclaim the gospel to more than 6 billion people. To help present the gospel throughout every country, the staff actively pursue ministry partnerships with churches, organizations, agencies, and individuals.

The following statistics track our progress toward our New-Life 2000 goals. All glory and praise goes to our great God and Savior for what He has done and is doing through the ministry of Campus Crusade for Christ/NewLife 2000.

Ministry Summary as of December 31, 1998

- Campus Crusade for Christ has 20,514 staff members and 663,612 trained volunteers, with either full-time staff members or a ministry presence in 181 countries, which represents 99.2 percent of the world's population.

- In 1998, more than 851.8 million exposures to the gospel took place through ministry and partnership activity, and 54.5 million people indicated decisions for Christ through "live" evangelism situations.

- Since 1951, approximately 3,399,946,000 exposures to the gospel occurred worldwide through ministry and partnership activity.

- A Campus Crusade ministry is active in 3,254 Million People Target Areas (MPTAs), in 390 Strategic Urban Centers, and on 1,085 Priority University Campuses.

- The *JESUS* film has been translated into 535 languages and viewed by more than 2 billion people in 223 countries.

Contents

Acknowledgments 7
Preface: Join Me for the Journey .9

1   The Whirlwind 13
2   When God Became Personal 21
3   The Night That Started It All 31
4   Our UCLA Beginnings 41
5   The Little Booklet 51
6   You Shall Receive Power 63
7   To Possess the Land 73
8   God Had a Better Way .83
9   The Birth of Other Ministries 93
10 Special Projects and Events 107
11 Going International 117
12 International Projects and Events 127
13 The JESUS Film 143
14 Into the 21st Century 159
15 On the Front Lines 173
16 World Impact 189
17 International Ministries 199
18 Living the Adventure .227
19 What an Adventure! 237

Appendices
A   Ministry and Project Profiles 245
B   Ministry and Project Directory 289
C   Paul Brown Letter 303

Acknowledgments

The growth and influence of Campus Crusade for Christ International as one of the world's premier non-profit, evangelistic missions organizations is much more than the work of its co-founders and president. Millions of people have been involved as staff, employees, volunteers, donors, board members, and support resources in accomplishing our simple strategy: Go, Win, Build, and Send. Remembering and thanking all these people who have helped shape and propel this ministry since 1951 would be impossible for my limited ability. Thankfully, God knows everyone who has helped to birth, build, expand, and accelerate this ministry around the world. I publicly want to salute and thank each one of you!

I would like to acknowledge with deep gratitude my most sincere appreciation and thanks to the following people:

The godly, gifted men whom I directly serve in this ministry:

Dr. Steve Douglass, Executive Vice-President and U.S. Director; Dr. Bailey Marks, Executive Vice President of International Ministries; Paul Eshleman, Director of the JESUS Film Project; Dave Hannah, Director of History's Handful; Stan Oakes, President of International Leadership University; Marvin Kehler, Director of Campus Crusade for Christ, Canada; Sid Wright, Chief of Staff for the President of Campus Crusade for Christ International; El Ridder, National Development Coordinator

I also look to the members of the President's Cabinet to give me wise counsel. They are:

Thomas Abraham, Steve Douglass, Paul Eshleman, Dave Hannah, Susan Heckmann, Kathryn Kehler, Marvin Kehler, Bailey Marks, Stan Oakes, Roger Randall, El

Ridder, Steve Sellers, and Sid Wright

I am especially fortunate to work with a godly and able Board who bring years of distinguished and successful experience to this ministry:

Bill Armstrong, Edward (Skip) Ast, Elliot Belcher, Clarence Brenneman, Vonette Bright, Bruce Bunner, Barry Cannada, Steve Douglass, Leroy Eger (emeritus), Edward Johnson, Mike McCoy, Arlis Priest (emeritus)

To help me tell this marvelous story, I am indebted to researchers and writers Dan Benson, Bonnie Porter, Jim Bramlett, and Bailey Marks. My sincere appreciation also goes to our *NewLife* Publications staff: Dr. Joe Kilpatrick, publisher and general editor; Joette Whims, substantive editing and polishing; Tammy Campbell, editorial assistant; and Michelle Treiber, cover coordination and print brokering. My gratitude also goes to Lynn Copeland of Genesis Publications for her design, typesetting, and copyediting.

Finally, I save my dearest expressions of love and appreciation for my beloved wife of more than fifty years, Vonette. She has labored with me in this movement throughout these years and her love, patience, and dedication to the Lord have helped further the impact of this ministry around the world.

To God be all the glory for the great things He has done!

Join Me for the Journey

This book tells the incredible story of how God raised up, blessed, and multiplied the ministry of Campus Crusade for Christ International. I do not, and cannot, claim one ounce of credit for what He has done. As a ministry, we have come a long way, learned through our victories and mistakes, and seen miracle after miracle. I am convinced that our most exciting and fruitful days lie ahead—just around the corner!

Come Help Change the World is my merely human attempt to document some of the wondrous things God has done through men and women of this movement who want to help change their world through His message of love, forgiveness, peace, and eternal life. I wish I had the vocabulary to convey my deep sense of awe, reverence, and love for our Lord, or to describe His supernatural working in the hearts of people with whom we have come in contact. But I have tried in these pages to share some benchmarks of the journey with you. Hopefully, you will catch at least a taste of the adventure that my dear wife, Vonette, and I have experienced, along with our devoted fellow staff, since we began in 1951. As you read, you will observe how exciting it has been for my associates and me as we have gone along for the ride of our lives.

When our Lord first revealed the vision for Campus Crusade for Christ to me, I believed Him for great and mighty things. But I never imagined the pathways His leading would unveil. How could I have ever dreamed that, through the efforts and prayers of ordinary people like you and me, He would work in most countries of the world to bring hundreds of millions into His kingdom?

When God gave me the vision for this ministry, He also gave Vonette the heart to respond. Since that day, she has been a vital part of everything we have done. She plays a major role in much of my decision-making and in helping establish godly policies, and I consider her the co-founder of Campus Crusade for Christ. Over the years, she has been essential in developing many important strategies, including the training for staff, our emphasis on evangelism, and the ministry's worldwide prayer thrust. In the process, Vonette and I have not only drawn closer to Christ, but also to each other. I continually thank God for the many wonderful years of marriage and fruitful ministry we have enjoyed together.

Vonette also provides a leadership role in her own right. In the early days of our ministry, she founded the Great Commission Prayer Crusade. She also served for fourteen years as chairman of the Intercession Working Group for the Lausanne Committee for World Evangelism, and as chairman of the National Day of Prayer for eight years. Because of her heart for prayer, millions of believers all over the world have learned the importance of prayer. She also founded Women Today International, which includes her daily radio broadcast, aired from coast to coast, and nationwide conferences. She and her staff are making a tremendous difference in women's lives across our nation.

In 1994 the Lord led me to fast and pray for forty days for national and world revival and the fulfillment of the Great Commission. Each year since then, He has led me to fast and pray for forty days for a mighty move of His Holy Spirit. Vonette joined me on three of these forty-day fasts as together we sought God's face and desired to be drawn closer to Him and to each other. I am so grateful for the role she is playing to help bring the world to Christ and to help fulfill the Great Commission. No one could have a better partner in this exciting adventure than I have had with her, the darling of my heart.

Through the years God has graciously worked mightily through Campus Crusade for Christ. I share this story for two reasons: to give God praise for what He has done, and to encourage you to ask God how He wants to use you to make your mark for eternity. In light of the vision and strategies He has given Campus Crusade for Christ for the next decade, we are praying for 100,000 sharp Christian men and women to join us full-time in the task of saturating our neighborhoods, cities, countries, and continents with God's message of love and forgiveness. I am believing God for one million full-time staff and trained volunteers to help us reach that vision and strategy.

So I give you fair warning: As you read the Campus Crusade story, you just might catch a bit of the personal excitement that our enthusiastic staff, Vonette, and I have felt during this miraculous ministry since its birth in 1951. You may find yourself wanting to inquire how your own background, skills, and education can be used by God in a cutting-edge outreach such as one of the many He has entrusted to us. Others may be ready to invest more time, talent, and treasure in this part of the Lord's vineyard. If so, some of the most outstanding Christian men and women in the world stand ready to train and assist you. All we require are a genuine commitment to Jesus Christ as Savior and Lord, a heart for God, a teachable spirit, and a desire to make your life-skills count for eternity.

As our Lord said, the fields are ripe unto harvest. There is growing evidence that revival fires are starting to flare across America and around the world. Millions of people are realizing the futility and emptiness of life apart from God. More people are turning to God today than ever before in human history. As we humble ourselves before God and obey His command to share Christ in the power of the Holy Spirit, I am convinced that revival fires will burn even brighter in the days ahead.

Your world is primed and ready for the good news of Jesus Christ. But, as the apostle Paul asked, "How can they believe in Him if they have never heard about Him? And how can they hear about Him unless someone tells them?" (Romans 10:14, TLB). There is no nobler calling, no better investment of one's life, than telling others how to know God personally and enjoy Him forever.

I trust that you will catch that excitement as you read how God is at work in our neighborhoods, on our campuses, in our businesses, and at countless venues around the globe. It is the journey of a lifetime, one that I would not trade for all the wealth in the world. I am both humbled and grateful that the King of kings invited me to join Him along the way.

I urge you to also find the excitement, joy, and sense of purpose that my associates and I have discovered as we surrendered our wills to God and became slaves to Jesus Christ, our Lord. He has promised that nothing we do or say will be wasted when it is done in the power of His Holy Spirit and in line with the principles and commands in His Word. I have found that promise to be absolutely true.

The best days for this ministry—and I trust for your life as well—are yet to come. God wants to share His work with you. Ask Him to reveal what part He would have you take in helping to fulfill His Great Commission. You will never regret for a moment that you willingly started on the adventure of a lifetime to *come help change the world!*

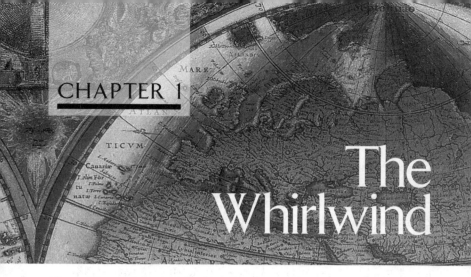

CHAPTER 1

The Whirlwind

MARCH 6, 1996. New York City. The United Nations. Vonette and I were at a press conference for the announcement of the 1996 Templeton Prize for Progress in Religion. As we listened to the remarks of the presenter, a wealth of thoughts and emotions flooded my mind.

The Templeton Prize is regarded by many as the most prestigious award given in the world—even more so than the Nobel Prize. Begun in 1972 by renowned global investor Sir John Templeton, the prize is awarded each year to a living person who has "shown extraordinary originality in advancing humankind's understanding of God and/or spirituality." Templeton endowed the prize so that it would always be the world's largest annual award, and that year it was valued at 700,000 pounds sterling, more than $1 million. Previous winners include Mother Theresa, Aleksandr Solzhenitsyn, Dr. Billy Graham, and Charles Colson.

Although I was aware of the purpose for this press conference, my heart was beating faster than usual as the presenter listed several of the benchmarks of Campus Crusade for Christ's history and concluded:

"…This year, as Campus Crusade for Christ celebrates its forty-fifth anniversary, Bill Bright continues his work with the same steadfastness with which he began. Indeed, though actually reaching the world's six billion people

would certainly be an amazing feat, there is also glory in setting it as a goal. For his efforts, Bill Bright has been awarded
the 1996 Templeton Prize for Progress in Religion."

Strobe lights flashed and camera auto-winders whirred as I
moved forward to accept a plaque commemorating the award.
Sir John Templeton shook my hand and posed beside me for
photos. Vonette, my dear wife and co-laborer since day one of
Campus Crusade's ministry, awarded me with a spontaneous
hug and kiss that was documented in newspapers worldwide.
The formal presentation would take place in a private ceremony in Buckingham Palace on May 8, with a public ceremony
the following day at the Church of Santa Maria near Rome.
But at this press conference, I felt deeply honored to accept
the Templeton Prize on behalf of my Lord Jesus Christ—whose
cause I serve—and on behalf of my beloved fellow staff, board
members, and financial supporters—all of whom He has used
so mightily in helping spread the gospel worldwide through
the ministry of Campus Crusade for Christ International.

Five Incredible Decades

Who could have imagined, when in 1951 I felt God prompting
me to leave my business and seminary studies and obey His
Great Commission to "go into all the world, and preach the gospel to every creature," that we would be where we are today—
poised to help take the wonderful news of God's love and forgiveness to the entire world by the end of the year 2000?

Who would have thought, during Campus Crusade's humble beginnings on the UCLA campus, that forty-eight years
later God would have enabled us to develop more than fifty
specialized ministries in 181 countries of the world, staffed by
more than 20,500 incredible full-time staff and more than
660,000 trained volunteers?

I am often asked the question, "Aren't you surprised at the
mighty way God has blessed the ministry of Campus Crusade
for Christ?" Grateful beyond words, I humbly answer, "Yes."

But the original vision God gave for this ministry is vastly greater than what we have already experienced. The best is yet before us.

When we began the ministry, the vision was gigantic, but the strategy was simple: reach the college campuses for Christ, and you will reach tomorrow's men and women of influence in all of society. Multiply this strategy to as many campuses as possible, and you can influence the course of an entire nation or even the world.

We have never abandoned that core strategy, but in the course of building evangelism and discipleship ministries on more than 790 university campuses in the U.S. and 370 campuses abroad, God has revealed hundreds of other key ways to spread His message throughout the world. He has brought us the full-time staff and volunteer help needed, and blessed their faithful efforts as literally hundreds of millions of people worldwide have indicated that they have received Jesus Christ as Savior and Lord through this ministry.

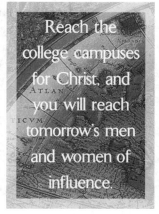

Reach the college campuses for Christ, and you will reach tomorrow's men and women of influence.

Indeed, it had been almost five incredible decades. Yet I knew that without God's supernatural guidance, empowerment, and blessing, all of our labors would have been in vain. If Vonette and I had not consciously turned every thought, possession, and desire over to Him, we surely would have followed our own materialistic path instead of His way of true abundance. Had we not built the ministry on a strong foundation of God's Word and prayer and continued to emphasize the importance of humbling ourselves before God and obeying His Word, we surely would have realized neither the positive results nor the multitude of blessings with which He has enriched our lives.

In the Name of Our Wonderful Lord

Since I was aware that the Templeton Prize press conference would receive global coverage, I had prayerfully considered my acceptance statement. I wanted my words to bring honor and glory to God, to briefly explain why I count it a privilege to serve Jesus Christ by telling others about Him, and to make clear that I wanted to donate the financial award to help bring spiritual revival to the United States and the world:

> I am deeply humbled and greatly honored to receive this prestigious Templeton Prize which, to me, because of its nature, is to be desired above every other prize given for whatever purpose.
>
> I would like to thank and commend Sir John Templeton for establishing the Templeton Prize, which emphasizes the most important aspect of life—the spiritual dimension—upon which all other considerations of life find fulfillment.
>
> I receive this prize in the name of our wonderful Lord, whom I have served for more than fifty exciting years, and on behalf of my beloved wife, Vonette, our wonderful sons, Zac and Brad, fantastic fellow staff members, board of directors, and a great army of faithful and generous supporters. I feel that I am the most privileged and fortunate man in the world to be associated with such a remarkable team.

After two years of marriage, Vonette and I began this now worldwide ministry on a modest scale. We both had been very materialistic in our youth. But we soon came to the conclusion that serving Jesus was the most important thing in the world. So on a Sunday afternoon in the spring of 1951, Vonette and I, in our home in the Hollywood Hills, got on our knees and prayed, 'Lord, we surrender ourselves completely, irrevocably, to you. We will go wherever you want us to go and do whatever you want us to do.' And we did something very unusual. I'm not saying that others should do it, but we decided that it was what God wanted us to do. As a businessman, I had signed many contracts. So we literally wrote and signed a contract with the Lord, committing our entire lives to Him. On that spring day in 1951, Vonette and I began the most exciting adventure one can experience: we made a decision to relinquish all of our rights, all of our possessions, everything we would ever own, and give them to our Master and Lord. In the words of the apostle Paul, we became slaves of Jesus [Romans 1:1].

Through December 31, 1995, by God's grace, Vonette and I have had the privilege and excitement of seeing Campus Crusade grow to nearly 13,000 full-time and more than 101,000 trained volunteer staff members with ministry in 165 countries. We have had the thrill of helping to take the good news of Jesus Christ to well over two billion people, and hundreds of millions have indicated their desire to follow Him as well. Our *JESUS* film alone, a full-length movie on the life of Christ, has been viewed by more than 750 million people in 355 languages in most countries of the world.

Deeply concerned over the growing decadence of our great America and the necessity of following the Lord's command to proclaim the gospel to all nations and peoples, I felt led of God in 1994 to fast and pray for forty days. I called upon godly men and women all over the world to fast and pray with me for a spiritual awakening in America and in the world and for the fulfillment of the Great Commission. For this purpose, we have held five such gatherings with millions of people joining us via satellite cable and other means, all for the purpose of fasting and praying for an outpouring of God's Spirit in revival power upon the United States and the world. Historically, we know that on four separate occasions God has graciously and remarkably visited America with great blessings to our nation. It is our prayer and expectancy that God will visit us again.

This money from the Templeton Prize will be used to educate leaders of the church worldwide to the spiritual benefits of fasting and prayer. I believe that fasting with biblical prayer is the most enriching and energizing of all the Christian disciplines and can accomplish more for the glory of God, and ensure His blessing upon the peoples of the earth, than anything else we can do.

Again, I am deeply grateful and honored for this recognition, and I give all the honor and glory to the One to whom it is due—our Lord and Savior Jesus Christ, who is risen, and who lives today in the hearts of all who love, trust, and obey Him.

I invite all others who share my hopes and concerns for the world to join with me in proclaiming His great and desperately needed message of love, forgiveness, peace, and eternal life to the ends of the earth.

That evening's TV and radio news, and the next day's newspapers carried the story of the Templeton Prize. Paul Harvey featured it on his news radio broadcast. Congratulatory phone calls and letters poured in to our ministry headquarters in Orlando, Florida. In the whirlwind weeks that followed, dozens of media requested follow-up interviews.

At Buckingham Palace

On May 8, Vonette and I were flown to London, treated as royalty, and presented the actual award in a private ceremony with Prince Philip at Buckingham Palace. Then it was on to Rome, where on the evening of May 9 close to 900 dignitaries and guests gathered for the public convocation at the Church of Santa Maria, Trastevere. On this worldwide platform, I was privileged to present a formal acceptance address in which I sought to share the gospel and give God all the honor and glory. Considering the influential worldwide audience, the speech was one of the most important messages and testimonies I have ever given. As I spoke, I sensed a special strengthening within me. Afterward I learned that 102 of our staff back in Orlando, and hundreds more around the world, had been on their knees praying as I spoke asking God to anoint me in a special way.

Another rapid succession of luncheons, receptions, and meetings followed. Finally, Vonette and I boarded our plane for the trip home to Orlando, exhausted but overjoyed at the experiences of the past several days. As we jetted across the Atlantic Ocean, I settled back in my seat, closed my eyes, and contemplated the incredible things God had done—not just in the past few days, but over the past five decades. My mind drifted back to Southern California, where God had used the lives of several loving, caring people to motivate Vonette and me to devote our lives to Christ—a decision we have never once regretted.

CHAPTER 2

When God Became Personal

WHEN I MOVED to California in 1944 to build my business, with dreams of making big money and enjoying all the material trappings of success, I had no clue that God had a far better plan for me.

I have not always cared about the will of God. I grew up on a ranch near Coweta, Oklahoma, with a mother who was a saintly Christian and a father who was not a believer. I tried to take on the "macho image" of my father and grandfather, thinking Christianity was for women and children but not for men. I was determined that, in spite of my shy nature, I would be strong and self-reliant and accomplish everything I set out to do.

I went away to college determined to become student body president, editor of the college yearbook, named to *Who's Who in American Colleges and Universities*, and graduate as the "Outstanding Student." In four years, I accomplished each of these objectives and more. Spiritually, I was an agnostic, not knowing whether God existed and not really caring if He did. I believed that "a man can do anything he wants to, on his own." My father and grandfather had modeled that philosophy for me and I had proven it to myself in college.

Following a short stint on the faculty of the Oklahoma State University extension, I decided to move to Los Angeles to start my own business. I rented an apartment from a charming, elderly couple in Hollywood and began pouring my life into building a new fancy-foods enterprise, Bright's California Confections.

Momentous Change

Little did I know how God would use this dear couple to turn my life around. "Will you come to church with us?" they repeatedly asked. For a long time I would smile, thank them for the invitation, then come up with an excuse. I had seldom attended church since I left home for college. I preferred to spend my Sundays doing an amateur radio broadcast and going horseback riding in the Hollywood Hills.

We lived right down the street from First Presbyterian Church of Hollywood, and I noticed that this loving, white-haired couple took delight in attending the services. "We have a great preacher by the name of Louis Evans," they persisted. "You'd love Dr. Evans."

I could not imagine loving any preacher, but God was using this couple to sow a seed. One Sunday evening as I returned from an afternoon of horseback riding, I decided to drop in on the evening service. I arrived after the program started, sat by myself in the back row, and left before the service was over so no one would see me.

So much for church. Or so I thought.

Apparently, my landlords had given my name to someone in the college and young adult department at the church. A few days later, I received a call from a young woman inviting me to a party, and since I couldn't think of an excuse not to go, I accepted. I was in for quite a surprise. Gathered were three hundred of the sharpest young adult men and women I had ever seen. They were happy, having fun, and obviously loved the Lord. In one evening, my notion that Christianity was a women-and-children-only religion was really shaken. I had never met people like this before.

Although very busy with my business, I started attending

the group's meetings at the church, along with regular church services. My shyness prevented me from mixing very much, and I always sat on the back row. But I listened to what the leaders were saying, and when I arrived back at my apartment, I fished out my long-unused Bible—a gift from my mother—from a box of books and began to read it on my own.

A number of successful businessmen in the church, including a prominent builder, would invite small groups of young people to their homes for picnics and swims in the pool. During one of those popular events, I asked the builder about his business and what it was like to be so successful. His answer startled me. "Material success is not where you find happiness," he stated firmly. "There are rich people all over this city who are the most miserable people you'll ever meet. Knowing and serving Jesus Christ is what's important. He is the only way to find happiness."

I recalled that my godly mother had exemplified this same principle. She had not been able to verbalize it in a way that made me realize my need to receive Christ as my Savior and Lord, but she had lived it. And now I was meeting sharp young adults, successful men and women, who were living what my mother had lived.

Over a period of months I began to be greatly impressed with the eloquence and personality of the pastor, Dr. Louis Evans. He presented Jesus Christ and the Christian life in an attractive way I had never known before. So, as a matter of intellectual integrity, I was forced to begin an in-depth study of the life of Jesus. The more I read and studied, the more I became convinced that He was more than just a great historical figure. Over the months I concluded that He was truly the Son of God.

One Sunday evening in 1945, Dr. Henrietta C. Mears, director of Christian education at the church, spoke to our college and young adult group about Paul's conversion experience on the road to Damascus. I had read the account before, but Dr. Mears made it come alive as she told of this ambitious man who was committed to ridding the world of the new heresy called Christianity. She told how Paul (then Saul of Tarsus) had been blinded by a bright light. Saul then asked, "Who are You, Lord, and what will You have me do?"

"This is one of the most important questions you can possibly ask of God, even today," Dr. Mears told us. "The happiest people in the world are those who are in the center of God's will. The most miserable are those who are not doing God's will.

"Paul deceived himself into thinking he was doing God's will by persecuting the Christians. In reality, he was pursuing

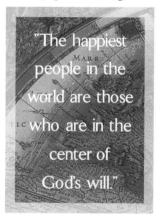
"The happiest people in the world are those who are in the center of God's will."

his own ambitions. So God set him straight with this dramatic experience on the road to Damascus."

As Dr. Mears spoke, I was deeply aware of her wisdom, her boldness, and her love for us. She was another proof that my stereotype of Christianity had been wrong. She spoke with authority, yet I saw a genuine concern for each of the young men and women to whom she spoke.

"Not many of us have dramatic, emotional conversion experiences as Paul did," she continued. "But the circumstances don't really matter. What matters is your response to the same question: 'Who are You, Lord, and what will You have me do?'"

She challenged each of us to go home, get on our knees, and ask God that all-important question.

As I returned to my apartment that night, I realized that I was ready to give my life to God. I was not really aware of being lost because I lived a relatively moral, ethical life. I didn't feel that I had an unfilled need. (In retrospect, I realize I was indeed lost and needed Jesus Christ to fill the "God-shaped vacuum" in my life.) What attracted me was God's love, which had been made known to me through my study of the Bible and through the lives of the people I had met at Hollywood Presbyterian Church.

That night I knelt beside my bed and asked the question with which Dr. Mears had challenged us: "Who are You, Lord, and what will You have me do?" In a sense, that was my prayer for salvation. It was not theologically profound, but the Lord knew my heart and He interpreted what was going on inside me. Through my study I believed Jesus Christ was the Son of God, that He had died for my sins, and that, as Dr. Mears had shared with us, if I invited Him into my life as Savior and Lord, He would come in according to His promise in Revelation 3:20.

Although nothing dramatic or emotional happened when I prayed, I know without a doubt that Jesus did come into my life. I accepted Him and He accepted me. Asking Him that question, "Who are You, Lord, and what will You have me do?" did not seem very dynamic at first, but as I began to grow in my new commitment and love for the Lord, I became more and more aware of what a sinner I am and what a wonderful, forgiving Savior He is.

Courtship in Southern California

In time, I was elected president of the Sunday school class and was privileged to meet regularly with Dr. Mears and other officers to pray together and discuss the profound truths of God's Word. The more I learned about God, the more I wanted to learn—so much that I decided to enroll in Princeton Theological Seminary in the fall of 1946.

A partial year studying at Princeton on the East Coast while maintaining my business in Southern California convinced me that I was spreading myself too thin. In 1947 I transferred my academic credits to Fuller Theological Seminary in Southern California, where I continued working toward a seminary degree. I was a member of the first class of 37 students. During my travels from coast to coast, I had been able to stop in my hometown of Coweta to visit my dear parents. There was another reason I enjoyed visiting Coweta; her name was Vonette Zachary. We had grown up together in this small Midwest town of 1,500, and although I was several years older, I had always considered Vonette attractive, talented, smart, and a delightful young lady. After I was established in business in Hollywood, I began corresponding with Vonette while she was attending Texas Women's University. Our friendship blossomed into romantic love. On our first date at the Rose Bud Ball, I proposed to her, and she accepted.

I had been growing in my new walk with the Lord for several months when I proposed to Vonette. Since she had been active in her church and came from a fine church family, I assumed that she was a vital Christian. The night we decided to become engaged, I told her, "I love you and want to spend our lives together. And I know you will understand that our Lord will always come first in my life, and in our marriage."

She didn't say anything at the time. Several months later, however, when I repeated this commitment, Vonette spoke up. "I'm not sure that's right," she bristled. "I think a man's family should be his first concern." I started to argue, but let the subject drop, knowing we would have plenty of time to work things out.

As Vonette's lack of a personal relationship with Christ became apparent, it began to trouble me deeply. I had been so sure that she was the one for me. We loved each other and wanted to build a life together. Yet, she simply could not accept the fact that the Christian life was more than mere church activity—it required a personal commitment of her life to Jesus Christ.

Upon her graduation with a home economics degree from Texas Women's University in 1948, I suggested that she visit her brother, who lived near me in Southern California. Vonette thought the visit might be a good idea, a kind of last chance for our relationship when we would decide for certain whether to proceed with a wedding. I learned later that Vonette confided to a friend, "I am either going to rescue Bill from this religious fanaticism or come back without a ring." As I look back on that visit and realize how close we came to breaking our engagement, I thank God for how He intervened on one critical afternoon.

That All-Important Meeting in the Cottage

I had taken Vonette to a meeting of several hundred college and career students at Forest Home Christian Conference Center. While Vonette seemed to enjoy the fellowship with the other young adults, she remained skeptical about the depth of their Christian faith. "Bill," she told me one evening, "I respect your commitment, but this just isn't for me."

Her words hit me hard. I had prayed so fervently for her. I cared deeply for her, romantically and spiritually. I wanted her to experience the joy of a personal walk with the Lord to whom I had made a total commitment for the rest of my life. But she was rejecting Him, and in so doing, it seemed that she was rejecting me. It was very clear to me: if she did not receive Jesus Christ, we could not be married.

"Are you sure?" I asked.

"I'm sure," Vonette whispered, her voice choking. "I just don't think all this personal relationship talk about God and Jesus Christ is real or necessary. But I can see that it's important to you, and..."

Tears came to her eyes and she struggled for words. I could feel my heart pounding as I sensed what was coming.

"...and it's built a barrier between us. Maybe it would be best for us to call off our engagement."

A lump welled up in my throat as I realized what was happening. I wanted her for my wife, but we were worlds apart. I could not give up my faith in Christ, and she could not embrace it.

I took her hands in mine and looked directly into her moist eyes. "Vonette, you told me you respect my commitment. I also respect you for the way you've weighed this carefully. Before we make a final decision, would you do one more thing?"

"What?"

"Talk with Dr. Henrietta Mears. I think you'll like her. She has an inquiring, scientific mind like you. She can explain these spiritual concepts much better than I can."

Dr. Mears, who had been so instrumental in my decision for Christ and my growth in Him, had founded the Forest Home Christian Conference Center and was one of the main speakers at the gathering. Reluctantly, Vonette agreed to meet with her. I arranged the meeting, and the following morning Vonette entered Dr. Mears' cottage thinking, *It won't do any good, but I want Bill to know I gave it every possible chance.* While Dr. Mears and Vonette talked, I paced back and forth outside the cottage, praying my heart out.

Time dragged. Fifteen minutes. Half an hour.

Forty-five minutes. An hour.

I continued pacing and praying.

Ninety minutes.

Suddenly the door to Dr. Mears' cottage burst open, and Vonette Zachary, the wonderful young woman with whom I was so much in love, came bounding into my arms. Tears of joy streaked her face and her smile seemed brighter than the sun. She didn't say a word. I knew what had happened, and tears of gratitude filled my eyes too.

Gaining Everything

With fondness and joy, Vonette recalls her visit with Dr. Mears. "Dr. Mears was one of the most vibrant, enthusiastic personalities I had ever met. She was waiting for me. The entire conference staff, without my knowledge, had been praying for my conversion. Dr. Mears explained that she had taught chem-istry in Minneapolis, and that she could understand how I was thinking. I had minored in chemistry in college, and every-thing had to be practical and workable to me. This was one of the reasons I had questioned the validity of Christianity.

"As Dr. Mears explained simply to me from God's Word how to receive Christ into my life and how I could be sure that I had become a child of God, she used terminology very familiar to me. She explained that, just as a person going into a chemistry laboratory experiment follows the table of chemi-cal valence, so it is possible for a person to enter God's spiritual laboratory and follow His formula for knowing Him.

"During the next hour, she lovingly proceeded to explain who Christ is and how I could know Him personally. 'Dr. Mears,' I said, 'if Jesus Christ is the way, then how do I meet Him?'

"Dr. Mears responded, 'In Revelation 3:20 Christ says, "Behold, I stand at the door and knock. If anyone hears My voice and opens the door, I will come in to him and dine with him, and he with Me." Receiving Christ is simply a matter of turning your life—your will, your emotions, and your intel-lect—completely over to Him. John 1:12 says, "But as many as received Him, to them He gave the right to become chil-dren of God, to those who believe in His name."'

"When Dr. Mears finished, I thought, *If what she tells me is absolutely true, I have nothing to lose and everything to gain.* I accepted her invitation to pray together and asked Jesus Christ to come into my life. As I look back, my life began to change at that moment. God became a reality in my life. For the first time I was ready to trust Him. I became aware that my prayers were getting beyond the ceiling. No longer did I have to *try* to love people; there just seemed to be a love that flowed from within that I did not have to create.

"God had added a new dimension to my life, and I found myself becoming as enthusiastic as Bill, Dr. Mears, and the other students—and as eager as they to share Christ with others."

Vonette and I were married December 30, 1948. I continued conducting my business and studying at Fuller Theological Seminary; Vonette secured a teaching position in the Los Angeles school system. We attended First Presbyterian Church of Hollywood and took part in various volunteer ministries, leading teams of young adults in outreaches to local hospitals, jails, and skid row missions. Although the response varied, we were always thrilled when God used us to help others find new life in Him.

We did not know what specific plans God had for us, but we had an increasing desire to live in a way that would please Him. Little did we know that, as I studied for a seminary exam late one night, something would happen that would change our lives forever.

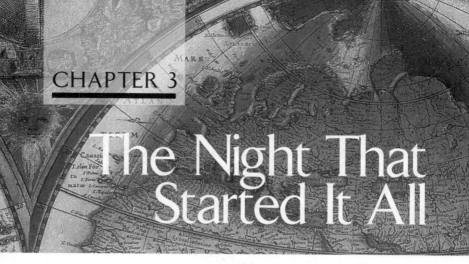

CHAPTER 3

The Night That Started It All

VONETTE AND I BOTH held very materialistic goals in life before our commitments to the Lord. Our dreams had included the finest European honeymoon money could buy; a home in the fabulous Bel Air district of Los Angeles; securing the region's finest voice teacher to develop Vonette's already-beautiful singing voice; expensive new cars for each of us; and all the other things that typically accompany wealth.

But after we decided to make Jesus Christ the Lord of our lives, we found ourselves beginning to respond to His command: "Seek first His kingdom and His righteousness" (Matthew 6:33). We realized that the more we learned of God's love and provision for us, the more we could trust Him. Every day, in some new and exciting way, we were learning that God's will was better than our own. We no longer had a great appetite for the materialistic goals that had previously driven us.

Since we both wanted our lives to count for eternity, we believed in setting goals—only now we desired to do so with God's guidance to make sure our goals were His. One Sunday afternoon in our home in the Hollywood Hills, we were talking about how our trust in God had grown, wondering aloud what new goals we should place before Him. Vonette, always practical, came up with an excellent suggestion: "Why don't we go to separate rooms and make a list of the things that are important to us? Then we'll compare notes and agree on a final list."

Vonette went into one room and I went into another, where we each prayed for God to show us what He wanted us to do, then wrote our ideas on paper. When we came back together, our lists were different, but after a time of discussion we agreed on the following items:

1. To live holy lives controlled and empowered by the Holy Spirit

2. To be effective witnesses for Christ

3. To help fulfill Christ's Great Commission (His command to "Go into all the world and preach the gospel to every creature") in our generation

4. To have a loving, Christ-centered, nurturing home

5. To have two to four children

6. To have two cars for getting around sprawling Southern California

7. To have a house nice enough for entertaining the President of the United States but modest enough that a person from skid row would feel comfortable

Admittedly, Vonette and I were young and naive when we established our new goals and signed a contract to be "slaves of Jesus" following the example of our Lord (Philippians 2) and the apostle Paul (Romans 1:1). However, it is fascinating to look back over the decades and see how God has not only met every true need in our lives, but He has also brought about every goal we listed that Sunday afternoon.

The first three goals have become the values by which we live and to which we have devoted our lives. We are humbled and consider ourselves privileged that God would use us. He has enabled us to live in the power of the Holy Spirit, witness exciting results as we share our faith with others, and lead a worldwide ministry dedicated to helping give every person on earth the opportunity to say yes to His Son, Jesus Christ.

We were blessed with two wonderful sons, Zachary and Bradley, and enjoyed nurturing them in an atmosphere of Christian values and unconditional love. Both now have fine families and are involved in Christian ministry. Zac is a Presbyterian minister, and Brad, a Campus Crusade staff member, gives staff leadership to Pinnacle Forum, a ministry to world leaders.

Regarding housing, we have never owned a home of our own, but God has always provided a comfortable place that met our criteria. Whether at our former headquarters in Arrowhead Springs, California, or at our new headquarters in Orlando, Florida, Vonette and I have been able to rent lovely, gracious accommodations where we have hosted visitors from all walks of life.

Our goal of two cars was not as crucial or strategic as we first thought. In recent years we have not owned any cars, but God has provided us transportation through the generosity of friends of the ministry. God's plans are always wiser, always better investments, than our own, and He provides for every true need when our hearts are centered on Him. As Christian author and speaker Ron Dunn says, "What you do not have, you do not require."

The Contract

On that Sunday afternoon in 1951, as Vonette and I compared notes and agreed on our goals, we both sensed the Lord leading us to make an uncommon commitment. As a businessman, I was accustomed to signing contracts to signify agreement with someone regarding terms of a working relationship. "What if," I suggested to Vonette, "we put what we have written in the form of a contract with the Lord, and surrender our lives, our goals, our material possessions, and our future completely to Him?"

Keep in mind that if this idea had been presented to us several years earlier, we both would have scoffed at it. This just was not the typical Southern California, college graduate, ready-to-conquer-the-world approach to life! I am not suggesting that every Christian do something like this. Such a transaction is strictly between an individual and God, as it was for us. But we sensed the Holy Spirit at work in our hearts, maturing our value system, and showing us a deeper meaning to life.

Vonette readily agreed that this was something we should do together. Prayerfully, we signed our names to the contract as a formal act of our commitment to Christ and His cause. It was not an emotional undertaking, but a transaction of the will.

To this day, almost fifty years later, we are convinced that our early "contract with God" commitment prompted our Lord to entrust us with the vision a short time later for Campus Crusade for Christ—first the contract of surrender, then the vision. The contract has also been a lifelong key to many of the spiritual blessings the Lord has bestowed upon us and to maintaining the financial integrity of a growing worldwide ministry. Whenever the temptation has arisen to "store up treasures on earth," our written agreement with God has come to mind and, with His guidance, steered us away from wrong choices. We agreed in writing to seek first His kingdom and His righteousness and claimed His promise that "all these things will be given to you as well" (Matthew 6:33).

We did not know what was to happen as a result of our commitment to become "slaves of Jesus," but I know God did. He was preparing our hearts to be receptive to an even bigger idea a few months later—an idea that came on a night I will never forget.

The Birth of a Ministry

It was spring 1951, my senior year in seminary. After signing our contract with God, Vonette and I continued seminary studies, teaching, volunteer work, and business. As we studied the Bible, prayed together, and fellowshipped with other believers, our love for God seemed to be growing each day.

One night I stayed up late studying for a Greek exam. Vonette, having prepared her lessons for teaching the following day, was asleep in the next room. Suddenly, I sensed the presence of God in a way I had never known before. I laid the textbook down, closed my eyes, and uttered a quick prayer: "Lord, do you have something to say to me?"

There was no audible voice; no heavenly choirs singing; no bright lights or bolts of lightning. However, the presence of the Almighty seemed so real that all I could do was wait expectantly for what He had to say. Within moments, I felt an amazing combination of peace and excitement, for I had the overwhelming impression that God had flashed on the screen of my mind His instructions for my life and ministry.

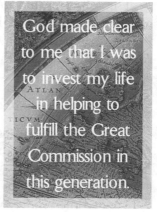

God made clear to me that I was to invest my life in helping to fulfill the Great Commission in this generation.

It is difficult to talk about such experiences for fear of being misunderstood or causing others to seek similar experiences. But this is the way it happened to me. There are no human words to describe what took place, other than to say that in a very definite way, God made clear to me that I was to invest my life in helping to fulfill the Great Commission in this generation. I was to begin by helping to win and disciple college students for Christ, since they are the leaders and influencers of tomorrow. How to carry out this calling was not spelled out in detail for, as we would soon discover (and have relied upon ever since), God would provide the insights and strategies as we moved forward in obedience to Him.

How would Vonette respond? Trembling with excitement

over what had just happened to me, I went into the bedroom, awakened Vonette, and told her everything. Without a moment's hesitation, she acknowledged that this was undoubtedly of the Lord and that she wanted to be part of it. Together we praised God for His direction and promised that, with His grace and strength, we would obey His call.

The next day I went to see one of my favorite seminary professors, renowned Bible scholar and author Dr. Wilbur Smith. As I shared with him what God had revealed to me, Dr. Smith got out of his chair and paced back and forth in his office. "This is of God," he said, over and over. "This is of God. I want to help you. Let me think and pray about it."

The following morning I hurried to Dr. Smith's early English Bible class. Before he began his lecture, he beckoned me into a small side room, fished a piece of paper from his suit pocket, and handed it to me. On the paper he had written:

CCC
Campus Crusade for Christ

"God has provided the name for your vision," Dr. Smith told me. "He has called you to this. Obey His call. Let me know how I can be of help."

Campus Crusade for Christ was born.

We had the vision. We had a name. We had a wise man of God willing to stand beside us with counsel and prayer. What should our next steps be?

The First Steps

After much prayer, thought, and counsel, I became convinced —and remain convinced today—that God did not want me to be ordained. While I hold deep respect and admiration for godly clergy, it became clear to me that the young men and women with whom we would be sharing the gospel on the college campus were likely to be more receptive to Bill Bright as a layman than to Bill Bright as a professional minister. So the first major decision I made was to drop out of seminary, although I had just a few units remaining before graduation. I will always treasure my seminary experience at Princeton and Fuller; what I learned there has proven invaluable as we minister to Christians and non-Christians alike. But I have never regretted the decision to leave seminary because my lay status has often worked to great advantage in our ministry with students, business people, and national leaders.

Our next move was to set up an advisory board that would enable us to seek the ongoing counsel of mature Christians. Dr. Wilbur Smith was the first person I asked to serve on our board, and he readily accepted. Encouraged, I then met with several other outstanding Christians, described what God was leading us to do, and asked if they would be part of the advisory board. In addition to Dr. Smith, our first board included:

- *Dr. Henrietta Mears*, one of America's leading Christian educators, who had been so influential in leading Vonette to Christ and influencing my life in a very meaningful way
- *Bill Savage*, a godly friend from First Presbyterian Church of Hollywood
- *Billy Graham*, who was on his way to becoming the most respected worldwide evangelist of our generation and who remains a beloved, trusted friend
- *Richard C. Halverson*, a Presbyterian minister and later Chaplain of the U.S. Senate
- *Dawson Trotman*, founder of the worldwide Navigators ministry
- *Dr. Ralph Byron*, leading authority on cancer
- *Cyrus Nelson*, President and co-founder of Gospel Light Publishers
- *Dan Fuller*, son of Fuller Seminary founder, Charles E. Fuller
- *J. Edwin Orr*, Bible teacher and foremost authority on revival

We were delighted that these fine Christian leaders agreed

to serve as advisors to the fledgling ministry of Campus Crusade for Christ. We remain indebted to them for their time, their encouragement and counsel, and their earnest prayer support during the early years of our ministry.

As spring turned to summer, Vonette and I and our friends undergirded the ministry in constant prayer. We often found ourselves praying, "Lord where do You want us to launch this ministry?" We knew we were to begin on a college campus. As we prayed and weighed the possibilities, the University of California at Los Angeles (UCLA) became the focus of our attention. UCLA was a large, influential campus of worldwide repute. In 1951 it had a strong, radical minority which exercised significant influence and was causing a number of disturbances. Ministering among students at UCLA would be a challenge, but we felt that if our new venture for Christ could succeed there, it would likely succeed on any campus.

We met with university officials to describe our plans and request necessary permission to work with the students. Approval came quickly. UCLA was indeed where we would begin!

The First Headquarters

We then searched for a house to rent, one that would be close to the campus and suitable both as our residence and as a place for student meetings. After carefully assessing our present and future finances, we felt $200 per month was our limit. Vacancies were slim, and on the few houses available, rents were higher than our tiny budget allowed. One vacancy did catch our attention: a large house located approximately one block from sorority row with a living room ideal for our needs. But the monthly rent was $450, an outrageously high sum in 1951. I decided to step out in faith, explaining to the owners our desire to help reach the students of UCLA for Christ and that we could afford only $200 per month rent.

"We'll think about it," the owners responded, and we said our good-byes.

Later that evening, the owners called to report that they were impressed with our mission and wanted to be a part of it. "We'll accept your offer of $200 per month, if you will pay an additional $20 per month for the gardener."

We readily agreed. We now had a vision, a ministry name, an advisory board of godly men and women, our first mission field, and our initial headquarters.

There was one more foundational piece of the ministry that God led us to put in place as we geared up. We knew from the start that we would be only as effective as God allowed us to be and that our new ministry must be bathed in constant prayer. We were aware that we would quickly get in trouble if we did anything outside of God's will and guidance; we wanted His Holy Spirit to precede us in every contact we would make. Our desire was to bring honor and glory to Him in everything we did.

To this end, we organized a 24-hour prayer chain, dividing each day into 96 fifteen-minute segments and inviting our church friends, advisory board members, and other caring Christians to sign up for one or more segments each week. How encouraging it was to know that Christians were praying around the clock for God to do a unique thing on the UCLA campus!

Their prayers would soon be answered—and in ways none of us could have imagined.

CHAPTER 4

Our UCLA Beginnings

FOR MORE THAN a year prior to founding Campus Crusade for Christ, Vonette and I and other volunteers from the church had gone into fraternity and sorority houses to speak with college students about Jesus. While we may have planted a seed or two, we never saw anyone commit his or her life to the Lord as a result of these meetings.

So it may have seemed presumptuous that our initial strategy at UCLA called for meeting with the leaders of fraternities and sororities and securing invitations to speak in their houses about spiritual matters. Yet as we planned and prayed, we felt certain that this was where God wanted us to begin—to "influence the influencers" and, with His guidance and strength, train them to influence those around them.

Our first campus meeting was scheduled to be held at the Kappa Alpha Theta sorority. However, the radical left controlled the student government and newspaper, and there was active Communist recruiting on campus. As I prepared to speak, we prayed that God would break through this tense atmosphere and reach at least one or two of the young women.

The sorority was nicknamed "the house of beautiful women," and indeed they were. Sixty women gathered in the living room for the meeting, and when I finished my message I said, "If you would like to know Jesus Christ personally, come and tell me."

We had prayed for one or two. But at least thirty of these beautiful college women stood in line to tell me they wanted to become Christians! Since this was my first group meeting and since so many people wanted to receive Christ, I did not know what to do. So I did what any good businessman does when he's unsure what to do—I called another meeting.

"Vonette and I would like to invite all of you to our home tomorrow night," I announced. "We will talk more about how you can know Christ personally. Please come and bring your boyfriend."

Each of the women agreed, and most of them came—some with boyfriends. Most of those young women and several of their boyfriends prayed with us that evening, yielding their lives to Christ.

One of the boyfriends in attendance was the star running back of the UCLA football team. After the meeting, he approached me privately. "I've never heard anything like this before," he confided. "I want to talk with you some more." The following Sunday, aching from a bone-crunching victory on the gridiron the day before, this young man and his girlfriend accompanied Vonette and me to church. Afterward as the women prepared lunch, he told me, "You know, all my life I've played football so I could be an All-American. But it occurred to me as you spoke earlier this week that if I broke my leg and couldn't play anymore, I wouldn't have anything to live for. I realize that I need God."

We got on our knees and prayed. As we stood up, he smiled and announced, "Now I want to be an All-American for God."

Donn Moomaw was an All-American on the football field for three years at UCLA and, along with several others from that first sorority meeting, served as part of the nucleus during Campus Crusade's initial years of campus ministry. As he confidently shared Christ with his teammates and other students, he lead many of them to the Lord. He would go on to become an influential pastor, and I was honored to be present when he gave the invocation at Ronald Reagan's 1981 presidential inauguration.

Positive Results

The positive response of so many sharp young women at the sorority gathering was a humbling experience—a dramatic confirmation in my heart that the vision to help fulfill the Great Commission, starting with the collegians of the world, was truly from God. Until then we had been cautious, unsure, stepping carefully and speaking reservedly; but God seemed to be urging us forward, filling us with much-needed confidence and the assurance that He was with us.

We began meeting regularly with those who had made personal commitments to Christ to teach them key principles from God's Word. Gradually, they realized the assurance of their salvation and began growing in their knowledge and appreciation of God's love and truth.

At the same time, we recruited established Christian students who were interested in ministering to their peers and trained them so they could join us in visiting fraternities, sororities, dormitories, athletic groups, and student leaders. At most meetings, two or three students presented short testimonies of how their faith in Christ had helped them in life, then I gave a brief message explaining who Christ is, why He came, and how we can know Him personally.

In meeting after meeting, the response was similar to that of the Kappa Alpha Theta sorority—between 25 and 50 percent of those attending indicated a desire to receive the Lord. Over our first few months on campus, more than 250 UCLA students—including the student body president, the editor of the campus newspaper, and a number of top athletes—committed their lives to Jesus Christ. So great was their influence that the campus chimes began to play Christian hymns at noon!

I must pause here to remind the reader that we did not for a moment think this positive response was our own doing. It definitely was not due to anything special about me. By nature I have always been a bit reserved—even shy—and I have never been a particularly dramatic or highly entertaining speaker. After many years of high school and college debate and oratory, I dreamed of becoming a great pulpit orator. But one day a wise seminary professor admonished his class: "When you speak, do you want people to marvel at what a great speaker you are, or at what a great God you serve?" That challenge convicted me, and ever since I have always sought to communicate as simply and directly as possible, praying that God will speak to the hearts of the audience and that His wonderful plan will be made clear to everyone. I say this to underscore that no one, especially me, can claim any human credit for what we saw God do in those early days at UCLA.

I am convinced that the positive results we witnessed were due to two things: First, we were simply being obedient to God's obvious direction in our lives; and second, through the 24-hour prayer chain and many other hours of fervent prayer, we surrounded everything we did with constant prayer for God's guidance and blessing. Campus Crusade for Christ was His ministry, not ours, and we knew that we would bear fruit only if we remained humble and obedient before Him. Our task was to take the initiative to share His love and forgiveness in the power of the Holy Spirit and leave the results to God, giving Him all the glory.

Recruiting the First Staff

News of what God was doing at UCLA had begun to spread to other college campuses. We began receiving letters and calls from Christian students, faculty, pastors, and businessmen in other cities asking, "Will you help us? We would like to start Campus Crusade at our school."

I had an important decision to make. The vision God had given me had embraced the whole world, beginning with the university campus and specifically UCLA. If I were to stay at

UCLA and devote all of my personal energies to reaching one campus, I would be disobedient to that heavenly vision. I loved the students there and could easily have spent my entire life serving Christ on that one campus. Yet, I felt strongly that God was leading us to take what we were learning at UCLA and establish similar outreaches on other campuses. To do so, I would have to begin recruiting and training other believers to join us full-time in helping to reach collegians of the world with the good news.

The standards we established for new, full-time staff were high. First, they needed to already be effective witnesses for Christ; second, we wanted them to be seminary graduates; and third, they needed to be concerned—even passionate—about winning, building, training, and sending men and women to help evangelize the world and thus help fulfill the Great Commission.

We surrounded everything we did with constant prayer for God's guidance and blessing.

After much prayer, Vonette and I agreed that Vonette would remain in charge of the work at UCLA while I went on a recruiting tour of many of the Christian colleges and seminaries in the nation. It was a tour that proved disappointing; in those days there just were not many individuals, with or without seminary degrees, who were fruitful witnesses for Christ or who wanted to be part of a brand-new ministry like Campus Crusade for Christ.

This forced us to carefully reevaluate. Did God want us to expand Campus Crusade to other campuses? Yes, we were convinced of that. To do so, we needed qualified, full-time staff members to help direct each campus's outreach. After careful consideration, we revised the requirements for our new staff—a move that, in retrospect, we believe was God's sovereign hand at work. In order to join Campus Crusade full-time, a person must: 1) be a dedicated Christian with a heart for God and His Word; 2) have a college degree; 3) have a teachable spirit; and 4) have a desire to learn how to introduce others to Christ and disciple them in the Christian faith.

After considerable recruiting, six choice people agreed to join us. Three were seminarians: Dan Fuller, Calvin Herriott, and Roe Brooks. The other three were college graduates: Gordon Klenck, Roger Aiken, and Wayne Arolla. They came one at a time with the few possessions they had, and our family table seemed to shrink as each new staff member joined us.

"Family" is the operative word, for we were indeed a family—not only in Christ, but also in experience. Quite often some or all of the six young men were in our home. We ate together, prayed together, and worked together. Our love for each other and for what we were doing was very real. I still do not know how Vonette managed to cook for us, since she never knew who would show up for dinner. But her home economics degree came in handy and we always seemed to have enough for everyone.

First Steps in Organizing the Ministry

From the very beginning, we considered initial and ongoing staff training to be vitally important. Vonette and I designed and implemented an intensive program that included everything from personal etiquette and hygiene to how to give an effective testimony. We especially emphasized training in the Bible, the lordship of Christ, assurance of salvation, and the ministry of the Holy Spirit (how to appropriate by faith His power for a holy life and effective witness). We studied subjects like methods of personal outreach, how to give an evangelistic presentation in a group setting, how to lead a Bible study, and how to train others to share Christ. Our approach used "learn by doing" labs, in which we would share what we had learned from our outreach experiences then take the men with us to see it happen for them in real life. After they ob-

served me a few times, I gave them the opportunity to conduct an outreach interview or group meeting while I observed
them. All of these aspects of training, especially the "learning
by doing," would become hallmarks of Campus Crusade's
new-staff orientation and ongoing staff training for years to
come.

In the fall of 1952, with the help of our first "class" of new
staff, we established the ministry on additional campuses,
including San Diego State, the University of Southern California (USC), the University of California at Berkeley, Oregon State, and the University of Washington.

In those days, staff members were paid a salary of $100 per
month for nine months only. During the summer months
they would receive no remuneration. Obviously, they had not
come because of the financial rewards, but because they wanted
to be part of something bigger than themselves. They wanted
to make their lives count for God, to help change their world by
showing college students how to find new life in Jesus Christ.

I am so grateful to those six young men who joined us in
the very beginning to help that vision become a reality. In a
very real sense, we were "making it up as we went" in those
days, and these men put their faith on the line in many ways!
God used their love for Christ and dedicated spirit of adventure to help lay the foundation from which Campus Crusade
for Christ International has been built.

Personally, Vonette and I drew no salary in the early years.
I had divested myself of my business and, as long as those
funds lasted, we drew from them to cover our living expenses
and to help accelerate and expand the ministry. As with any
ministry, more funds would be needed to cover staff salaries,
operating expenses, and growth, so I began letting interested
churches and individuals know about Campus Crusade's
financial needs. We never had more money than we needed,
but we always had just enough. Anything that came in was
applied directly to ministry opportunities rather than to build-

ing reserves—a practice that we continue today. I have always wanted to be dependent upon the Lord rather than upon a ministry bank account, keeping funds active in meeting actual, real-time ministry opportunities instead of building a reserve for "someday." Whenever a need has arisen with no obvious funds to meet it, we have placed that need before God, informed our ministry friends about it, and trusted God to provide as He desired. Whatever we have needed, He has supplied; whatever did not come in, we did not need!

We knew from the start that, in obedience to God and our desire to honor Him, our motive for ministry could never be that of personal gain. To that end we established modest standards of staff remuneration and have kept them to this day.

We knew from the start that our motive for ministry could never be that of personal gain.

All staff, including myself, are compensated by the same standards. We also determined strict procedures of financial stewardship to ensure that all funds would be used as wisely as possible toward the mission of helping fulfill the Great Commission. Believing in total transparency and total disclosure, we pioneered annual financial reporting.

Some years ago several organizations, concerned over financial abuses in Christian ministries, established the Evangelical Council for Financial Accountability (EFCA) to help ensure fiscal integrity among non-profit ministries. Campus Crusade for Christ became a charter member and continues to maintain membership. We have pledged to abide by the council's strict code of ethics and financial accounting practices. For several years in a row, *Money* magazine and other respected publications have ranked Campus Crusade among the very top of all non-profit charitable and religious organizations for financial efficiency, specifically the percentage of funds raised that go directly to ministry versus funds used for administration. While we do not maintain our high standards for the applause of men, it is reassuring to know that even the most careful scrutiny verifies our commitment to financial integrity.

A New Headquarters

As we began to grow, we had many opportunities to trust the Lord. One day a wire came from the owners of the home we had rented; they were returning early from overseas and asked if we would be willing to relinquish the house. Although we were only six months into a one-year lease, they had rented the house to us at less than half the original asking price and I did not feel we should deny their request. As I sat reading the wire, wondering what to do, the telephone rang. Dr. J. Edwin Orr, the internationally known evangelist and author, was calling to ask if I knew of anyone who would be interested in living in his home during the next year while he was on a worldwide speaking tour. It just happened that I did know of someone!

Dr. Orr's house became our home and headquarters for the next three semesters. As we continued to hold many fraternity, sorority, dormitory, and other group meetings, by now confronting thousands of students with the claims of Christ, so many were responding that we were again pressed for space.

Each day on my way to the campus, I passed a large Moorish castle-style home with a "For Sale" sign on the lawn. The home happened to be located in the Bel Air district of Westwood Village, directly across from the UCLA campus. An inquiry revealed what I had suspected: the price was far more than we could afford. I decided to put the idea out of my mind.

A short time later, our good friend Dr. Henrietta Mears learned of my interest in the property. "I was interested in that house several years ago," she told me. "In fact, I actually negotiated to purchase it. It just didn't work out at that time." Dr. Mears went on to explain that, after the recent death of her sister with whom she had shared a home, her present two-story house was now too large for her. "What if I purchase the new house, and you and Vonette come to live with me and share expenses?"

The three of us visited the "castle" together and unanimously agreed that it would be ideal for us and for the growing ministry of Campus Crusade. The house was large, ideally located, and designed so that we each could have the privacy we needed. With furniture pushed aside, as many as 300 students could be packed into the spacious living and dining rooms for meetings. And soon, they were!

It is impossible to count the number of college students who came to that house for evangelistic meetings or for discipleship training, but we know that hundreds were introduced to Christ there as Vonette, Dr. Mears, our growing team of Campus Crusade staff, and I conducted numerous gatherings each week. Once again, God had proven a faithful provider for our needs. In the process, He arranged even closer fellowship with a dear friend. How we treasure those times with Dr. Mears! She was one of the most brilliant Bible teachers and effective witnesses for Christ I have ever known. She loved God and served Him faithfully. Now she is enjoying eternity with Him. For all of us, Dr. Mears helped make those early years special with her godly wisdom, her lively personality, her faithful prayers, and her deep personal interest in the spiritual lives of the students of UCLA.

CHAPTER 5

The Little Booklet

T HE NEXT SEVERAL years of the ministry seem like a blur to me now, but as Vonette and I look back we can see God's hand in everything that happened. Each summer more and more college graduates, sharp young men and women who wanted to make their lives count for the Lord, joined us for training in personal evangelism and discipleship. Each fall we sent them to additional university campuses, where they employed a basic but effective strategy to increase their outreach among students and professors.

First, through surveys, meetings, and personal visitation, they sought to identify students and professors who were already Christians and witness to those who were not. Both believers and nonbelievers were invited to join together in College Life fellowship groups for Bible study, prayer, mutual encouragement, and training in personal outreach. While the ultimate purpose of these groups was serious, meetings were a joy to attend because our creative staff built lots of singing, laughter, skits, and wholesome comedy into each program.

Second, we as a staff sought invitations to speak to student and faculty groups, fraternities and sororities, athletic teams, student newspaper staff, and student governments. Here we would present our personal testimonies and the claims of Jesus Christ, inviting interested students to meet individually for more discussion. Quite often, the Christian students previously identified would take part in these meetings as part of their ongoing training in outreach. Such gatherings resulted first in dozens, then hundreds, and eventually thousands of students and professors accepting Christ as Savior and Lord.

Third, from the very beginning we placed a high value on follow-up and discipleship. Whenever young men or women indicated decisions for Jesus Christ, members of our staff would meet with them individually or in small groups to help them understand the essentials of their new faith. They covered subjects like assurance of salvation, how to be filled with the Holy Spirit, how to pray, how to read and benefit from God's Word, how to trust God, and other key concepts to help them build a strong foundation for a growing faith.

All of us sensed God's guidance in this approach. As important as each individual soul is to Him and to us, we felt that His command to help fulfill the Great Commission would be slow going if we sought mere spiritual addition. Winning men and women to Christ was the essential starting point, but we did not wish to stop there. By investing the time to help build these new believers in their faith and to train them to share their faith with confidence, they would then repeat the process within their own spheres of influence—with or without our presence. The result would be not only spiritual addition, but also spiritual multiplication—the potential for exponential growth in the kingdom of God.

A New Conference Center

Our staff was growing. So were the number of students coming together during the school year and during the summer months for training in Christian growth and personal evangelism. Even the large "castle" in which Vonette and I lived with Dr. Mears was strained to capacity from all the activity. But the Lord knew far better than we did what the future held and what our needs would be. In 1956 I received a call from Bill Greig, Jr., then chairman of Midwest Keswick, a large coalition of Christian camp meetings, asking if Campus Crusade would be interested in receiving a gift of land. The five-acre tract was in Mound, Minnesota, on the shore of beautiful Lake Minnetonka. His group could no longer use the property and they were looking for an organization that could use it effectively for the glory of God.

"Come out and look it over," Bill invited. "If it fits your needs, it's yours."

I was thankful for the offer, but it wasn't until I saw the property that I fully appreciated the gift. It was a breathtakingly beautiful location. The buildings were old and mostly decrepit and there was only a foundation for a future chapel-dormitory building, but the land offered wonderful promise. As I toured the grounds, I imagined the buildings spiffed up with renovations and fresh coats of paint, the chapel-dormitory complete, and hundreds of students and laypeople gathering for Christian training and fellowship in God's magnificent outdoors. We gratefully accepted title to the property, and during the next year friends of the ministry donated funds to help us complete the chapel-dormitory complex and remodel the other buildings. Although our headquarters was still in Southern California, Mounds became our conference center.

Completing the renovations came right down to the wire. We had scheduled our first training conference at the new site for the summer of 1958, and more than 150 students arrived to see workmen and volunteers scurrying about the grounds, still hammering nails and painting walls. In fact, many students joined the workers to help finish the job. It was chaotic but fun, and we all rejoiced at how God had provided us with a beautiful retreat where Christians could gather from across the country.

The Basic Message

Prior to this summer training conference, something else happened—an event that would prove pivotal not only in the ministry of Campus Crusade for Christ but eventually in the personal outreach of millions of Christians around the world. I must confess it began because I took personal offense at something a guest speaker said to the conferees—about me!

He was an outstanding Christian sales consultant and friend. In his talk he emphasized that a successful salesman must develop a clear, simple, understandable presentation that he can use over and over again. Salesmen call this the KISS principle: Keep It Simple, Stupid. He warned us that when a salesman grows tired of hearing himself give the same message and develops "presentation fatigue," he often changes the presentation and loses his effectiveness.

His next statement startled me. "In sharing Christ, we need to develop a simple, understandable, logical presentation just like the successful salesman does. We need to stick with that message and not yield to presentation fatigue."

I did not agree with him. I felt that God honored spontaneity—sharing as the Holy Spirit leads instead of giving a prepared, "canned" approach. But if the speaker's first statement startled me, the next remark almost knocked me from my chair.

"Your leader, Bill Bright, thinks he has a special message for each of the different groups to whom he speaks. He has ministered on skid row, in prisons, and now to college students and laypeople. I have never heard him speak, but I would be willing to wager that he has only one message for everyone. Basically, he tells them all the same thing."

I squirmed in my seat and hoped that my resentment did not show on my face. How could I, or anyone else truly committed to serving God, not be led by Him to speak with originality in every situation? How could this speaker have the audacity to embarrass me like this in front of my fellow staff?

When the meeting was over, I was still feeling irritated over the speaker's message. But as I began to reflect on exactly what I did say in various witnessing opportunities, I asked myself: *Do I share the same basic message with everyone? Is my message really that simple?*

I retreated to my quarters, asked the Lord what He wanted to teach me, and picked up a pen. For the next two hours, I wrote down my basic presentation and was amazed to discover that our guest speaker had been right. Without realizing it, I had been saying basically the same thing in every witnessing situation, whether to men in the Bowery or men in business suits, university students, professors, or laypeople. With just a few variations to relate to their personal situations, the gospel message itself was basically the same every time I talked with someone. In most situations my approach was effective.

What I wrote that day was known as "God's Plan for Your Life," a positive, twenty-minute presentation which I asked the staff to memorize and use in their evangelistic speaking opportunities. Within one year, our combined effectiveness in sharing Christ dramatically multiplied. The salesman had been right!

Soon we felt the need for a shorter version of God's Plan, so I prepared an outline, complete with key Scripture verses and diagrams. Again, we had the staff memorize it. For several years we actually wrote it out on the back of the Van Deusen Letter, a letter with an evangelistic emphasis that I wrote. We used these to share Christ with others. But as more students and Christian adults became involved in our training conferences, it became apparent that we needed to make the presentation available in printed form.

Thus, in a roundabout way, that one guest speaker's remark (and my reaction to it) led to the birth of an evangelistic tract for which Campus Crusade may be best known today: the *Four Spiritual Laws* booklet. As of January 1, 1999, we estimate that approximately three billion copies have been printed in over 200 languages of the world.

Obviously, we had no idea back in the 1950s what kind of impact this simple publication would have. We simply wanted a brief, distilled essence of the gospel message to assist in our outreach among non-Christian students and adults, something that would also serve the layperson who may not have much training or confidence in personal evangelism.

The title of the booklet, *Have You Heard of the Four Spiritual Laws?*, came from our emphasis on four fundamental principles in the gospel. Just as there are physical "laws" governing the physical universe (such as the law of gravity), so there are spiritual laws that govern the spiritual universe. These four laws are:

1. God loves you and offers a wonderful plan for your life.

2. Man is sinful and separated from God, thus he cannot know and experience God's love and plan for his life.

3. Jesus Christ is God's only provision for man's sin. Through Him you can know and experience God's love and plan for your life.

4. We must individually receive Jesus Christ as Savior and Lord, then we can know and experience God's love and plan for our lives.

Each principle is validated by key Scripture passages and further explanation.

The presentation then provides a suggested prayer by which the reader can thoughtfully invite Jesus Christ into his life according to our Lord's promise in Revelation 3:20. A few final pages provide information on the assurance of salvation, Scriptures to read, how to grow in one's new relationship with Christ, and the importance of getting involved in a good church.

I still rejoice as I reflect on the first printing of that booklet and how, at the last second and with God's guiding hand, we avoided a critical mistake. Originally, our first principle emphasized man's sinful nature; the second then underscored God's love. I had completed my final edit and, tired from a great deal of traveling, went upstairs to bed while Vonette and some staff women finished the typing. Just as I was drifting off to sleep, I sat straight up in bed. I thought, *There's something wrong about starting this written presentation with the negative note about man's sinfulness.* I flung the covers aside, got out of bed, and paced the carpet, repeating those words in my mind. *Something's not quite right...*

Why not start where God Himself starts, with His love? I remembered being drawn to Christ myself when I was overwhelmed with God's love for me. Would other people want to know more if they first hear the positive affirmation that the Creator of the universe loves them personally? How could anyone say no to Christ if they truly understood how much He loves them?

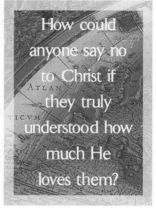

We needed to start with the positive! I went to the head of the stairs and called down to Vonette and our associates to reverse the sequence of laws one and two, which they did. It seemed like a simple adjustment.

It was years before I learned how this change had traumatized one of the staff women working with Vonette that evening. "Bill," she confided, "I was so distressed over your last-minute change that I cried that night. I was afraid you were beginning to dilute the gospel because you placed such a strong emphasis on God's love instead of on man's sin. Now, in retrospect, I realize that this is one of the greatest things that has ever happened to the Campus Crusade ministry."

Stories of Excitement and Fruitfulness

I could fill volumes with stories of how God has used this simple little booklet to reach men, women, boys, and girls around the world. And just as significantly, He has used it to help encourage Christians, who sometimes were skeptical or fearful, to share their faith with confidence. I remember one Christian leader who introduced himself to me after one of my speaking engagements. "I've been witnessing for years," he told me, frustration tinging his voice. "But I've seen very few people receive Christ as a result of my efforts. Can you tell me what I'm doing wrong?"

"What do you say when you seek to introduce a person to Christ?" I asked.

He explained his presentation, which was long, complicated, and sermonic. I sensed that the large number of Bible verses he used and his lengthy commentary on each verse confused most people and hindered them from making an intelligent decision.

"Let me encourage you to try an experiment," I challenged him. "Let me give you a gospel booklet that is concise, to-the-point, and focuses on Jesus Christ. Use it in all of your witnessing opportunities for the next thirty days, then let me know what happens."

He could not wait thirty days to call me. Just two weeks later, I answered my phone to hear his ecstatic voice. "Bill, I can hardly believe it! By simply reading through the booklet with others, I've seen more people come to Christ in the last two weeks than I had previously seen in several months."

Frank, a layman in his mid-thirties, told me about his cousin, a computer whiz who likes to think everything through in scientific terms. One day the young man mentioned to Frank that he wondered about the existence of God and about the role of a Creator. "You know," Frank replied, "I believe that just as there are physical laws that govern science, there are also spiritual laws that govern man's relationship with God. Here's a booklet that explains it."

Frank read aloud through the *Four Spiritual Laws* booklet as his cousin looked on. It made sense to the young man. He eagerly prayed the suggested prayer to ask Jesus Christ into his life, then took the booklet and led his fiancée to Christ.

A few years ago I was visiting some dear friends, a doctor and his wife, and they asked if I would talk to her brother about Christ. He is a respected economist and one of America's foremost businessmen. "He's not a Christian, but he's a wonderful person," they explained. "We'll setup an appointment for you."

A few weeks later when I met her brother, we chatted for a few minutes about world conditions and the urgency of the moment in which we live. "You know," I offered, "I think the only one who can help us solve these crises is Jesus Christ."

I watched his face for a response. "I sure agree with that," he nodded.

"I have something I want to show you." I pulled out a *Four Spiritual Laws* booklet, held it so he could read along, and read through the gospel presentation. After each principle, he commented, "That makes sense. I agree with that."

We read through the suggested prayer. "Does this prayer express the desire of your heart?" I asked.

"It sure does."

"Would you like to pray it right now?"

"I sure would."

So together we prayed asking the Lord to come into his life. About six months later I visited him at his office in New York City. "You know, my life has made a 180-degree turn since I met you," he smiled.

I recall one of the most famous pastors in America. I am sure thousands have received the Lord through his church, and his television and writing ministries, but he had never experienced the joy of personally leading someone to Christ. His daughter had taken our training on how to use the *Four Spiritual Laws* booklet, then passed her training on to him. Very late one night, he called me rejoicing that, for the very first time, he had just led someone to a personal relationship with Jesus Christ. I'll take late calls like that any time!

Former U.S. Senator Bill Armstrong recalls how the booklet was a factor in his own decision for Christ:

"After a few years in Washington, my wife, Ellen, began to seriously study the Bible, meeting with dedicated Christians who led her to a relationship with Jesus Christ. As she explained her new relationship to me, I realized that she had discovered something worthwhile and meaningful that could also become meaningful for me. For the first time I understood that being a Christian is far more than merely belonging to a church or trying to live a good life.

"In November 1975, through the encouragement of one of my colleagues, I heard Bill Bright speak. Later, Dr. Sam Peeples, one of Bill's associates from the Christian Embassy in Washington, took me through the *Four Spiritual Laws*, explaining how I could receive Christ. As we prayed together, I asked Jesus Christ to forgive my sins and to be my Savior and Lord. It was an easy decision to make because I knew that something vital was missing in my life—something only Christ could provide.

"My life began to change immediately, not in a single moment, but gradually each day. Most significantly, Christ became the center of our family life. I desired to be an example to my family of trusting the Lord with all of our day-to-day concerns."

The Work of God

The stories go on and on, from high school and university campuses to the halls of Congress; from office break rooms to the beaches during spring break; from neighborhoods to locker rooms; from large gatherings to two friends visiting over coffee—city to city, country to country, continent to continent. We have never contended that this portrayal of the gospel is the only way to present Christ, or that it is the best way. There is no magic in the *Four Spiritual Laws* booklet. God blesses its use because it contains the distilled essence of the gospel, presented in a logical, easy-to-understand manner.

When we went to press with the first edition, we had no clue how powerfully He would use our small effort. Approximately three billion copies have been printed in every major language in the world as well as in hundreds of smaller languages. Scores of other Christian organizations and denominations have adapted it for their own use, and hundreds of similar evangelistic booklets have sought to duplicate its effectiveness. To our Great God and Savior be all glory and praise.

Many are the times I have thanked God for His leading in the development of this outreach tool—a simple little booklet that would become a cornerstone in the growing outreach and effectiveness of Campus Crusade for Christ. Because the gospel is always contemporary, the *Four Spiritual Laws* presentation remains to this day a key component in our U. S. and worldwide evangelistic strategies.

CHAPTER 6

You Shall Receive Power

L EADING A GROWING organization brings dozens of challenges each day—some small, but many of them daunting. An ongoing challenge, of course, was raising funds to keep the ministry going and to expand it to other campuses as well as to additional target groups. As we continued to grow and train new staff, I found that raising the funds to cover staff salaries, modest as they were, was consuming a significant amount of my time and energy—commodities that I would much prefer to focus toward direct evangelism and training opportunities.

I thought and prayed about this for several months, consulting with Vonette and our board about possible alternatives. Of course, we wanted to be sure that our staff received enough remuneration to provide their basic needs of housing, food, clothing, transportation, and the other necessities of living and raising families. At the same time, we were funding the upkeep of our conference center, renting other facilities, transporting staff and guest speakers to various training conferences, printing ministry materials, and paying for the myriad miscellaneous costs that any thriving organization encounters.

After much prayer, I sensed the Lord leading me to suggest a dramatic shift in remuneration for our staff. They were on the front lines of ministry, and most of them had already cultivated a team of prayer supporters in their hometowns and churches, and with family and college friends. Often our staff would write to their support teams to report how God was honoring their faithful prayer by changing hundreds of lives each year through the outreach of our staff. So the thought occurred to me: *Why not have each staff member raise his own financial support?* We would have the leadership of Campus Crusade determine a fair level of remuneration for everyone, with prorated adjustments to allow for the difference in need between single and married staff. Additional adjustments could compensate for the number of children in a staff couple's family. Each staff member would be responsible for developing his own team of prayer and financial supporters to pray for his ministries and fund his salary and work expenses.

The board of directors approved the plan, and we began the transition. Our existing staff began raising their own financial support. As part of our new staff training, we provided sessions and materials to help our new men and women develop their own support teams. Following their intensive three-week summer training program, new staff returned home to speak before church and civic groups, visit interested individuals, and write to their mailing list of friends and families, telling of Campus Crusade's goal of helping fulfill the Great Commission in this generation. Potential supporters were invited to make a personal investment in the ministry of the new staff member by committing to pray regularly for that individual and to make a monthly investment in his or her personal front-lines ministry. All funds would come through the national headquarters as tax-deductible donations to Campus Crusade for Christ. Our accounting department would keep careful track of each staff member's account and debit the account bi-weekly for salary checks.

New Kinds of Fund-Raising

While somewhat intimidating at first, the process of developing one's personal support team has proven to be one of the greatest blessings God provides in the first months of ministry for our new staff. As new staff members report to their assignments with their support team in place, they are consistently amazed and excited at how God has provided for them. Some support team members may be able to pledge prayer support only—but all of us consider a pledge of prayer far more valuable than finances. Others may be able to pledge as little as $10 or $20 per month or as much as $1,000 or more. Other interested parties may not be able to make a monthly commitment but give a quarterly or annual gift. Other staff have entire churches supporting them through their annual missions or outreach budget. Every individual team member or group, no matter how little or how much they can give, is highly regarded because we know that their ongoing prayer is crucial to God's supernatural work through our staff.

New staff members are consistently amazed and excited at how God has provided for them.

Another decision we made at this time was that, in the process of raising their financial support, each staff member would help fund the ongoing administrative efforts of the ministry—efforts that provide either direct or indirect support to their ministry in the field. We determined that 17 percent of incoming funds from ministry supporters would be designated to help with ongoing administrative expenses of the international headquarters, which in turn served the worldwide staff.

We made this applicable for all staff, including Vonette and myself. As a result we have all raised funds and been remunerated according to the same salary structure. This not only made a significant difference in the funding of the ministry, but it also dramatically broadened our base of prayer as literally thousands of ministry supporters pledged ongoing prayer support for the effectiveness of their personal "missionary" on the front lines of ministry.

Stories of Fruitful Ministry

As word continued to spread about the impact of Campus Crusade for Christ, more and more invitations and opportunities came our way. While we continued to recruit and train new staff to expand the outreach to other university campuses, we also received invitations to train groups of adults in how to live in the power of the Holy Spirit and how to effectively witness to others. As we traveled to churches and conference centers, and brought in groups to our own training facilities, we realized that God was opening up a whole new area of opportunity for helping to fulfill the Great Commission.

Eventually we developed the Lay Ministry, a big part of which was the Lay Institute for Evangelism, held at various locations across the country. At these weekend seminars, Christian adults, often frustrated by a lack of joy or fruitfulness in their walks with God, learned how to appropriate and live in the power of the Holy Spirit and how to share their faith. Part of each weekend's training was an actual witnessing experience where pairs of participants would go door to door, sharing Christ in neighborhoods using witnessing tools such as the *Four Spiritual Laws*.

Often these laypeople would feel anxious about their first witnessing experiences. But after training and prayer, they would embark on an afternoon of sharing, then return with glowing faces and gather to testify of what God had done. "I was so nervous," their stories would usually begin, "but the Lord gave me courage..." They would go on to tell how they had had the privilege of introducing someone to Jesus Christ that day.

One such story represents the hundreds of thousands that have been shared over the years. Sara, in her mid-thirties, teamed up with another woman to do neighborhood visitation as part of a Lay Institute weekend. We had provided our conferees with a simple survey in which they ask residents a few questions about the role of spiritual faith in their lives. If the resident expressed interest in hearing a brief presentation of how they can know God personally, conferees shared the gospel with them using the *Four Spiritual Laws* booklet.

"We were both extremely nervous when we began," Sara reported, "and we were actually relieved when there was no answer at the first house we visited! But at the second house, a young woman answered the door and invited us in to take the survey. When we asked if she would like to hear how she could have a personal relationship with God through Jesus Christ, she said yes.

"So, just as we had been trained to do, I held the *Four Spiritual Laws* booklet so she could see it and began reading it with her. Meanwhile, my partner prayed silently. When we got to the suggested prayer, I asked, 'Does this prayer express the desire of your heart?' Our host said, 'Yes, it does.' I asked, 'Would you like to pray this prayer, right now, to receive Jesus Christ as your Savior?'

"And you know what? She did! It was a beautiful experience to lead her in that prayer and to see the joy in her eyes as she gave her life to Christ. We went through the follow-up material, gave her some more literature to help her in her new commitment, and asked for her name and address so we could send her additional follow-up material and encouragement.

"My partner and I left rejoicing. We had had the incredible experience of helping someone receive Christ as Savior and Lord. It was the first time for both of us—but it will not be the last!"

I rejoice every time I hear stories like Sara's, and I have heard thousands. Most Christians just do not realize what God wants to do through them, if only they will obey His call to share the gospel with all who will listen. In recent years I devoted a full book to helping individuals learn how to share

Christ with others: *Witnessing Without Fear: How to Share Your Faith with Confidence.* With a foreword by Billy Graham and dozens of true stories and step-by-step instructions, it is designed to help even the most timid Christian effectively lead others to Jesus Christ. We were thrilled and humbled when it was awarded the Gold Medallion Award for Excellence by the Evangelical Christian Publishers Association. God has used it mightily in helping individuals and church groups learn to share their faith.

The Power of the Holy Spirit

While practical training in witnessing is important, there is a far more essential component to successful outreach: being filled and empowered by the Holy Spirit. Vonette and I have always been aware that we can do nothing for God in our own power; in fact, if we are not fully yielded to Him and His guidance, we could actually do His cause more harm than good.

Early in my Christian walk, I sought for many years to understand the Person and work of the Holy Spirit. I had on numerous occasions enjoyed wonderful fellowship with the Lord and even had several experiences when I knew the Holy Spirit had touched my life and used me. Yet I knew nothing of how to live under His control. Hungry for all God had for me, and longing to be a man of God whatever the cost, I made a special study of the Person and work of the Holy Spirit. My search included not only God's Word but nearly every book I could find on the subject.

I discovered that our Lord Jesus Christ said, "You will receive power when the Holy Spirit comes on you; and you will be My witnesses..." (Acts 1:8). I realized from the very beginning that we needed power from God, through His Holy Spirit, every waking moment to live lives pleasing to Him and to be effective witnesses for Him. Paul wrote, "The fruit of the Spirit is love, joy, peace, patience, kindness, goodness, faithfulness, gentleness and self-control" (Galatians 5:22,23).

Why, then, were more Christians not experiencing true joy in their lives? Why were they struggling with anxiety, impatience, a lack of love, and the desires of the flesh?

The words of W. A. Criswell underscore an important point:

> Without the presence of the quickening Spirit there is no conviction, no regeneration, no sanctification, no cleansing, no acceptable works. We can perform duties without Him, but our service is dull and mechanical. Life is in the quickening Spirit.

Indeed, we did not want our service to be dull and mechanical, but to be brimming with life and joy and effectiveness.

As a result of my study, the Lord impressed me that in order for Christians to be effective, bold witnesses for Him, and thus help fulfill the Great Commission in this generation, they need to understand who the Holy Spirit is and how to appropriate and walk in His power every moment of every day. If Christians are not living in victory and do not have a passion for souls, it is likely that they are not walking in the power of the Holy Spirit. Instead of giving Christ the throne of their lives, they allow their own self-interests and egos to dominate the throne.

I began speaking about this, and we began to incorporate the ministry of the Holy Spirit into our ongoing training. However, it was not until late one night in Newport Beach, California, that the concept came together in a way that would revolutionize the ministry of Campus Crusade for Christ, as well as the lives of countless individuals in the coming years. Dan Fuller invited Vonette and me to spend a few days in the beach home of his parents, Dr. and Mrs. Charles Fuller. Dr. Fuller conducted the world-famous radio program, "The Old-Fashioned Revival Hour," and was the founder of Fuller Theological Seminary. Vonette and I were both very tired. Our schedules had been extremely busy and crowded with no vacation for several years, and we could think of nothing more inviting than having a few days to sleep, lie in the sun, and swim in the Pacific Ocean.

The midnight hour had come and gone by the time we arrived and unpacked. Sometime near 1 a.m., we wearily climbed into bed, fully expecting to be asleep by the time our heads hit the pillows.

But God had other plans—as He so often does. As I turned over to go to sleep, my mind was suddenly flooded with the wonderful truths I had been reading about the role of the Holy Spirit in the life of the Christian. I tried to fall asleep,

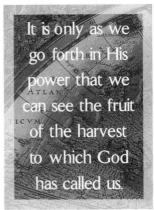

It is only as we go forth in His power that we can see the fruit of the harvest to which God has called us.

but could not. Finally, all that I had been studying and speaking about was becoming clearer and more practical to me than ever. Fearful that I might forget these thoughts if I did not write them down, I got up to look for pencil and paper. There was no paper! Among our clothing, I located several shirt boards, the kind laundries use to wrap cleaned-and-pressed shirts, so I began writing on them. After filling the shirt boards, I found some brown wrapping paper and continued to write furiously. The result was "You Shall Receive Power," an article explaining in layman's terms the role of the Holy Spirit in the life of the believer.

The essence of this article became another foundational cornerstone to the ministry of Campus Crusade for Christ, something we emphasize in our ongoing training in evangelism, discipleship, and Christian living. The material has been incorporated in our popular Bible study course, *The Ten Basic Steps Toward Christian Maturity,* and *The Transferable Concepts* series—brief self-contained studies on key components of the successful Christian life. I have also written two books, *The*

Holy Spirit: Key to Supernatural Living and *The Secret: How to Live With Purpose and Power.* I recommend them to anyone who would like to better understand how to appropriate daily the power of the Holy Spirit.

We later condensed the material into a brief presentation the same size as the *Four Spiritual Laws* booklet and titled it *Have You Made the Wonderful Discovery of the Spirit-Filled Life?* This booklet has now been printed in the tens of millions and is being used all over the world to help lead worldly, fruitless Christians into an abundant and fulfilling life in the Spirit.

The moment-by-moment ministry of the Holy Spirit is something that we continue to strongly emphasize among our staff. It is only as we go forth in His power, and under His guidance and control, that we can truly see the fruit of the harvest to which God has called us.

With this foundation, God began leading us into another adventure that would once again change our ministry for His glory.

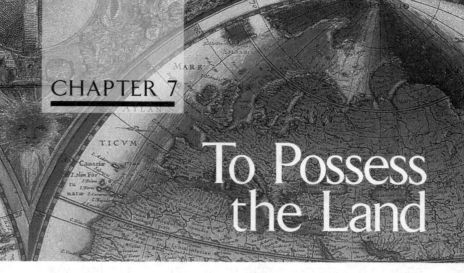

CHAPTER 7

To Possess the Land

B Y 1960 OUR STAFF numbered more than one hundred, and we were serving Christ on forty campuses in fifteen states. By then we had also established ministries in Korea and Pakistan.

With the growth of the ministry, we had also outgrown our conference facilities at Mound, Minnesota, and we began to intensify our search for a solution to our expansion problem. We knew that we must either build or purchase larger facilities in the Lake Minnetonka region or find more adequate facilities elsewhere. It was then that word came from a long-time friend, George Rowan, president of the R. A. Rowan Company in Los Angeles, that the famous Arrowhead Springs Hotel and Spa, which had been closed for most of the last four years, was for sale at a "greatly reduced price."

I agreed to look at Arrowhead Springs in the foothills above San Bernardino, California, assuming that this beautiful hotel would have deteriorated considerably from the lush days when it hosted some of the biggest names in the entertainment and business worlds. To my surprise, it was all in amazingly good condition. Except for some peeling paint on the outside of the building, there seemed to be little wrong with it. One could not haggle too much over a little paint!

"This is a fabulous place, and it would be an ideal headquarters and training center for us," I told George, "but I am sure that the price is far beyond our means. What is the lowest price the owner would take?"

"He's asking $2 million, firm," George replied. I swallowed hard. This was an incredible amount for our organization, which had never had an extra dollar in its ten years of existence. Although we had expanded to the point that we had to have larger facilities, I could not truthfully conceive of any way to raise the kind of money that would be needed to make such a large purchase.

The $2 million figure was a good one—only a fraction of the property's appraised value of $6.7 million. The beds were even made; spare linens were in the closets; china, silverware, and cooking utensils (about $450,000 in inventory) were ready and waiting for guests. *All we would have to do would be to move in*, I thought. The place did not look as though it had been closed for much of four years.

The History of Arrowhead Springs

I did a little research and learned several interesting things about the famous resort. For example, various Indian tribes had come to this spot through the centuries, bringing their sick and wounded for healing in the natural hot mineral springs. They called the place "Holy Land," and all weapons of warfare were laid aside here.

Dr. David Noble Smith built the first hotel and spa on the property in 1854, and it was widely advertised as a health resort. When the original hotel was destroyed by fire, two others followed.

They in turn were destroyed by fire, and the present structure of concrete and steel was built in 1939, financed by a group of Hollywood film stars. Arrowhead Springs became a popular retreat for the movie colony and for top executives in the business world. Only a short distance from the heart of Los Angeles, world-famous movie stars streamed to Arrowhead Springs for relaxation and revelry.

When transportation developed so that the stars could easily travel further afield, they were attracted to Las Vegas and Palm Springs, and the Arrowhead Springs resort turned into something of a white elephant. Several different owners tried to restore the property to the status it had once enjoyed, but without success. Finally, Benjamin Swig, owner of the Fairmont Hotel in San Francisco and the historic Mission Inn in Riverside, California, bought it from the Hilton Foundation. He operated it briefly before concluding, as had his predecessors, that it had limited profit potential. After he closed it down, different groups tried to purchase it from him, and one or two parties used it for a brief time.

The remoteness and beauty of the Arrowhead Springs property immediately enchanted me.

The remoteness and beauty of the property immediately enchanted me. As we followed a winding road in the hills above San Bernardino, I reeled with the grandeur of this famous place before I ever stepped out of Mr. Rowan's automobile. I was even more impressed as we toured the spacious property—1,735 acres in all.

The grounds were beautiful and quiet. In a way, an ethereal quality permeated the place, and more than once I found myself almost whispering to Mr. Rowan as we walked among the many buildings. The caretaker showed us the ten private bungalows, dormitory facilities for several hundred, an auditorium that could accommodate 700 people, a recreation house, four tennis courts, a stable, two large swimming pools, and the 136-room, six-story, concrete-and-steel hotel. Without too much imagination, I could see as many as a thousand people here at one time. This was breathtaking compared to Mound, where our capacity was approximately 150 guests.

Could this be the answer to our dilemma—our need for larger training facilities? I wondered. Desiring to be alone to talk with the Lord, I asked Mr. Rowan and the caretaker to excuse me while I went into the hotel to pray.

Lord, Is This Your Will?

I moved past the unattended reception desk, through the empty lobby, out into the glass-enclosed Wahni Room, the click of my shoes echoing as I walked. There was a shiny bar, empty of customers. Behind it, glasses were neatly stacked, awaiting business. The shelves, where a good supply of bottles once stood, were now empty. Tables and chairs were grouped in intimate clusters so holiday visitors could look out on the city, which I could imagine would be a starry wonder at night. But it was broad daylight at that moment, and I had not come there for a drink or to see the panoramic view, but to share with the Lord the dream that was working overtime in my head.

At the entrance to the Wahni room, I fell to my knees. I bowed my head and began praying and listening, "I am overwhelmed, Lord. This place is so big and beautiful. True, we've been asking You to direct us to new facilities, the best place in the country, and I know that You will; but if this is it, where will we get $2 million to buy it? It seems too impossible to even consider. Yet I keep hearing in my heart Your voice, and it suggests that this is the place You have chosen for us. If it is, then You are going to have to make it crystal clear. How can I know for sure?"

Then, though not in an audible voice, God spoke to my heart as clearly as if there had been a public address system in the room. Unmistakably I heard Him say, "I have been saving this for Campus Crusade. I want you to have it, and I will supply the funds to pay for it."

With tears running down my face, I said, "God, I don't know how You intend to work this miracle, but I know You can, and I thank You for this gift. I claim this property in Your name and for Your glory."

I came away from that memorable visit to Arrowhead Springs convinced that Campus Crusade would one day occupy those beautiful facilities. The impression that God wanted this facility for Campus Crusade was so real that almost every day I found myself expecting a telephone call from some person telling me that he had heard about our interest in the property and would purchase it for us.

I felt certain the Lord did not want me to write letters inviting people to invest, believing instead that God had a plan already working. Vonette and I and other members of the Campus Crusade staff purposely limited our concern to prayer. For fourteen months we prayed that if God wanted us to have Arrowhead Springs, He would provide the funds in some supernatural or unusual way.

Increasingly, I knew that God wanted us to move to Arrowhead, though there was no tangible evidence of that fact. That is not to say that our faith never wavered. Sometimes I thought, *What if someone else buys the property?* Then deep down in my heart I was convinced that God would not let us have Arrowhead Springs unless it was His perfect will for us. I knew that unless this was truly God's will, to become involved in raising money for such a big project could well sabotage our spiritual ministry and destroy Campus Crusade in the process.

Making an Offer

While we were praying, we were also working. We did a feasibility study of the property, a cost analysis of what was involved in operating the grounds, figuring the cost of maintenance and repairs and the operation of the various facilities. After several weeks of careful analysis, various factors convinced us that if money could be raised for the capital investment, we could carry the load and operate in the black from the very beginning. The factors included such items as our office rental in Los Angeles, our expenses for the various training conference grounds that we rented from time to time, and the fact that the headquarters staff would live on the Arrowhead Springs campus and pay rent. A dedicated staff willing to work long hours without thought of personal pay or reward strengthened our conviction.

Then the telephone rang. Henry Hanson, the father of two students who had been influenced for Christ through our ministry, was on the line. Through him negotiations were begun with the owner, Benjamin Swig.

Though we had not asked our supporters to help us purchase the property during the fourteen months of waiting and praying, I now felt, after my conversation with Mr. Swig, that the Lord wanted me to share this opportunity with some of my close friends. Outstandingly successful men who were also dedicated to Christ and vitally interested in the ministry of Campus Crusade came to look over the property and give me their counsel. Many of our close friends, however, were far from being of one mind concerning the wisdom of making the purchase. Some were convinced that it would be a foolhardy move and poor stewardship of the Lord's money, while others believed that Campus Crusade needed training facilities such as Arrowhead Springs would supply. A few individuals supported their convictions with offers to help make the down payment.

After careful and prayerful consideration of loans and gifts, acting on the advice of these men who were interested in helping us, we decided to make an offer to Mr. Swig. The offer was a $15,000 deposit toward a $2 million purchase price, with an additional $130,000 to be paid within thirty days after we signed the contract. Amazingly, the offer was accepted. With an empty bankbook, we were buying a $2 million property! It was the greatest act of faith I had ever seen or in which I had ever had a part. We borrowed the $15,000 needed for the deposit, and on December 1, 1962, Campus Crusade for Christ International moved from its UCLA headquarters in Los Angeles to Arrowhead Springs.

We still did not have the remainder of the down payment, but thirty days later at the last minute the necessary $130,000 had been donated by interested friends. I dashed off to San Francisco to see Mr. Swig and make the payment to consummate the purchase. The monthly payment schedule was a stiff one, and there followed a series of financial cliffhangers that forced us to depend wholly upon the Lord. Every financial move was a prayerful one because we did not want the raising of funds for the new headquarters to hinder in any way the ongoing ministry of our staff across America and in other countries.

The Challenges in the First Months

From the start, God blessed and used Arrowhead Springs in a spiritual way that surpassed all of our expectations. Hundreds of young men and women and adults came for training that first year, and their lives were transformed. We envisioned the day when God would send a thousand people per week to Arrowhead Springs for training. That goal was quickly exceeded, and so many staff, students, and laymen began to respond to our training that scores of conferences eventually were held each year, not only at Arrowhead, but also on university campuses, in conference facilities, and in hotels across America.

Prior to the purchase of the new property, Arlis Priest, an outstanding Phoenix businessman, visited the grounds and volunteered, "If God should make this property available to you, I would like to give my services for one year without salary to help you get the headquarters operating efficiently." His life had been greatly affected in one of our daylong lay institutes in Phoenix and this was his way of thanking us. Imagine his surprise a few weeks later when I took him up on the offer. "How soon can you come?" I asked over the phone. "We are now ready to move to Arrowhead Springs, and we need a manager."

"I'll call you back later today and give you an answer," he replied. Within a matter of days he was with us; God used him mightily to help organize the offices and get the long-closed facilities operating efficiently. I do not know how we would have done it without him and his lovely wife, Nadine, who was not only a great help herself but also was willing for Arlis to work day and night to help us get into operation.

May 17, 1963, found several hundred friends of Campus Crusade gathered for the dedication of Arrowhead Springs as our international headquarters and conference center. One of my favorite speakers, Dr. Walter Judd, brought the dedication address, which was one of his characteristically inspiring and challenging messages. The mayor and many outstanding local officials were present. The mayor stated, "The finest thing that has ever happened to the city of San Bernardino is the coming of Campus Crusade for Christ to Arrowhead Springs." Many leaders of other fine Christian ministries graciously accepted our invitation to the ceremonies.

We were confident that if we sought first the kingdom of God, He would meet our financial needs.

Also present that day were Mr. and Mrs. Guy F. Atkinson. He was one of the world's leading builders of roads, dams, bridges, and other multi-million dollar construction projects. He was then 89 years of age—sharp, alert, and very astute— and had come primarily to hear Dr. Judd. He inquired what we planned to do with the property and asked more questions about the ministry of Campus Crusade than anyone had ever asked me in our history.

He expressed interest in helping, but he first wanted to send his attorney to look over our financial records and our non-profit corporate structure, including the bylaws. We were happy to allow him do this. After several days of careful study of the organizational structure, polices, and financial records, Mr. Atkinson announced he would like to donate $300,000 if we would raise the balance of the $1,570,000 still due. This was an exciting challenge. He gave us exactly one year to raise that amount, and we set forth with enthusiasm and determination to raise a sum so great that I could hardly comprehend the amount. It might as well have been a billion dollars, yet we were confident that God would help us.

With the passing months, however, it seemed we were not going to be able to reach our $1,570,000 goal to qualify for Mr. Atkinson's $300,000 pledge. We had an additional challenge of an offer from Mr. Swig to discount $100,000 from the balance due, plus a savings of $120,000 in interest. With Mr. Atkinson's pledge of $300,000, this amounted to a savings to the ministry of $520,000—over half a million dollars! But we were becoming aware that we were faced with an impossible task. We asked Mr. Atkinson if he would still pledge his $300,000 if we raised part of the balance by selling some of the land. He agreed to do this with the understanding that we would not sell more than 400 of our 1,735 acres.

Arlis Priest and I had interested a group of twenty laymen in the idea of purchasing $1 million worth of our land from us. We estimated that by selling approximately 400 acres we could raise that amount. With Mr. Atkinson agreeable to this, we gained new courage and approached the deadline of June 30, 1965, with confidence. In the meantime, we contacted potential contributors in an attempt to raise the balance.

In spite of the additional encouragement, we found that we would still fall short of the amount needed. I had made a commitment to the Lord that I would not allow Arrowhead Springs or the raising of funds to interfere with my personal ministry or the ministries of any of our campus staff. In fact, none of the field staff were ever asked to become involved in raising funds at any time, because we felt that it was a tangible expression of our trust in the Lord to put our spiritual ministry first. We were confident that if we sought first the kingdom of God, He would meet our financial needs.

The Deadline Arrives

In the last week prior to the deadline, Dr. Raymond V. Edman, president of Wheaton College, came to speak for an educator's conference at the same time a Campus Crusade student conference was in session. He shared with Vonette and me a very meaningful verse that God had given him that morning while he was praying for our needs. The verse was especially appropriate: "He who puts his trust in Me shall possess the land, and shall inherit My holy mountain" (Isaiah 57:13, NKJ). We will always be grateful to Dr. Edman for his special encouragement and prayers for us during those urgent days, as well as for the great ministry of his life and witness with us.

On the evening of the deadline, I met with Arlis Priest, just before I was to bring a message to the conference then in session. He informed me that we still needed $33,000. Every possible source of revenue had been exhausted. There was nothing more, humanly speaking, that we could do. After the completion of my message at about 9 p.m., I inquired again as to our progress. Though several members of the staff were gathering and praying, working and hoping, the situation remained unchanged. I assumed that there was nothing more I could do personally so I went to our cottage, too weary to give further thought to the matter.

I was dressing for bed when Vonette returned from a youth meeting with our two sons, Zachary and Bradley. "All the money must be in or you wouldn't be going to bed," she said.

I told her that was not the case, adding, "I've done all I know to do. I will have to leave the rest in the Lord's hands."

"Honey, I have never seen you give up so easily," Vonette said.

"If the miracle is going to happen, the Lord will have to do it right away," I replied.

It was 10 p.m., only two hours before the deadline.

God Had a Better Way

WE HAD BEEN PRAYING for months, but now the deadline was just two hours away and Vonette, our sons, and I prayed with a new urgency. I prayed first, then Vonette and then Zac. But it was Brad's prayer that I remember. He was only seven years old, but he spoke to the heart of the matter: "Lord, we need this money and ask You to send it right away."

After all of us had prayed and the boys had gone to bed, I reached for my Bible to read before turning out the light. As I did so, I saw a scrap of paper I had brought home from my office. I had read only one side; now I saw the other side. A friend of the ministry, Gerri von Frellick, had called me the day before and asked me to call him back.

I checked my watch and by now it was 10:30, which meant that it was 11:30 at his home in Denver, Colorado. I debated whether I should return his call at such a late hour. "Maybe Gerri wants to help," Vonette suggested. I finally decided to call him even though it was late. He answered the phone sleepily, and I apologized for waking him up. "How are you getting along with your fund-raising campaign?" he asked.

I told him that we had an hour and thirty minutes to go and still lacked $33,000. He said he wanted to send us $5,000 if it would help us meet our goal and would send it the next morning. Gerri had already given generously when we first moved to Arrowhead Springs; now he was giving again. At that point, I did not think $5,000 was going to make much difference, but I was encouraged and thanked Gerri warmly.

"You were right, Vonette," I reported. "He did have some money for us. Now we need only $28,000."

Suddenly it occurred to me that a month or so before, a businessman in Arizona had given us a piece of property not far from Denver for which we had been offered $17,000 by a local attorney. If he would pay $20,000 for the property, that would reduce the balance we needed to $8,000, and there might still be a possibility of meeting that amount. The more I thought about it the more excited I became, so I placed the call to the attorney in Colorado, who I realized was also probably in bed asleep.

I reminded him that a month ago he had offered $17,000 for the property and that we would be willing, because of a particular need, to take $22,000 for it. He countered with $18,000 and said he would wire it the next morning. I accepted his offer. Now we were within $10,000 of our goal.

I called the switchboard at the hotel and reported the news. I heard a big cheer in the background when staff and friends who had gathered to pray learned that we were within sight of our goal. With less than thirty minutes before the deadline, we had $10,000 more to raise. We were all getting increasingly excited. Surely God was going to answer our prayers and meet our need.

Dr. Walter Judd, congressman from Minnesota and former medical missionary to China before the Communist takeover, had come to Arrowhead Springs to address one of our conferences. He had just returned from speaking at a local medical association meeting and called to inquire about the progress toward our goal. "Have Bill call me," he told the switchboard operator at about fifteen minutes before midnight.

When I called, he said that he would like to give the last

$5,000, and I should call him back if his money was needed. In the meantime, Vonette's mind was working overtime. She reminded me that Al Curtis, our business manager, had set aside a $5,000 gift several months previously, money that had been given to be used wherever we felt it was most needed. We had agreed then that the money should be held for this very deadline in case of need. Yet, in the excitement of the moment I had forgotten about it. I called Al, who had just returned from Los Angeles from a futile attempt to raise funds. He verified that we had $5,000. "Get it ready," I told him.

This meant that we needed only Dr. Judd's gift of $5,000. At two minutes till midnight, I called him to be sure I had understood his offer. "I will pledge that amount," he repeated, and a minute later I called the hotel lobby and an anxious, waiting staff to announce that God had worked another miracle.

By this time Vonette and I and the members of the staff were so excited and filled with gratitude to the Lord that we decided to meet immediately in the International Theater to thank Him for the miracle. We quickly dressed and rushed to the hotel, where the auditorium was packed to overflowing with grateful staff and friends.

Never did the lyrics, "Praise God from whom all blessings flow," hold so much meaning.

For the next couple of hours, our headquarters staff, other workers, and faculty who were there for the educators' conference all joined together in singing and worshipping the Lord. It was a beautiful experience, one of the highlights of my spiritual life. Never have I heard the doxology sung with such vigor. Never did the lyrics, "Praise God from whom all blessings flow," hold so much meaning.

The good news of what God had done had to be told. Soon a letter was dispatched to thousands on our mailing list and to our personal friends and supporters, telling them that the deadline had been met and that Campus Crusade had been able to pay off the total indebtedness against the Arrowhead Springs property.

Major Trial of Faith

But the story was not ended. Less than two weeks later, a major trial of faith turned our miracle upside down.

Just ten days after I mailed the letter to our constituents, announcing the miracle, the appraisers announced that the acreage required for the $1 million sale of property was approximately 120 acres more than we had thought would be needed. The twenty businessmen headed by Jess Odom, under the leadership of our long-time friend, Roy Rogers, had agreed to purchase the land. They had planned to borrow the money from an insurance company, purchase the land and later sell it or develop it, and give the profits to Campus Crusade. But to borrow that amount, the value of the land had to be at least double the amount of the loan, which meant that $2 million worth of land had to be made available to the men to secure a $1 million loan.

When I informed Mr. Atkinson of these developments, he was disturbed and wanted to see me immediately. When he arrived at my office, he reminded me that his original agreement called for our raising in contributions and pledges the entire amount of $1,570,000 to match his contribution of $300,000 in cash. When it was discovered that we were not going to be able to raise that amount, he had agreed to our selling 400 acres of land.

"I remember when land in nearby Orange County was selling for a few dollars an acre and some of it is now selling for as much as $50,000 an acre," he said. "You would be foolish to sell at this price. Whatever you do, don't sell it. And if you do, I withdraw my pledge of $300,000."

I realized that Mt. Atkinson, because of his warm friendship and interest in the ministry, was seeking to prevent us from making a terrible mistake. Nevertheless, this was a crushing blow, and after Mr. Atkinson left I closed the door behind me, fell on my knees, and wept.

The miracle had become a mirage. All of our hopes and dreams had suddenly crumbled. In the attempt to meet the challenge of Mr. Atkinson's pledge, most of our fund-raising efforts during the previous year had been focused on raising the money for Arrowhead Springs. Now since we had failed to meet this goal, we were in an impossible position financially. Not only could we not write off the debt, but we would also lose the property unless God intervened immediately. Furthermore, I would have to write the thousands of our friends who had read only a few days before that God had worked a miracle and tell them that there had been no miracle at all. There was personal humiliation involved, of course. But worse than that, the cause of Christ would suffer, and many Christians would be confused.

What was I to do? I got out my Bible and looked for help and assurance. I turned to Romans 8:28 and read, "In all things God works for the good of those who love Him, who have been called according to His purpose." Then I turned to Hebrews 11:6: "Without faith it is impossible to please God," and Galatians 3:11: "The righteous will live by faith."

Then I remembered a command from God which I had discovered some years before and which on various occasions had proved very meaningful to me: "Give thanks in all circumstances, for this is God's will for you in Christ Jesus" (1 Thessalonians 5:18).

Since the righteous are to live by faith and since "in all things God works for the good of those who love Him," I did not know of a better way to demonstrate faith than to say, "Thank You." So again I knelt to thank God for what had happened, even though I could not, on that discouraging day, see or understand His purpose in what had happened. By faith,

I thanked Him through my tears. I thanked Him that in His wisdom and love He knew better than I did what should be done, that out of this chaos and uncertainty would come a far greater miracle. There on my knees, while I was giving thanks for this great disappointment, by faith God began to give me the genuine assurance that a greater miracle really was going to happen.

Even so, the next day I began drafting the letter that would inform our friends that "our miracle" had been only a mirage. For some reason, however, I felt strongly impressed to delay mailing the letter.

A week passed. Ten days. Then Mr. Atkinson called and said that he had been talking to Arlis Priest and had an idea

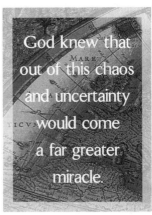

God knew that out of this chaos and uncertainty would come a far greater miracle.

he thought might solve our problem. As soon as he arrived at Arrowhead Springs, he came directly to my office. "I would like to suggest," he said, "that Campus Crusade borrow the money as an organization from the same insurance company that had offered to loan the money to the original twenty men. We should invite the men who had originally agreed to purchase the land to sign the note as guarantors. If you like this idea, I will still give Campus Crusade the $300,000 originally pledged."

I was overjoyed at his offer. This meant that we would not have to sell our acreage, which we would need one day to accommodate our rapidly expanding training program. God, in His sovereignty, knew how important that property would be to us during the next thirty years!

The twenty men, who had no interest in personal financial gain but wanted to further this ministry, readily agreed to this new arrangement and signed the note. Jess Odom, the president of the insurance company and a wonderful Christian friend of Campus Crusade, approved the loan at the lowest legal interest rate allowable. Mr. Swig, the seller of the Arrowhead Springs property, still gave us a generous discount on his note. So I tore up the letter of apology to our constituents and in its place sent another explaining how God had provided in an even better way.

I shall be forever grateful to the Lord for Mr. and Mrs. Atkinson and for their encouragement in so many ways. After Mr. Atkinson went to be with the Lord, memorial gifts from his family and friends were used to build the beautiful Guy F. Atkinson Memorial Chapel at Arrowhead Springs, which served for many years as a quiet, peaceful place of prayer for our headquarters staff and many thousands of conferees.

Expansion Plans

The purchase of Arrowhead Springs was a giant leap of faith. In addition to providing office space for our growing headquarters staff, the facility accommodated several times as many as could be housed at our training grounds in Minnesota. The first summer of 1963 found the big hotel and most of the other facilities filled, and by the second and third summers, we were overflowing during the summer peaks. By 1966, projections indicated that we would one day be training thousands each week during the summer months.

What were we to do? By the following summer we would be in the awkward position of having to turn people away—something we did not want to do. I called together a group of outstanding businessmen, planners, and builders for counsel. Norman Entwistle, our very able architect, drew up elaborate plans. One member of the board of directors agreed to chair an emergency fund-raising campaign called Operation Explosion. Warren Bradley, an outstanding Los Angeles building contractor and dedicated Christian, agreed to construct whatever facilities we chose to build without profit to himself or to his company.

Mr. Entwistle designed a beautiful complex of four dormitories and a dining-auditorium area that would accommodate a minimum of 480 and a maximum of 640, depending on the number of people assigned to each room. We were under pressure of deadlines. If we did not start building at once, it would be impossible to complete construction in time for the summer invasion of thousands of students. Though no funds were available for the construction of these buildings, the urgency of their completion was upon us and, after much prayer, we felt impressed to proceed with the building in the assurance that God would supply the funds to pay for their construction.

The bulldozers had cleared the site, the foundations were being poured, and some of the walls were beginning to rise when a newcomer (who has since become a very good friend and strong supporter of Campus Crusade) appeared on the scene. He and Arlis Priest visited the building site, and as they surveyed the hustle and bustle of busy workmen hastening the construction of the urgently needed facilities, my friend turned to Arlis and said, "Who is going to pay for these buildings?"

Arlis said, "God impressed me to share this need with you."

Our friend dropped his head as if in silent prayer and meditation and then replied, "I think I would like to be responsible to provide the funds for the building of the four dormitories. I need to talk with four of my associates and see if they are in agreement."

A short time later he came excitedly into my office to share his idea. He explained that they had been down to look over the site of the new Arrowhead Springs Village and that he had felt impressed by the Lord to encourage his associates to join with him in paying for the project. "How much money will it take?" he inquired.

"Approximately $550,000," I responded.

"I think we can swing it," he said, "if we can work out a

plan that will enable us to pay a certain amount each month over a period of years."

Soon he was on the telephone contacting his associates, and before long they were in unanimous agreement that this was a good investment of the Lord's money, which He had so graciously given them. Here they saw a chance to multiply their dollars a hundredfold so that the tens of thousands of men and women who would be trained in this new addition could help take the claims of Christ to the entire world. This gift was a true example of Christian stewardship—an inspiring example to all of us to "store up for yourselves treasures in heaven, where moth and rust do not destroy, and where thieves do not break in and steal" (Matthew 6:20).

Later, I said to my friend, "What you are doing is such a challenging and inspiring example of Christian stewardship. We would like to prepare a plaque so other friends of Campus Crusade will see what God has done through you and your associates. How would you like the plaque to read?"

My friend thought for a moment, then answered, "My associates and I want to give God all the glory for the gracious way He has blessed our business. So we would like the plaque to read: *Arrowhead Springs Village, donated by five businessmen who want to give God all the glory.*"

Later, the beautiful dining-auditorium building, also underwritten by our anonymous friends, was added to the Village. Over the years, tens of thousands of students and laypeople from across the country and around the world were trained to be disciples for our Lord Jesus Christ in these facilities.

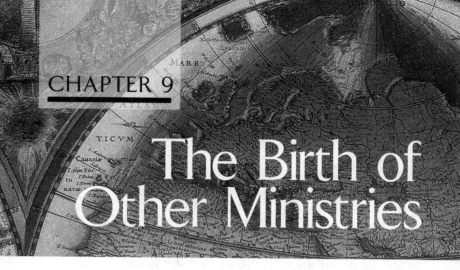

CHAPTER 9

The Birth of Other Ministries

As CAMPUS CRUSADE staff, we have discovered that when we truly train people, they are inspired to a higher dedication that inspiration alone cannot sustain. In fact, I have found that true inspiration results from a strong training program. Therefore, from the beginning our major thrusts have always been to first build disciples, then train them and send them forth to win, build, and send others for Christ and His kingdom.

Training alone cannot achieve a purpose; it must have the right focus. I believe God has blessed our ministry in such a phenomenal way because we remain focused on the following four points:

1. We are dedicated to exalting Jesus Christ and His cause in everything we do.

2. We maintain a strong emphasis on the ministry of the Holy Spirit in the life and witness of the believer.

3. We give special, detailed, comprehensive training to every staff member, student, and lay volunteer in how to live holy lives and share their faith in Christ with others.

4. We insist that each of the fifty-plus ministries are particularly dedicated to the fulfillment of the Great Commission.

Although our ministry experience and our tested methods are transferred to each type of outreach we do, each ministry is also unique with its special appeal to the group of people it serves. Let me describe our methods of training those who join our organization as full-time staff. In Chapter 10, I will explain the way we train our ministry volunteers.

New Staff Training

Our commitment to training led us to establish two types of training—first for our staff, especially new staff, and second for volunteers and laypeople who are discipled by our staff.

New staff training used to take place every summer and winter for about seven weeks. The timing was to benefit those who were graduating from college and wanted to join our staff immediately.

> Our goal is to help train tens of millions of Christians to experience and share abundant life in Christ.

who were graduating from college and wanted to join our staff immediately.

But today, God has blessed us with many mid-career applicants whose schedules and family obligations do not permit them to leave their homes for extended periods. Therefore, we have added shorter versions of new staff training in the fall and spring.

At this training, each new staff member learns the basics of the Christian life: how to walk in the power of the Holy Spirit, how to love by faith, how to witness in the Spirit, and so forth. Though many have had prior training in these concepts, they review them as a refresher course. We feel that these messages are so vital to a fruitful life and ministry that we must be sure that our staff members know these concepts thoroughly.

Each person who goes through new staff training enjoys the privilege of trusting our Lord for the personal support of their ministry. Staff members are trained in how to raise their personal support for ministry. The training Campus Crusade offers is based on research and the experiences of senior staff who have seen God use these principles to help thousands of our staff raise their own personal support.

Transferable Concepts

Our basic training methods are based on an essential biblical principle that Paul gave Timothy, his son in the faith, when he wrote, "You must teach others those things you and many others have heard me speak about. Teach these great truths to trustworthy men who will, in turn, pass them on to others" (2 Timothy 2:2, TLB). Through the years, we have developed a series of how-to's or "transferable concepts," which have helped us base our training methods on Paul's admonition. A transferable concept is a biblical truth that can be communicated to someone else, who in turn will communicate that same truth to a third person. This process goes on spiritual generation after generation without distorting the original truth. The transferable concepts we use in our training contain the basic essence of the Christian life for spiritual growth.

A "transferable technique" is the vehicle—such as a book, booklet, audiotape, videocassette, CD, DVD, and so forth—which is used to communicate a transferable concept. For example, the *Four Spiritual Laws* booklet is a transferable technique and the message it contains (how to receive Christ through faith) is a transferable concept. Although no one can ever completely master these concepts, our experience has shown us that we can teach a transferable concept in a short period of time to any sincere Christian who wishes to know it. We do this by using a transferable technique. Christians, with training, can quickly learn these concepts well enough to make them a part of their life, then pass them on to others. Our goal is to help train tens of millions of Christians around the world to experience and share the abundant life in Christ so they can help fulfill the Great Commission generation after generation.

The transferable concepts established training as an essential part of our ministry. As we began to see the need for expanded and specialized ministries beyond the college campus, our organization began to grow. What about high school students? We could train them to reach their generation. The military needed a strong witness, as did executives and laypeople. Dynamic Christian athletes could use their national platform to win others to Christ. What about prisoners? And how could we reach the masses who live outside the United States? In response to so many needs, our field ministries have grown from our beginning on the college campus to ministering across cultural boundaries to internationals, the military, women, children, inner-city areas, and cross-cultural outreaches.

Modern-Day Prodigal Son

This training and consequent ministry outreach goes hand-in-hand with Campus Crusade's commitment to aggressive evangelism. The goal is to reach people where they are with the good news of our living Christ and His love and forgiveness. In our enthusiasm to reach out and love those who do not know Christ, we do not use argumentative tones or high-pressure techniques, but take the initiative to tell people everywhere about Christ. The results are amazing.

God does miracles through any Spirit-filled Christian who is available, moment by moment, to be used by Him. For example, each year the Campus Ministry plans a spring break outreach to college students at various locations around the country. Many times I speak at these events. During one event in Daytona Beach, I heard a knock on my door in my second-floor hotel room. When I answered it, I saw a young man who asked if he could retrieve his key. He quickly explained, "I tried to toss my key from the patio area on the ground to someone on the third-floor terrace. My throw missed the third floor and the key fell on your terrace instead."

Since I firmly believe that God does not make mistakes in timing, I sensed that He had prepared this young man for this moment. I invited him in and he found his key. Then I asked him if he had a few moments to talk. As we chatted together, I explained to him the love and forgiveness that God offers through faith in Jesus Christ. We went through the *Four Spiritual Laws* together.

When we finished, he told me his story. "I grew up in the church," he said. "My mother and father are very devout Christians, but I have rejected Christianity. For some reason, I have not found satisfaction and fulfillment in the church. My parents did not want me to come to Daytona. They knew I would be involved with the wrong crowd. In violation of their wishes, I came anyway. And now, of all the places in the world, you should be here to confront me with what my mother and father have told me all these years. Surely, God has arranged this meeting."

We knelt together and prayed, and this young modern-day prodigal who had been running from the Lord surrendered his heart to the Savior.

Spiritual Multiplication

This story, which has been repeated millions of times in countless situations, shows how anyone, using a transferable vehicle like the *Four Spiritual Laws*, can simply and clearly transfer the concept of salvation to someone who is hungry to know God. This kind of transfer happens over and over in the many ministries of Campus Crusade. We call our overall training methods the "win, build, train, and send" process. In the power of the Holy Spirit, we *win* others to Christ; we *build* them in their faith through discipleship; we *train* them to share their faith and disciple new believers; then we *send* them out to reach others for Christ and train them to share their faith to begin the process all over again with the people won to Christ.

This method uses what I call *spiritual multiplication*. This biblical concept, modeled by our Savior and Lord, has made our methods much more effective. Let me explain. Usually, we think of a Christian witnessing for His Lord by winning people to Christ one at a time. That is spiritual addition. Perhaps this person is able to win three hundred people to Christ within a year. (That would be close to one person each day!) We would consider that a pretty good record. In spiritual multiplication, however, a Spirit-filled believer introduces someone to Christ, helps that new believer begin his Christian adventure, and teaches him how to share his faith effectively. Right away, the number of people witnessing has doubled. Then both the trainer and the trainee go on to each win someone to Christ and repeat the training process. Now there are four people reaching out to unbelievers with the good news of Jesus Christ. Soon the four become eight, eight become sixteen, and so on. The efforts of the first person who won his friend to Christ are multiplied many times over through effective training. As you can see, the results of spiritual multiplication are exponentially greater than that of spiritual addition. And training is the key.

The beauty of the transferable concepts (which I first wrote in the 1950s and 1960s) is that they can be adapted to fit the needs of many different types of people in any place in the world. After all, the win, build, train, and send strategy is the method Jesus and the apostles used to reach others and to train them to go out and share their faith with others. The early Church spread the good news to the then-known world during the first few centuries. This strategy also helps us expand what we are doing for Christ in each generation.

Reaching Out to Laypeople

As I mentioned earlier, after our work on college campuses was well established and flourishing, God began to lay ministry needs outside the campus on the hearts of godly men and women. As God continued to do a mighty work in the lives of thousands of students on many college campuses, laymen began to ask, "Can't you give us the same kind of training you give your staff and students?" In 1959, I began to speak at many daylong Lay Institutes for Evangelism in various cities throughout the United States. From early morning to late at night, I presented basic messages and seminars on how to live the Christian life and share one's faith in Christ more effectively. Hundreds of laypeople and pastors came for the entire day. The daylong institutes soon became weeklong and spread citywide, involving hundreds of churches and thousands of laymen and women.

The greater the response to the training, the more we realized the need for our Lay Ministry to become more than a training institute. We became even more committed to the fact that local pastors and laypeople are the key to evangelizing communities.

Eventually, the Lay Ministry served in two areas. First, the staff assisted churches (pastors and laypeople) to develop discipleship ministries. Second, the staff developed movements of spiritual multiplication within leadership groups in the community, such as business and professional people, lawyers, doctors, educators, and entertainers. The LIFE (Lay Institute for Evangelism) seminar and conference training grew out of these areas.

An integral part of the LIFE training is practical, real-life experience in how to witness. Within twenty-four hours after conference attendees arrive, they have already been trained in how to witness and have spent a few hours in the field seeking to communicate their faith to others. Today, our lay ministry is called ChurchLIFE. The methods we developed in those early years are still effective in changing the lives of laypeople and helping them minister in their communities.

As we continued to grow over the years, God began to give dedicated Christians a vision to use their talents, abilities, and concern for people in many different ways. I want to mention a few of the earliest ministries to show you how God led us to expand our efforts from the college campus to almost every area of life.

Andre Kole Ministry

In the early 1960s, Andre Kole, America's leading illusionist and foremost creator of magical effects, made a two-day visit to Arizona State University. He was only twenty-five years old, but he was already financially and professionally successful with a wonderful family. From the campus director and the work at ASU, Andre caught a vision of an intriguing new life that lay open to him. Within a short time, he developed a presentation to illustrate the *Four Spiritual Laws* through illusions. He joined our staff in 1963, and has been serving our Lord in a fruitful evangelistic entertainment ministry ever since. As of this writing, Andre's ministry continues to take him to most countries of the world, where he has presented the gospel to many millions with remarkable results.

Josh McDowell Ministry

In 1964, another talented young man joined our staff and began reaching large audiences on college campuses. Josh McDowell's insightful message to students about well-documented historical, scientific, and biblical evidences for the Christian faith produced amazing results. In addition to campus lectures, Josh wrote several books that shot onto the Christian best-seller list, including *Evidence That Demands a Verdict* and *More Evidence That Demands a Verdict*. These books are still in print today.

Because the issues that college students face have become prevalent at younger and younger ages, Josh extended his ministry from the college campus to high schools and then to junior high students. Josh has also had an impact overseas. Most recently, the Josh McDowell ministry has been involved in Operation Carelift, a humanitarian outreach to Russia and Belarus and campaigns such as "Right From Wrong" and

"Why Wait," which target the sexual attitudes of young people in America. Tens of millions have been confronted with the claims of Christ through Josh's ministry.

Student Venture

In 1966, we began to see the need for reaching high school campuses as well as older students. At this time, many college students who returned to their home communities wanted to start Campus Crusade meetings among high school students. Across the nation, unofficial Campus Crusade high school groups were springing up. To avoid conflicts and misunderstandings, I met with the presidents of Young Life and Youth for Christ who already had ministries to this age group. They informed me that they were reaching only about 1 percent of American high school students and invited us to help them. With this encouragement, we expanded our campus ministry to include high school campuses. First called the High School Ministry, Student Venture under the leadership of Chuck Klein targets high school student leaders for Christ, which results in many other students following their example.

> Often entire families are influenced for Christ through the faith of their teenagers.

Often entire families are influenced for Christ through the faith of their teenagers. For example, in 1984 Student Venture sponsored a performance by Andre Kole in San Diego. Hundreds of people indicated that they had received Christ during the event. One of those was Rob, a high school junior. When one of our staff followed up on Rob's decision, he discovered that Rob's mother and two sisters had also indicated decisions to receive Christ that same night. Student Venture staff are experiencing the same ministry results across the nation and in other countries.

The Military Ministry

In 1966, I was invited to address a community church in Atlanta established by a local businessman. This gracious southern gentleman was Col. John M. Fain, USAF, Retired. During World War II, he had served on General Douglas MacArthur's 5th Air Force staff in the Pacific, and now he was devoting most of his energies to introducing others to the Savior. Sensing his love for our Lord and his understanding of the military, I invited him to start a military division of Campus Crusade for Christ.

Today, the Military Ministry has a worldwide impact through military installations as staff and volunteers take the gospel to America's servicemen all over the globe. Under the leadership of General Dick Abel, trained men and women in the military become overseas missionaries at the government's expense as they reach beyond their bases to the world.

Music Ministry

In 1966, two hundred of our staff and students convened at Ohio State University for Operation Otherside, which was designed to saturate the campus with the claims of Christ. There I heard an outstanding singing group known as the Christian Minstrels, who had come from the University of Minnesota. The members asked me if there might be a place for them in the ministry of Campus Crusade. As we talked and prayed together, I felt impressed to invite the entire group to come to Arrowhead Springs for training that summer.

During the course of that summer, the group changed its name to The New Folk. After their training was completed, they took off for their first year of touring. From that beginning, the Music Ministry grew to include more than ten singing groups, which performed not only in the United States, but overseas as well. Each group developed a different style to communicate with various audiences such as laypeople, high school and college students, military personnel, and prison inmates. This method of presenting the ageless love of God and the exciting message of Jesus Christ has an appeal that crosses cultural barriers and communicates throughout the world.

Music evangelism is still one of the most effective ways to touch the hearts of people for our Lord. Under the name Keynote Communications, our music ministry directed by Randy Ray provides additional ministry opportunities by providing musicians and producing musical tapes, CDs, and videotapes.

Athletes in Action

Athletes have a unique platform from which to influence people and to give their testimonies. Of the first few new believers at UCLA, most were athletes—several were All-American and some nationally and internationally known. In 1967, we gave the Christian athletes a permanent place in our ministry by forming the athletic ministry that later became Athletes in Action.

I asked Dave Hannah, who had played football for Oklahoma State University, to direct the ministry. He began putting together an amateur Christian basketball team that would play other major sports teams. This provided a platform before ready-made audiences for AIA athletes to share their faith at the games.

To play major colleges and universities as an extra game in their season, Dave had to get permission from the NCAA. Then he had to find schools willing to play an unknown, untried team of former college ballplayers. Against all odds, permission was granted by the NCAA and Dave scheduled 29 games. Fortunately, no one asked Dave how many players he had or who his coach was. At the time, he had only one player and no coach! By the time the season opened, the Lord had brought together the right people. Today, AIA has a fine reputation as athletes are continuing to share their faith with millions all over the world through many types of sporting events. Under the leadership of Wendel Deyo, AIA anticipates presenting the gospel to over 1.5 billion people worldwide through athletic events in 1999.

Paragon Productions

In 1970, a ministry was formed to reach large groups of people with multimedia productions. The Paragon Productions staff developed slide shows which they presented to large crowds through simultaneous use of nine projectors and three screens. At these showings, an average of 25 percent of the viewers responded to Christ. Over the years, Paragon has continued to use technology to present the claims of Christ. In 1991, Paragon became a part of Keynote Communications and continued to serve other ministries by producing culturally relevant projects to present the gospel through music, media, and various dramatic formats.

The Great Commission Prayer Crusade

If you recall, Campus Crusade began in 1951 with a twenty-four hour prayer chain. People were praying around the clock. Year after year, we have witnessed miracles as a result of prayer.

In 1972, Vonette felt impressed to launch the Great Commission Prayer Crusade to unite women in praying for worldwide revival and for the fulfillment of the Great Commission. Women such as Mrs. Billy Graham and Mrs. Harold Lindsell, wife of the editor of *Christianity Today*, and Mrs. Fred Dienert, whose husband is a speaker with the Billy Graham Evangelistic Association, joined Vonette in addressing audiences at citywide prayer rallies. The response was tremendous, not only among women, but also among men.

The movement spread beyond the borders of our country to many parts of the world. In 1978, a personal prayer diary was developed to help Christians pray for specific concerns and areas of the world. Today, more than 100 countries of the world have Prayer Coordinators.

In 1983, the Great Commission Prayer Crusade was divided into two ministries: the U.S. Prayer Ministry and the International Prayer Ministry. These two ministries play a vital role in bathing our efforts in prayer and bringing crucial concerns before our Lord. These prayer efforts have been led by Earl Picard, E. V. Davis, and Ben Jennings since 1983. Dan Peterson was appointed director of the worldwide prayer and fasting ministry in 1998.

The Ever-Expanding Vision

The expansion continued. From the '60s to today, staff men and women have translated their visions of reaching the world into practical ministries that touch the lives of people where they live and work. Chapter 15 includes "bios" of major ministries within our organization, and the Ministry and Project Profiles in Appendix A provide brief descriptions of our other ministries. The Ministry and Project Directory in Appendix B provides more information, phone numbers, and E-mail addresses for all our ministries. I urge you to take time to read about these ministries and pray about what God would have you do to help fulfill the Great Commission in our generation. If He is leading you to join us in reaching our world for Christ, we have a place where you can use your talents and abilities.

Next, I want to give you a glance at some of the amazing things that were happening during the '70s and '80s which helped the ministry see explosive growth. In the following chapter, we will explore a number of special projects and events that helped us bring the gospel to millions of people across the country. Once again, God led our staff to step out in faith—and see Him work in wondrous ways.

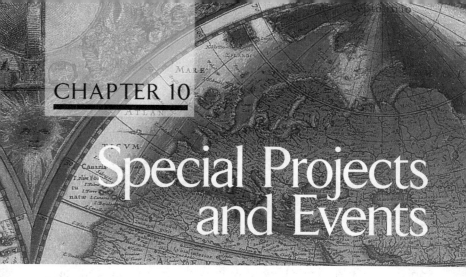

CHAPTER 10

Special Projects and Events

F ROM THE BEGINNING, as staff of Campus Crusade, we have tried to maximize the opportunities God has given us to help reach others for Christ. We believe deeply that God will always work His miracles if and when we truly make ourselves available to be used by Him. The history of Campus Crusade has borne out that truth. One proof is how God has used the ministry to launch a number of special projects and events in our country and throughout the world. Each project had its own unique strategy, but with the same purpose—to help fulfill the Great Commission. Only the methods and the timing change. Some events have been one-time efforts, others have continued year after year.

In this chapter, I would like to describe several of the major events and projects that our U.S. staff has coordinated over the years. Only the Lord knows the tremendous results that have occurred through these projects. I thank God that He provides the leadership, finances, and opportunities to accomplish what He lays on our hearts to do for His kingdom. I sincerely believe that since the Great Commission is His plan, He will always provide the necessary finances, materials, and everything we need to accomplish any task. Of course, we must keep our hearts and motives pure and do everything for His glory.

Spring Break Outreaches

One of the first strategies began during "Bal Week" in 1965. Throughout Easter vacation, about 30,000 students from California and surrounding states crowded the sunny beaches at Balboa and Newport Beach in Southern California. For years, Bal Week had been one of the biggest headaches for local police as thousands of students became involved in all kinds of delinquent behavior.

Our staff believed that something could be done to take the claims of Christ to these students. A strategy was developed to train students how to walk in the power and control of the Holy Spirit and to communicate their faith in Christ with thousands of beach-goers. The training took place in the mornings; the afternoons and evenings were spent at the beaches in personal and group contacts with students.

The results were startling. Many students had time to sit and listen. Trained students sat down with a sun-baked coed and shared the *Four Spiritual Laws* booklet or another ministry tool. The impact was so great that delinquency and vandalism were greatly lessened, and before the end of the week, the police were giving violators an alternative of either going to jail or talking with a member of the Campus Crusade team.

In a converted bar called The Hunger Hangar, several members of our team provided refreshments and personal counseling to hundreds of lonely students. Hung across the front of the temporary summer headquarters was a banner: "Christ Is the Answer." On the other side of the street, a group of fraternity men hung a sign from their apartment which read: "Booze Is the Answer." But in the days that followed, these men made their way one by one to The Hunger Hangar. At first they came out of curiosity and then from a genuine interest that developed as team members talked to them about Christ and introduced them to the Savior. Eventually all the young men met Christ, and the "Booze Is the Answer" sign came down.

From its beginning at Balboa and Newport Beach, the ministry soon spread to other beaches. Daytona Beach, Ft. Lauderdale, Panama City, Ocean City, Lake Tahoe, Cape Cod, Santa Cruz, Colorado River, and other resort areas became the scene of Campus Crusade activity as thousands of staff and students invaded these areas each year to give witness to the living Christ.

The Spring Break outreach continues to be a big success with our U.S. Campus Ministry. Today the Spring Break location in Florida is Panama City Beach and it is called the Big Break, but the focus is the same. Students still come to the annual spring break conference to tell their fellow students about Jesus Christ. Eventually, the vision is that Big Break will not be hindered by location. Since Florida is a long trip for many campuses in the West, these campuses plan to organize a West Coast Big Break. Some campus ministries already do outreaches to the inner city or even take overseas trips to give students a broader vision of the needs of the world.

Summer Projects

The success of the Spring Break outreaches prompted us to expand the format to involve students in a similar type of program for an entire summer. The Summer Projects gathered students for training to help them grow in their Christian walk. The plan is simple. A selected team of students comes to a resort area, locates jobs, and settles into a normal work routine. At the same time, a Campus Crusade staff team arrives to live with the students. After work hours, the staff members spend time with the students, helping them acquire effective evangelistic skills. The constant influx of tourists and vacationers in most spots provided ample opportunity for students to practice one-to-one evangelism.

The Summer Projects have been so effective that church members in the area are ecstatic to see the students return each summer. Employers beg students to work for them because of the quality of life evident in the young people. And thousands of people on the beaches and in the parks come to know Christ personally through the witness of these students.

Some staff minister to international students. We have found that students studying in the United States are generally more open to the gospel than they are in their home countries. They represent the future leadership of the countries from which they have come. When those who respond to the message of Christ and receive training return to their homes, they often become powerful influences for Christ.

In recent years, we have added the inner cities and numerous international locations (which change every year depending on the political climate of each country), as well as internships at our international headquarters where students can enhance their professional skills while serving in the kingdom. We estimate that as many as 75 percent of our full-time Campus Ministry staff participated in a U.S. Summer Project as students. As you can see, recruiting future laborers for the harvest is an added benefit to the success of Summer Projects.

EXPLO '72

In 1969, I was sitting on the platform of the great City Auditorium in Minneapolis during the U.S. Congress on Evangelism. Together with evangelist Akbar Haqq of India, I was enjoying one of Dr. Billy Graham's messages. During the message, I leaned over and mentioned briefly to Dr. Haqq that I had a strong impression from the Lord that Campus Crusade should sponsor a congress on evangelism—primarily to train young people in how to share their faith.

"Bill," he replied, "I think you should do it and you should ask Billy to be involved."

After returning to Arrowhead Springs, I presented the idea to our ministry directors, some of whom were enthusiastic. Others were skeptical about undertaking such a big task. Finally after several months, we were in agreement to proceed. So we began talking and praying about assembling possibly 100,000 students in a major city in America for such a congress. The suggested time for the event was the summer of 1972.

Paul Eshleman, our campus director in Madison, Wisconsin, agreed to manage the project which we called EXPLO '72. In March, we worked out details with Dallas city officials to hold the event in their city. As Paul and I met with incredulous officials at the Dallas Convention Bureau and the Chamber of Commerce to discuss our plans, the task became realistically clear. We were going to be moving a city into a city! The responsibilities of the EXPLO staff were mammoth: building a national promotional strategy, including radio and TV spots, a promotional film, newspaper releases, inviting Christian leaders from across the U.S. to speak, arranging for rooms, transportation, and registration for 100,000 people. We prayed for every detail of the event, especially that the Lord would cause many thousands to see a need in their lives for a closer walk with Him, a desire to share His message of love and forgiveness with others, and practical ways of doing just that.

In February 1972, only four months before EXPLO began, only nineteen delegates had registered. But by the opening date, the total number of registered delegates swelled to about 85,000. They came from seventy countries, pouring into Dallas by plane, automobile, bus, bicycle, in campers, and hitchhiking. During the long hours of waiting to register that day, many of the conferees sat on their suitcases in the midst of the Dallas heat, studied their Bibles, sang, or prayed. Most of the delegates adopted the slogan, "You can't make it tough enough for me to complain." Their attitude was an inspiration.

EXPLO '72 was the largest week-long Christian training effort in the world up to that time. Specialized training for collegians, high school students, laymen and women, pastors, faculty members, military personnel, business executives, athletes, and 2,000 international delegates was held in 63 locations throughout the city. Workshops taught the basics of the Christian life: how to walk in the power of the Holy Spirit daily, how to experience God's love and forgiveness, how to know His will, and how to communicate His love and plan to others.

Each evening, the Dallas Cotton Bowl rang with praise to God as delegates united in song and listened to well-known speakers such as Billy Graham and E. V. Hill, who joined me as I spoke each evening. Delegates took advantage of opportunities to tell Dallas citizens that God had a wonderful plan for their lives. An estimated 25,000 people from the Dallas area indicated that they received Christ during that week.

> There is only one solution to these problems: faith in Jesus Christ and training in biblical principles.

A final rally in the Cotton Bowl was held on Friday night. It ended in a moving candlelight ceremony which symbolized the spreading of God's love from person to person throughout the world. On Saturday, the Jesus Music Festival held downtown drew an attendance of 180,000 people to hear well-known Christian musicians and messages from Billy Graham and myself. After Dr. Graham's talk, EXPLO delegates could be seen all across the long stretches of pavement sharing God's love through the *Four Spiritual Laws* with thousands of individuals hungry for a new life.

When the congress ended, 85,000 trained men and women, including thousands of students, left Dallas with a plan, resources, and a desire to capture their communities for Christ. As news reporters interviewed delegates about what the week had meant to them, the most common response was, "This week I learned how to witness for Christ." As a result, a new emphasis on evangelism with training materials was introduced to many thousands of delegates who took the materials back to their churches, youth groups, and communities all across our country. During the two months that followed, a three-hour EXPLO '72 special was broadcast over nationwide television with an estimated audience of 35 million.

Here's Life, America

One day in 1971, I was sitting with several staff members discussing the challenge of reaching our nation for Christ. We were dismayed over the increasingly obvious problems in American society, including crime, poverty, divorce, alcoholism, and drugs. We agreed that there was only one solution to these problems: faith in Jesus Christ and training in biblical principles. Yet how could we present the gospel to every man, woman, and child in our country? For several months we discussed and prayed about reaching our nation for Christ. During this planning period, eight principles emerged that became the foundation for a strategy to help reach our goal:

1. We must go where most of the people are—in the cities.
2. The resources needed were already available in and through local churches.
3. We needed local Christian leaders to commit their time and resources toward reaching their city for Christ.
4. Christians must pray and trust God for a plan to reach their city.
5. Christians would need to be trained to release their full potential for our Lord.
6. The entire city could be reached through mass media.
7. Each city must be broken down into "bite-size" pieces so individual Christians could be involved personally in reaching their city for Christ.
8. We must assist churches in developing ongoing discipleship and evangelism programs.

Through much prayer, we launched a movement that was eventually called Here's Life, America, and later, Here's Life,

World. This movement would ultimately help to introduce many millions of people to Christ.

The initial testing for the strategy was held in Atlanta, under the leadership of Bruce Cook. In February 1974, a prayer coordinator was appointed to organize a 24-hour prayer chain. But by November of that year, the Atlanta staff found themselves with no money, no computer system, no media plan, and worst of all, no committed pastors to lead a campaign scheduled to begin in five months! Then, after much prayer, Dr. Charles Stanley, pastor of the First Baptist Church, felt God leading him to assume a leadership role, and with the help of Bob Screen, an advertising consultant, we developed a campaign theme: "I found it! New life in Christ!"

By March 30, 1975, the movement included ninety churches with 4,000 trained workers, enough money to pay the early expenses for the campaign, including 122 billboards strategically located throughout the city. The billboards announced, "I found it!" After piquing the curiosity of many people, the billboards later revealed the answer: "I found it! New life in Christ! You can find it, too!" with a telephone number for interested people to call.

Miracles began to happen. The three-week city saturation campaign, in which more than 140,000 households were contacted, resulted in 25,000 phone calls from interested people. Of those, 10,000 people indicated salvation decisions for Christ!

What started in Atlanta continued for the next two years. Here's Life, America reached 246 major cities and thousands of smaller communities. Our marketing consultants estimated that 179 million Americans were exposed to the "I found it!" campaign. A total of about 7.7 million people were contacted personally and heard the message of God's love from 325,000 trained workers from 17,000 cooperating churches. More than 525,000 people indicated salvation decisions.

During those two years that the Here's Life, America movement was being planned and implemented, I lived out of a suitcase. I spoke in a different city almost every day, working with students, laypeople, and pastors. I also helped raise the necessary funds to saturate the United States with the gospel by the end of 1976. That was an exciting time as we saw God work across the land, including through multiracial and multi-denominational efforts. Let me give you some highlights:

- In Philadelphia, 430 churches cooperated in reaching the city, including 100 Black churches.
- In the greater Los Angeles area, 950 churches cooperated, including 35 Asian, 67 Hispanic, and 73 Black churches.
- In Portland, 230 churches of all denominations worked together to reach the city for Christ.
- In the Phoenix area, 5,800 people indicated that they had invited Christ into their life.
- In Miami, 2,240 people signed up for follow-up Bible studies, one of the highest responses in the nation.

Chain Reaction

Miracles happened in every city. Television station managers who refused to air paid commercials changed their policies. Inner-city residents who normally refuse to open their doors to strangers welcomed in Christian workers. Students became concerned about their fellow classmates and witnessed of their faith.

One thrilling story reflects the excitement and results of the campaign. Two workers made an appointment to follow-up with a new believer. When they arrived at his house, they discovered that the man had been called in to work. Only his teenage son was home.

As the two workers presented the gospel to the young man, he received Christ. Then he called five of his friends to come over. When they arrived, they too received Christ. One of the boys called his parents, and they said, "We want to see what's happening. We'll be right over." When that boy's parents arrived, the two workers shared the claims of Christ and the parents also made a decision to receive Christ as their Savior.

Seeing what happened, three of the other boys contacted their parents. Soon after arriving, these parents also received Christ. The final outcome of one follow-up appointment was that fourteen people entered God's family.

At the conclusion of the campaigns in most cities, praise rallies were organized to give glory to God for what He had accomplished. As I visited city after city to participate in these rallies, I was enveloped in joy and gratitude for the thousands who were introduced to Christ in each area. Here's Life, America was truly the most remarkable movement of its kind. During a single time span, more people in our country heard the gospel of Jesus Christ and made commitments to Him as Savior than at any other time. And thousands of people got involved in discipleship and evangelism training.

But God was just beginning to move in new and exciting ways. Another of the wondrous miracles I have seen God perform is the advancement of His kingdom overseas. He has led Campus Crusade to establish evangelism and discipleship in the world's remotest parts and in all its major cities. The next chapter explains how God led us to establish the international arm of Campus Crusade.

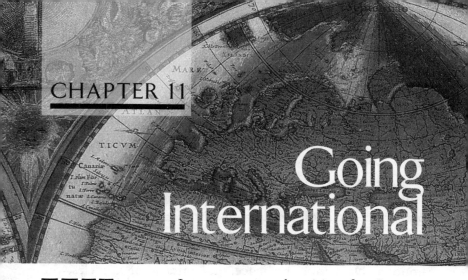

CHAPTER 11

Going International

W HEN THE LORD gave me the vision for Campus Crusade for Christ—a vision to help fulfill our Lord's Great Commission—it had a worldwide scope. There was never a doubt because the wording of the Great Commission confirms it. Our Lord commanded, "Go and make disciples of *all nations...*" (Matthew 28:19). Those words pierced my heart during the days when I began to believe God for the impossible. I reasoned that the Great Commission is His idea and He obviously has the power and wisdom to fulfill it through His disciples who trust and obey Him. The Great Commission became a personal command to me, not just a general one. He was telling me that our ministry was to go to *all nations*. I knew it was just a matter of time. But how and when was up to God.

A Milestone

God's perfect timing came in 1958 when a major milestone in our outreach occurred. By divine appointment, I was privileged to meet Dr. Joon Gon Kim at Fuller Theological Seminary. Dr. Kim is one of South Korea's outstanding educators and Christian leaders.

His tragic testimony deeply touched my heart. One evening in South Korea during the Korean War, Dr. Kim was with his family. Without warning, an angry band from the North

Korean Communist Army burst into his village, mercilessly slaughtering everyone in their path. Their trail of blood left behind the dead bodies of Dr. Kim's dear wife and father. The attackers thought they had killed him too, but he miraculously survived.

Being a man of deep faith in God and obedient to the Holy Spirit, Dr. Kim was reminded to love his enemies and to pray for them. Although hurt deeply, he felt the Lord leading him to return to the village, seek out the Communist chief who led the attack, and tell him about the love of Christ. God honored Dr. Kim's obedience, and miracle of miracles, the formerly bloodthirsty chief knelt in prayer with Dr. Kim, acknowledged his sin, and received Christ as his Savior. Years later he became a pastor in a village church in South Korea.

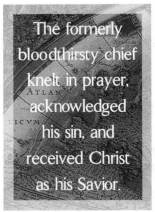

The formerly bloodthirsty chief knelt in prayer, acknowledged his sin, and received Christ as his Savior.

Dr. Kim became known and respected throughout South Korea. We met after he came to the United States to pursue an advanced degree in theological studies. His commitment, humility, and vision challenged me. Then I challenged him.

I carefully laid before him the vision for the world that the Lord had given me. Dr. Kim listened attentively. I was full of hope, but unsure of what his reaction would be. To my delight, as the Holy Spirit bore witness to his heart, Dr. Kim indicated full agreement! Then I boldly asked Dr. Kim if he would launch the ministry of Campus Crusade for Christ in South Korea. He agreed, becoming our first international director.

God has since used Dr. Kim and his ministry throughout Asia and around the world in astonishing ways. They have helped reach untold millions with the gospel, to the point that South Korea has now become a significant missionary-sending nation, with plans to send 100,000 missionaries to different parts of the world such as Japan and Russia. Equally important, with Dr. Kim's assignment a powerful leadership principle for missions was born.

God's Wisdom: Using Nationals

Through the wisdom and leading of God, Dr. Kim became the national and indigenous leader of a U.S.-based ministry in his own country. The appointment of a national leader to head the ministry was logical, yet such a practice was not generally accepted or followed at this point in missions history. Usually, an American would lead the outreach initiative in a foreign country. At the time, I did not fully realize just how profound this Spirit-led decision was. Therefore, at the outset, selecting and appointing nationals for leadership became a standard policy of Campus Crusade, and with only rare exceptions, we have continued this practice all over the world. But thousands of our American staff have played a vital role in winning, building, training, and sending nationals to reach their own people.

Here is the wisdom of using nationals. A national Christian does not have the same problems with language and culture as does a missionary from abroad. Nationals can do a better job of reaching their own people. We train and assist them, but they do the work, and for the most part, they do it marvelously. Dr. Kim—and the other national directors who followed him—recruit and train other nationals, who recruit and train others—in the pattern of spiritual multiplication. Over the years this multiplying effect has been astonishing.

More Nations Added

As time passed, the Lord allowed us to continue to expand abroad. By 1968, we had ministries in 32 countries. Then in 1972, shortly after EXPLO '72, God gave us the vision for the *Agape* Movement. (*Agape* is the Greek word for God's love.)

This was a project to raise up men and women to invest two years or more of their lives, like a Christian Peace Corp, to help take the gospel to the ends of the earth through meeting the physical and medical needs of millions. As I prayed, God confirmed in my heart that this was indeed His will, and the leaders of our movement responded favorably to the idea.

In the next few months, we put together the basic structure. In January 1973, we invited the leaders of several missions organizations to meet with us. Those who came were Dr. Clyde Taylor, general director of the National Association of Evangelicals; Dr. Edward Frizen, head of the Interdenominational Foreign Missions Association; Dr. Donald McGavran, Dean of the Fuller School of World Mission; and Cliff Barrows and Walter Smyth from the Billy Graham Evangelistic Association.

As we sat around our board room table, I shared with these men as fully as possible the direction my staff associates and I wanted the new movement to take. Then I asked these men, whose judgment I greatly respected, whether they thought we should proceed. For a moment, there was a breathless pause around the table.

Dr. Taylor broke the silence: "If you had asked me this a year ago, I would have said, 'No, you have no business attempting anything so large.' But EXPLO '72 changed my answer. When I saw how God used this organization to bring over 100,000 people together and solved the unbelievable logistical problems, not only do I think you should do it, I also think you are the only organization in North America that ought to attempt it."

Dr. Frizen spoke next: "I too feel you ought to proceed. My reason is not because of the magnitude of EXPLO '72, but because of the spirit of EXPLO '72. When I saw that you had invited 200 Christian groups together to present opportunities within their organizations, I knew that this is the kind of spirit it is going to take if we are ever going to see the world reached for Christ." (As an expression of our love and desire to help create a spirit of unity among different Christian groups, Campus Crusade had invited these Christian organizations to come to EXPLO as our guests to promote their ministries.)

The other men followed Dr. Frizen with statements of encouragement and support. This was a fruitful confirmation that the Lord was going to bless this new venture.

In time, thousands of believers committed themselves to serve the Lord for two years or more through the *Agape* Movement. They received regular staff training and the special 14-week *Agape* International Training. People from different vocations were sent, helping people professionally as well as sharing the gospel with them. The impact is still being felt in countries all over the world.

The Birth of a Strategy

Step by step, God gave us a strategy in tune with His Word to reach the world. Our international ministry is not just happenstance or an opportunistic effort, although we do look for opportunities as God keeps opening new doors. The ministry is conducted prayerfully and systematically. We continually ask for and rely upon the wisdom of God. This is the core of our strategy.

First, as described previously, God has led us to rely on nationals in the many nations where we minister. This aspect is no doubt the reason for the great explosion in Campus Crusade's worldwide ministry.

Second, we have a three-pronged, 1-2-3 approach:

1. *One movement:* Committed to helping fulfill the Great Commission in this generation

2. *Two ministries:* Campus Ministry and Community Ministry, both served by many strategies

3. *Three missions:*

   - Campus mission: to promote ministries at all of the

8,000 major universities of the world, representing 60 million students

- Community mission: to develop ministries in 1,215 communities of the world

- Coverage mission: to cover the whole world in the almost 6,000 Million Population Target Areas (MPTAs) into which we have divided the world

Let me explain what we mean by "campus" and "community." From the earliest days of Campus Crusade, our unofficial motto and rallying cry has been, "Win the campus today; win the world tomorrow." Our desire has been to win the future leaders of the world, who would in turn reach their families, their neighborhoods, their cities, and their nations. As we saw in the U.S. Ministry, what starts as a campus ministry soon spreads into the community. Within these two areas of focus, "campus" and "community," Campus Crusade has developed many unique and effective strategies. With the campus mission, we target *future* leaders; with the community mission, we target *present* leaders.

Worldwide Campus and Community Missions

University students represent about 1 percent of the world's population. They are a small but strategic resource of manpower for helping to fulfill the Great Commission. The beauty of a university as a resource, especially outside the United States, is that it selects and gathers into one place those students who show promise of becoming leaders within their society. In most societies, the university is a *narrow gateway* through which most people of influence pass.

Since the selection and gathering are already done for us, we simply seek to establish movements of evangelism and discipleship at these locations. We desire to mobilize these future leaders to have an effective lifetime of ministry in their various spheres of influence. Some graduates will become full-time staff with Campus Crusade and other ministries. Most will go back to their communities and provide leadership to help reach their country and the whole world for Christ.

Our desire is to help students who were trained on their campuses to continue their personal ministries in their neighborhood, church, and workplace. We call this our "Bridge Strategy."

We have divided the world's 8,000 universities into three levels of priority: Levels I, II, and III. The 2,307 Level I universities represent the largest and/or most strategic and are the ones where we hope to establish "direct ministries." The other two levels will be reached through our trained volunteers.

All segments of society are important, and all people need to be reached; however, there is a strategic value in targeting leaders to help facilitate reaching all others. Such leaders and influencers usually represent only a small percent of a nation's population, but as they are reached, trained, and mobilized, they can help reach the rest of the population, either through their personal witness or by using their influence to open doors for the gospel.

NewLife 2000

Campus Crusade's worldwide strategy to cover the whole world and give every person on earth the opportunity to say "yes" to Jesus Christ is called *NewLife 2000*. We have identified 1,215 regions of the world that have strategic urban areas as their centers of influence. In most areas of the world, several MPTA regions naturally cluster around these urban areas that serve as centers of political, educational, financial, and religious influence. Our goal is to have "direct ministries" in each of these regions. Most of these regions also have universities and their alumni, which will help us obtain manpower. Disciples from these movements can help us reach the remaining MPTAs.

NewLife 2000 has six goals:

1. Help present the gospel to more than six billion people using

the *JESUS* film, personal evangelism, and other evangelistic tools.

2. Help introduce one billion people to Jesus Christ as their personal Savior.

3. Help establish more than five million NewLife Groups, which will minister to as many as 200 million new believers.

4. Help provide training through New Life Training Centers in the almost 6,000 MPTAs and through 10,000 *JESUS* film teams to show the *JESUS* film in 1,000 major languages and dialects.

5. Help start ministries on the 8,000 college campuses in strategic metropolitan areas worldwide to present the good news to 60 million university students and their professors.

6. Assist all participating denominations with their church growth goals, resulting in one million new churches. As of this writing we have helped to start over 100,000 churches in 233 countries. None of these churches are owned or controlled by Campus Crusade for Christ or bear our name.

In the United States, the *NewLife 2000* strategy is implemented through the Campus Ministry and the many lay ministries. Nonbelievers are introduced to the gospel of Jesus Christ, then trained in Christian growth and evangelism. Overseas, the normal strategy would begin with a *JESUS* film team who would show the *JESUS* film in a village or urban area. Those who respond by receiving Christ as their Savior are encouraged to join NewLife Groups where they learn the basics of the Christian faith such as studying the Bible, witnessing, prayer, and growing in their faith. As these NewLife Groups grow, they are combined with other groups to form churches. Many of these churches are planted in areas where no churches exist and will come under the leadership of denominational leaders. In areas where sharing the gospel is not permitted, other strategies will help further the kingdom of God.

Campus Crusade for Christ Canada

One area to which I must give special recognition is Campus Crusade for Christ Canada. Although it is considered a part of the International Ministries, it has taken a direction separate from the U.S. Ministries and the International Ministries. When we first sent Campus Crusade for Christ staff from the U.S. to Canada in 1965, we had no grand plans for that great country. We were just trusting God for each day's guidance and provision. But with the passing of time, God raised up godly leadership to direct the movement. Under the strong directorship of Marvin and Kathy Kehler and their remarkable Board of Directors and dedicated staff, Canada became a spiritual force worldwide.

It all began on the University of British Columbia campus. Bob Horner and Jim Holt, at that time U.S. Campus Crusade staff, laid the groundwork for the new outreach. Bob Horner describes the exciting beginning: "Only the Lord could have begun what Campus Crusade for Christ saw that first year. For some reason, we ran across solid Christians, sold-out people. By Christmas, we had 90 students, some high school age, whom we took to Arrowhead Springs for a Christmas conference. When we returned, we had 40 to 60 students attending weekly leadership training classes."

In the fall of 1966, Josh McDowell, then a young, budding apologist, assumed the position as campus director. That year, 226 people traveled to Arrowhead Springs for Campus Crusade's annual Christmas Conference—the largest group ever from any one campus. Josh describes the amazing growth, "We had grown so large, so fast, the student union approached us and gave us an on-campus office with two telephones—free of charge."

Campus Crusade for Christ Canada was granted legal status in 1967 and expanded its ministry to the University of Toronto a year later. In 1970, a British Columbia businessman and denominational leader, Marvin Kehler, and his wife,

Kathy, attended a LIFE conference at Arrowhead Springs. When he learned that he had to go door-to-door sharing the *Four Spiritual Laws*, he almost refused. But that week, he led someone to Christ.

When Marvin returned to Canada, he enthusiastically started applying what he had learned. He and a friend began organizing Lay Institutes for Evangelism all over Canada—and the Lay Ministry of Campus Crusade for Christ was born. In 1972, he and Kathy joined our staff. In 1974, they accepted the director's position of Campus Crusade for Christ Canada. The evangelism skills he learned are still paying dividends today.

Campus Crusade for Christ Canada today is making a great contribution to the gospel in countries all around the world. It is hard to imagine that a country of 30 million people could have an impact in more than 100 countries. This has come about through innovative strategies, through translating and showing the *JESUS* film, and the tireless work of the staff and volunteers involved in the ministry. The scope of their efforts is outlined further in Chapter 16, "World Impact."

By God's grace, through the campuses, the communities, and the MPTAs, our international staff have been able to impact almost the whole world. As we continue to work with many thousands of churches and hundreds of missions organizations, every person on earth will, indeed, have the opportunity to say "yes" to our Lord.

With this strategy in place, we are now able to help win hundreds of millions and train believers to help fulfill the Great Commission. In the next chapter, we will see the international events and projects that followed the success of EXPLO '74 in South Korea. Some of these originated in the United States and were expanded to help reach the world for Christ; others are distinctly international. But in all cases, God worked in mighty ways to enable us, His servants, to spread His Word beyond our "Jerusalem" and to all parts of the world.

CHAPTER 12

International Events and Projects

J UST AS IN THE U.S. side of our ministry, the International Ministries have participated in major events and projects which have resulted in an expansion of our work around the globe. Thanks to the Spirit-filled leadership of our fellow staff overseas, strategies have been adapted to each area so that people could understand the claims of Christ through their own culture. Over the years, leaders have been developed using the principle of spiritual multiplication and the training provided through Great Commission Training Centers, New Life Centers, and Campus Crusade's seven International Schools of Theology. God has given us such prime leaders—humble, intelligent, and willing to do whatever God requires of them.

These national leaders deserve the credit for the miracles God has worked in so many places and under so many differing conditions. No one person or committee could accomplish what they have done through intensive prayer, cooperation, faith, and plain hard work. Some have sacrificed more than we in the United States can imagine as they have faced persecution and incredible hardships. Some risk death daily and others have died as martyrs. As you read the record of their successes, keep in mind the faith and courage these men and women have shown throughout these decades of service. I count it a great privilege to co-labor with them in this ministry.

EXPLO '74

EXPLO '74 in Seoul, South Korea, was one of the most exciting experiences of my life. As I began to speak on the first
night of the mass rallies in Yoida Plaza, I looked out upon an
ocean of people stretching as far as I could see. Officials estimated 1.3 million people had gathered for this international
congress on evangelism training sponsored by Campus Crusade for Christ.

After each sentence I spoke, I paused, allowing my transla-
tor to translate my statements into Korean. At the completion
of my message, I asked all of those who wanted to receive Christ,
or who, as a result of my message, had gained assurance of their
salvation, to stand.

As the 8,000-voice choir sang, hundreds of thousands of
people stood from where they had been sitting on the asphalt
of this converted airstrip. I wanted to make sure that everyone
understood what I had said, so I slowly repeated my invitation
again. Still more people stood!

About midnight, I answered a phone call from Dr. Kim to
report on the evening's activities. "I have exciting news," he
said. "When you gave the invitation tonight, our staff determined that at least 80 percent of the people responded. Do
you realize that more than one million people indicated tonight
that they received Christ or that, for the first time in their lives,
they were assured of their salvation?"

I was overwhelmed. I knew this happened only because of
God's supernatural, miraculous working, for what greater miracle is there than the new birth? I also knew that God was
honoring Dr. Kim, his great staff, and thousands of cooperating churches for their fasting, prayer, faith, and hard work.

Night after night I was filled with awe and praise to God
as I looked out over the sea of faces. I was deeply moved to
learn that these were the largest Christian, and possibly secular, gatherings in recorded history. According to police estimates, at least one of the evening mass rallies exceeded 1.6

million people.

Besides this amazing "first" in the history of the Christian church, Dr. Kim later told me of some 24 other "firsts" in connection with EXPLO '74, some of which remain unmatched. They included:

- The largest number of Christians trained in discipleship and evangelism during one week (a total of 323,419 registered, representing some 78 nations).

- The largest number of decisions for Christ in a single evening.

- The largest all-night prayer meetings in the history of the Christian church (prayer meetings occurred six nights in a row with several hundred thousand in attendance each night). The night before EXPLO began, Vonette spoke to more than 100,000 women gathered for prayer.

- The largest personal witnessing campaign ever conducted (more than 420,000 heard the gospel in one afternoon and a record 274,000 indicated salvation decisions for Christ) as trained workers witnessed for Christ throughout Seoul.

- The largest number of Christians to appropriate the filling of the Holy Spirit at one time (an estimated 70 percent of the 1.5 million audience one night responded to this invitation).

- The largest number of Christians to commit their lives to the fulfillment of the Great Commission at one time (a response of 90 percent was estimated among the final Sunday crowd of 650,000).

All the glory, honor, and praise must go to God.

Here's Life, World!

In 1977, Bailey Marks, now our Executive Vice President of International Ministries but then our director for Asia, invited me to help launch the Here's Life movement in a number of countries throughout the Asian continent. This movement incorporated much of the same strategy and concepts that proved so successful in the Here's Life, America campaigns.

Our efforts were received enthusiastically in other countries. Again and again, I heard the expression, "Nothing like this has ever happened in the history of our country." An unprecedented moving of God's Spirit was calling Christians from various organizations and denominations that do not normally cooperate to work in harmony and love.

When I arrived in Pakistan to help initiate the Here's Life movement in that country, Pakistan was in a state of political turmoil. Although riots were raging with buses and trains being burned and people being killed, Christians still came to the meetings. Sessions were held each morning and afternoon with as many as 1,200 present in a single meeting. Many of

the Christian leaders of Lahore and Karachi, Pakistan's two largest cities, met together for prayer, fellowship, and strategy sessions with a view toward launching Here's Life in those key cities. With such a large Muslim population, the campaign faced opposition on every side. Yet through it all, God blessed with reports of 1,000 decisions for Christ, an unprecedented result for Pakistan.

The media campaigns in Manila and Baguio City in the Philippines started in March that same year. Statistics showed that 1,971 workers and 102 churches participated in the outreach; 209,830 responses were received from various forms of media advertisements. In the first 13,000 times the gospel was presented as a part of the campaign, 9,242 people indicated decisions to trust Christ, a 70 percent positive response. More than half of those who received Christ as their Savior enrolled in Bible studies to be trained in the basics of Christian faith.

Although many of the strategies were the same as those used in Here's Life, America, cultural differences made alterations in the Asian campaigns a necessity. For example, the outdoor "I found it!" advertising was more prevalent in Manila and Baguio City than in American cities because Filippino shop owners were more willing to display banners and posters in their windows. Thousands of taxis—which dominate the streets in both cities—carried bumper stickers.

Since so few people had telephones in Manila and Baguio City, the main emphasis of the media campaign was to urge people who wanted more information about Christ to respond either by telephone or by filling out a coupon and dropping it into one of the 800 "I found it!" boxes located throughout the two cities. The strategy worked. More than 180,000 of the 210,000 responses that were received were retrieved from the boxes.

Let me mention other exciting things that happened during the numerous campaigns conducted all over the world:

- *Tijuana, Mexico*—Of those who made decisions for Christ, 89 percent enrolled in follow-up Bible studies.

- *San Cristobal, Dominican Republic*—The average response rate was 90 percent (10,260 recorded decisions from among the 11,400 people who heard the gospel).

- *Singapore*—By the beginning of the media campaign, prayer chains had been formed with almost 8,000 Christians. Campaign workers represented 100 of the approximately 180 churches.

- *Malaysia*—The law in predominantly Muslim Malaysia is clear: Christians are not allowed to approach Malays with the gospel. Therefore, Here's Life Malaysia represented a united effort to reach the 48 percent of the population that is Chinese. Although threatening telephone calls were received every day and vehicles bearing "I found it!" bumper stickers were maliciously damaged, campaign workers remained undaunted.

■ *Hong Kong*—A total of 359 churches were involved in the campaign, and 300 of these churches held evangelistic campaigns simultaneously with the Here's Life media campaign. Trained campaign workers numbered 15,000 while another 85,000 people participated in other ways. They represented about half the colony's Protestant population. By the close of the campaign, 28,174 people had indicated salvation decisions for Christ. One month after the campaign, 200 churches reported attendance growth of between 30 and 150 attendees.

■ *Nairobi, Kenya*—Some 15,000 decisions for Christ were recorded and six Baptist churches added 2,600 new members as a direct result of the outreach.

■ *Barcelona, Spain*—Thirty-five churches took part in the campaign, representing 75 percent of the city's evangelical population.

■ *Tampere, Finland*—Church attendance tripled in the first three Sundays following the start of the campaign.

Rural Strategies

The success of these campaigns in reaching cities around the world filled me with praise and gratitude to our wonderful Lord. Yet, at the time, an estimated 62 percent of the world's population did not live in cities, but in villages and rural areas. That's why I became so excited about what happened in the Kilungu hills, a rural area of Kenya.

Three-fourths of the people in Kilungu were non-literate, so a tape recording and a booklet of photographs was used to train pastors and laymen in evangelization. These trained pastors and laymen equipped their own churches by using the same tape packages.

Once the training was completed, four cars and a motorcycle equipped with loud speakers broadcast "I found it!" (*Niniwonete*) throughout the 100-square-mile section of the Kamba tribal lands. Soon the cars could not go anywhere in the area without being met by children singing the *Niniwonete* jingle. Churches set up bright yellow banners to help people locate places where they could find the new life in Jesus Christ or where follow-up Bible studies were being held.

An average of 50 percent of those who came to the information centers indicated decisions to receive Christ. In some places, where the terrain was most difficult, 75 percent of those who came accepted Christ as their Savior.

Other types of rural campaigns were used in India, Mexico, and the Philippines. One of the most spectacular results occurred in the Indian State of Kerala. Our national director in India, Thomas Abraham, believed God for the total saturation of this state of 22 million people by the end of 1976. From the busiest streets of sprawling coastal cities to remote mountainous tea plantations, trained workers went house to house communicating the good news of Jesus Christ. At the end of the campaign, 99 percent of the homes had been contacted. During the last three months of the campaign, large evangelistic meetings were held in all 11 districts of Kerala so people who were at work or school during the day would have a chance to hear the gospel.

During 1978, an estimated 65 to 86 percent of Colombia's 27 million people heard how they could have a personal relationship with Jesus Christ. Nearly 18 million people were directly contacted through personal presentations or in group meetings and millions of others were touched through mass media. More than 2.6 million decisions to receive Christ as Savior and Lord were recorded.

EXPLO '85

One of the greatest landmarks of our international ministry was a tremendous worldwide effort in 1985 which we called

EXPLO '85. Conducted December 28–31, it was the most ambitious training conference we had ever organized. Three hundred thousand believers from more than 160 nations at 94 sites all over the world worshiped God together, linked via television by satellites and sophisticated relay stations, providing simultaneous daily training.

The EXPLO broadcast network was one of the most complicated in history, involving eighteen different satellites. From our main studio in London, transmissions were sent to two large "earth stations," which beamed the broadcasts to orbiting satellites, which beamed the transmissions back down to selected ground stations in various parts of the earth. The signal then traveled overland via cable and microwave to the 94 sites.

According to technical experts, the project was a miracle because of the complexity and potential problems that could have occurred. It was also a spiritual miracle. It brought a spiritual unity transcending many nations and languages, reminding God's people in faraway places that they are not alone in their faith, but that they are a part of Christ's worldwide Body.

The Birth of an Idea

The idea of EXPLO '85 goes back to a meeting of Campus Crusade's international leadership in October 1982. We asked God to clarify for us the world plan for our movement. Our goal was to be used by God to help introduce one billion people to our Lord by the end of the year 2000.

After the meeting, Bailey Marks and I discussed the exciting possibility of bringing together 50,000 believers from around the world for training in prayer, evangelism, and discipleship. But when we did some calculations, we found that the cost would be about $150 million, or about $3,000 per person!

"For a few days, I lost my enthusiasm for the conference," Bailey said. "However, the Lord would not let me forget about it, and I continued to pray." One morning while shaving, the Lord gave Bailey the idea. Instead of bringing people to a conference, we would take a conference to the people—by satellite!

This is an example of how the Lord's plans are so much better than ours. Whereas our plan would have involved only 50,000 people at a cost of $150 million, God's plan involved more than 300,000 people with a cost of only $7.5 million— 600 percent more people at only 5 percent of the cost! With the miracle of electronics, God's plan bound together all the many people and nations into an unusual unity and awareness of the worldwide Body of Christ. But the logistics of the project were mind-boggling.

Thousands of Details

Bailey's able assistant, Jerry Sharpless, coordinated the massive project. Jerry and other EXPLO '85 organizers found many opportunities to trust God. And God never failed them. In India, importing satellite-receiving dishes was impossible, so the Lord raised up a man who built the needed dishes in his backyard. In Korea, we had to go all the way to the top—to the president—to get permission to use the Olympic Gymnasium for EXPLO '85 participants in Seoul. In Lagos, Nigeria, conference arrangements collapsed just three weeks before the event. Organizers had to quickly arrange an alternative site, Ife, 200 kilometers away. The list of challenges and God-provided solutions is endless.

Only God knows the full results of EXPLO '85. We know for sure that 300,000 lives were immediately and directly touched. I am confident that those in attendance have since touched millions of other lives.

But more than that, EXPLO '85 did something special to the whole movement of Campus Crusade for Christ. It gave us all new vision and new momentum and an international unity. Our international growth since that time has been exponential. More countries and staff were added. For example,

EXPLO '85 gave Campus Crusade for Christ in Africa much recognition and credibility with the churches, which opened many doors for training and mobilization. Just one year after EXPLO '85, 1,421 students participated in international summer projects in 16 countries. In 1990, we held a historic *New-Life2000* conference in Manila. Five thousand delegates came from 102 countries, and the gospel was presented to 1.3 million people.

International Special Projects

In addition to the worldwide events in which we are involved to help fulfill the Great Commission in all the countries where the Lord has sent us, He brings us special opportunities to spread the gospel in unique ways in specific parts of the world. We prayerfully pursue such special projects as the Lord leads us, and over the years these projects have proven extremely fruitful in reaching people for Christ. Following are some examples.

Easter in Moscow

During Easter 1990, I was invited to speak from the Palace of Congresses, the inner sanctum of Communism, on television to 150 million people throughout the Soviet Union. Only God knows how many responded to my televised invitation to receive Christ, but we saw phenomenal response among the Soviet people. The next year on April 26, 1991, hundreds of Americans and our staff assembled in Russia's Red Square to joyously celebrate the resurrection of our Lord Jesus Christ for the Russian Orthodox Easter, which is one week later than our own. This historic event came on the heels of the collapse of Soviet communism and the new climate of religious freedom. We found the Russian people hungry for spiritual truth after seventy years of state atheism and censorship of God's truths.

Our group included a 350-member choir from different

Christian churches and denominations in the U.S. and Russia, plus 42 American business and civic leaders. These leaders also met with their Russian counterparts during their stay.

In spite of the rain, Russian police estimated the Red Square audience possibly as high as 100,000. At one point, rain stopped the program. It was so bad that a cancelation notice was given. But everyone began to pray that God would intervene and allow the program to continue. God answered! He graciously lifted the rain, the cancelation was itself canceled, and the huge crowds sang the stirring streams of the song, *How Great Thou Art.*

After my address and invitation, at least 75 percent of the crowd responded, raising their hands to indicate their decision to trust Christ. This two-hour Easter celebration was carried live on television throughout the former Soviet Union to a potential audience of 60 million. It is possible that hundreds of thousands, even millions, received Christ that day, or at least had seeds planted that will someday produce spiritual fruit.

While there, the visiting Americans distributed 100,000 copies of the New Testament, the first to be printed in modern Russian language. The people in Red Square and the nearby subway and shopping area flocked to accept the Bibles.

Through the Military Ministry, we presented forty tons of baby food to destitute Russian military families living in tent areas around Moscow. I was able to visit Russian cosmonaut Igor Volk in a Moscow hospital. Volk was recovering from a recent automobile accident. He had recently received Christ and had been baptized in his own church. I encouraged him in his faith, and we prayed together.

Mission Volga '92
The largest evangelistic campaign in Russian history was held on the Volga River on the mission ship *The Alexander Radishev,* from August 23 to October 4, 1992. Called Mission Volga

'92, it included thirty meetings in twelve cities along 3,000 kilometers of the historic river. At each stop, the good news of Jesus Christ was shared by Finnish evangelist Kalevi Lehtinen, a staff member of Campus Crusade's Mission Europe. The combined attendance was close to 120,000. More than half of the people at each meeting indicated decisions for Christ, with some meetings having a response rate as high as 80 percent. I had the joy of speaking in Simbirsk, Russia, where Lenin was born. As in other cities, the response was phenomenal.

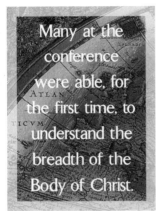

Many at the conference were able, for the first time, to understand the breadth of the Body of Christ.

An Institute for Evangelism was held aboard ship during the voyage where Russian pastors and laypeople received training in personal evangelism and discipleship. Television stations in the Volga cities broadcasted programs about the mission to about 25 million viewers. More than 3 million Mission Volga newspapers were distributed in the targeted cities.

Mission Volga '92 also brought food, medicine, hospital equipment, and supplies to the mission cities. Tens of thousands expressed their desire to know Jesus Christ as their Savior and Lord.

Rwanda Relief

When the Tutsi minority forces overthrew the ruling Hutu majority in Rwanda, Africa, in 1994, more than 2 million Rwandans fled to surrounding countries. Many Campus Crusade staff were among those forced into refugee camps.

Kulu Pauline, one of our staff members in Zaire, coordinated relief efforts within several refugee camps in Zaire and Tanzania. Tons of corn, wheat, Bibles, blankets, and clothing were provided for tens of thousands of people. In addition, Rwandan national staff members traveled daily to the camps, sharing the gospel through the *JESUS* film and the *Four Spiritual Laws* booklet. Hundreds of thousands heard the good news and tens of thousands indicated decisions to trust Christ.

International Year

In the summer of 1997, the ministry's broad-based leadership from 172 nations came together for International Year—the first in 30 years. The event was held at Colorado State University in Ft. Collins, Colorado, in conjunction with our U.S. Staff Conference. The meeting was in two segments. The first consisted of 859 national staff leaders from every corner of the globe. The second half of the conference included an additional 5,000 staff members from the United States and elsewhere.

The focus was the continuing development of the worldwide movement with: 1) a common vision; 2) a common commitment; and 3) an uncommon camaraderie.

Asians, Africans, Latin Americans, North Americans, Europeans, Middle Easterners, and Pacific Islanders spent time together in awe of God's power. Many were able, for the first time, to personally experience fellowship with fellow servants from other continents and to understand the breadth of the Body of Christ. Everyone returned home with a renewed confidence that God would, indeed, reach the people of their countries, and that, in spite of obstacles, the Great Commission would be fulfilled.

Strategy 100

Strategy 100 is an ambitious plan to send teams of national Christians with the *JESUS* film and Christian literature to cities throughout Russia and, working with local church volunteers, to give millions the opportunity to hear the gospel.

One of the team leaders, Viktor Neifeld, took his team to Krivoshenio, a city in central Siberia about 500 miles north of the Chinese border. Church volunteers from the team's home base in Tomakaya joined to help invite people to view the

JESUS film. Seventy people packed the theater and, at the end, more than half signed up for a Bible study formed by the team and volunteers. The Bible studies have continued each week, even though some in attendance have to travel 120 miles by train.

MIAMI *Strategy*

MIAMI (Millions In A Month International) is a cooperative strategy between Campus Crusade for Christ Canada and Latin American evangelical churches to reach millions in a specific geographic area with the gospel. The idea began with an outreach in the Volcano Region of Mexico. Because of the active volcano that threatens to erupt at any time, missionaries have found the Mexicans who live in this area very receptive to the gospel. In 1997, our staff worked with local churches to show the *JESUS* film throughout the region. More than one million saw the film and approximately 100,000 indicated decisions to trust Christ. This experience gave our Latin American staff the idea to reach other regions with a similar focused saturation over a single month.

In November 1997, our Canadian staff were committed to helping reach 1.2 million people in Nicaragua in partnership with our Latin American staff. The results were beyond expectation—about 3 million people were reached. Together, they then went to Bogota, Colombia, then to Venezuela, and on and on. God is greatly using the MIAMI Strategy to help fulfill the Great Commission among the people in Latin America.

Love South Africa

The purpose of the Love South Africa project is to saturate the nations of southern Africa with the knowledge of the love and forgiveness of our Lord Jesus Christ. An example of the dedication of our staff members was demonstrated when a 28-member team left Pretoria for a 1,500-mile journey to Lichinga in a northern province of Mozambique. This area has the largest concentration of unreached people in Africa south of the equator and many are Muslim.

Upon arrival, New Life Training Center (NLTC) training was given to numerous pastors and church members. The teams separated and went to different areas between 40 and 190 miles around Lichinga, where they worked alongside local churches. Thousands of Bibles were distributed and tens of thousands of people were exposed to the gospel. The Lichinga experience is just a sample of what God is doing through Campus Crusade staff with Love South Africa.

Youth at the CrossRoads

A powerful, new, innovative concept that is gaining acceptance and making an impact in nation after nation is a project we call Youth at the CrossRoads. Due to rampant secularism and humanism, traditional morality and biblical values have crumbled all across the globe. Many older adults are still guided by morals, but young people of most cultures enter a society virtually void of values, a dark world constantly dominated by an addiction to the culture's music and entertainment. Youth crime and immorality have skyrocketed across the world.

We have found that government and institutional leaders welcome help to solve this growing social crisis. Of course, we know the only answer is in the Lord Jesus Christ and in His holy, inerrant Word, the Bible. To that end, CrossRoads offers these nations and communities an outstanding curriculum called *Life at the CrossRoads*.

The *Life at the CrossRoads* curriculum provides thirty classroom lessons about right and wrong, morals, character, and establishing a personal value system. The lessons involve interaction among students, parents, and teachers, and include small student groups for discussion and accountability. Most importantly, the curriculum includes showings of the *JESUS* film and school rallies, which provide varied opportunities for evangelism, follow-up, and discipleship.

The story of our international ministries could continue for many more pages telling the great things God helps us accomplish through events such as the Barcelona Olympics, the Paris Olympics, the Egypt Book Fair, and others. As we have encountered new cultures and different ways of living, the Lord has enabled us to reach out to people in varied ways. Much of the success we have had worldwide has been due to the use of the *JESUS* film. This evangelistic tool has revolutionized the way individual Christians, churches, and denominations minister. In the next chapter, we will read the story of how the *JESUS* film came to be and how God is using it all over the world.

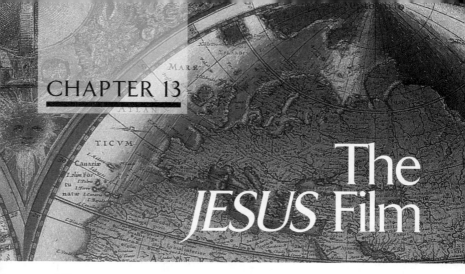

CHAPTER 13

The JESUS Film

O F ALL THE FILMS ever produced, which one has been translated more than any other film? Which film has been viewed by the most people? The *JESUS* film, sponsored by Campus Crusade for Christ! As of May 1, 1999, the *JESUS* film has been translated into over 500 languages and viewed by more than 2 billion people. Hundreds of millions of viewers have indicated salvation decisions in response to the closing invitation to receive Christ at the end of the film. To God be all the glory and praise for this remarkable and unprecedented demonstration of His love and grace!

The Dream

It all began in 1945 when as a young Christian businessman, I felt God impressing me to do a film on the life of Christ. Of course, I had no experience in film producing so I sought the counsel of one of the greatest film producers of all time, Cecil B. Demille. He had produced many great films, including *The Ten Commandments* and *King of Kings*. He was a Christian and came to Hollywood with the desire to produce only religious films. His father had been a Broadway actor who had received Christ and taught his children a chapter each day from the Old and New Testament and from an American history book.

I had hoped to finance the film from my own business, but the Lord led me to start Campus Crusade for Christ instead. The years passed, but the desire to produce the film on the life of Jesus remained and grew. Often in Campus Crusade board meetings, I would share the urgency of producing the film.

At that time, our ministry did not have the funds to produce such an ambitious film project. Yet I continued to pray with the board and staff about the need for the film as an evangelistic tool. We reviewed more than thirty films on the life of Christ, but most of them were not scripturally correct. We even seriously considered buying the rights to one of those films and reworking it to make it biblically accurate. But we were never able to raise the huge amount of money needed for production.

Thirty-three years passed, but that was part of God's divine timing. In 1976, I met John Heyman, a man who had an idea for an ambitious project—to put the entire Bible on film. As a movie producer with more than thirty feature-length films to his credit, he seemed like the person who could help me fulfill my dream.

I introduced John to Paul Eshleman, at that time our U.S. Field Ministry director. A few months later, Bunker and Caroline Hunt, long-time friends and generous supporters of the ministry, offered to provide financing for the film. God was opening the doors for a new venture.

Why did God wait so long, 33 years from when He gave me the vision, to provide the resources for producing and distributing the film? He was waiting for Paul Eshleman to be born and develop into a man of God. As a young man, he directed EXPLO '72 in Dallas, the largest week-long evangelism-training event in history. Later, I asked him to direct the U.S. field ministry. When Bunker and Caroline provided the finances and John Heyman agreed to direct the *JESUS* film, I asked Paul Eshleman to assist John and ultimately give worldwide direction to the entire *JESUS* film project. Under Paul's creative, aggressive entrepreneurship and his godly leadership, the film has been blessed by God in phenomenal and unprecedented ways. No one else I know would have been so successful.

Accuracy and authenticity were crucial as a team of researchers painstakingly produced a 318-page document giving the biblical, theological, historical, and archeological background of every scene as presented by the Gospel of Luke. Jewish actors played most roles, but the search for an actor to play the lead role took months. Finally, an Englishman and Shakespearean actor, Brian Deacon, was chosen to play the role of our Lord.

During the filming in Israel, John Heyman demanded excellence. For example, he stopped the cameras once when he noticed a ripple-soled tennis shoe print in the dust. But excellence was what we needed to produce a film that could touch the world.

The Results of That Dream

I prayed that the *JESUS* film would be mightily used by God, not knowing that it would eventually become one of the most revolutionary documentaries in history and have a worldwide impact for the glory of God. Even during the filming, the story of Jesus changed lives. One young college dropout worked a couple of days carrying props. While staying in a Tel Aviv hotel room, he picked up a Gideon Bible and began reading the Book of Luke for himself. As he finished, he slid to his knees and received Christ as his Savior. Five months later, he was studying at Dallas Bible College to become a minister.

When Eshleman was meeting with Hollywood executives to work out the film's distribution, a Warner Brothers executive asked him, "How would I begin, I mean, with a faith in Jesus?" Later, with a tear-choked voice, the executive bowed his head and asked Christ to come into his life. And these are only two isolated stories of the power of Christ's life and message.

Finally, the filming and production were wrapped up, and

JESUS opened in many theaters across America in the fall of 1979. By the end of the commercial run a year later, more than 4 million people had seen the film. The stories of changed lives began to come in from many places. For example, theater managers in Birmingham and Jacksonville gave their lives to Christ. At a special screening for college students in Sacramento, twenty-one viewers indicated their desire to follow Jesus.

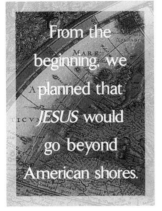

From the beginning, we planned that *JESUS* would go beyond American shores.

From the beginning, however, we planned that *JESUS* would go beyond American shores. The format of the film—its simple, straight narrative taken directly from the Book of Luke—made it easily adaptable for foreign translation. Today, a few simple steps help us bring *JESUS* to many diverse places and translate it into hundreds of languages:

1. Funding—A person or group funds a new translation at an average cost of $30,000.

2. Translation—The script is carefully translated so that it is doctrinally accurate, but conveys the meaning of the Scriptures in the new language.

3. Production—This includes directing and video fitting:

   ■ Directing—A native director is found who auditions voice actors for the 42 speaking roles and directs the recording.

   ■ Video fitting—Before taping the voices, the dialogue director reads aloud every line of the script while watching a videotape of the film to make sure each line of the new language version fits the picture. Careful recording, lip-synching, and mixing the recording with the film ensures that the new soundtrack exactly matches the picture.

4. Approvals—The language approval committee views the result on videotape to ensure an accurate translation and

correct pronunciation.

5. Distribution to film teams—16mm film copies and video-tape cassettes of the new translations are sent to film teams of indigenous missionaries. Each team is fully trained in how to use and maintain the equipment and in how to prepare counselors who will do follow-up care of the new believers.

6. Showings—We developed a strategy to bring the film to urban centers, rural areas, islands, mountaintop villages, hidden people groups, and countries where electricity is a rarity. Teams promote the coming showing throughout the surrounding area. An average showing attracts about 300 people, and each team shows the film to about 40,000 people each year.

   After a showing, a string of lights commonly illuminates the front of the viewing area. Viewers are invited to "come to the light" where counselors help each person who responds to understand how to receive Christ. Additional sessions for more instruction are announced.

7. Discipleship and church planting—Whenever possible, film teams conduct showings in cooperation with a nearby church. As part of the follow-up, New Life Groups are formed, often led by those potential leaders prepared and trained to give direction to the groups in a New Life Training Center. Many New Life groups eventually develop into new churches. We estimate that as of January 1, 1999, we have been able to help plant over 100,000 churches in 225 countries in cooperation with many denominations and national believers. None of these churches carry our name.

JESUS Film Teams

We have trained and sent out more than two thousand *JESUS* film teams, groups of men and women who show the film in places such as remote villages or in huge cities. You can imagine the excitement when a team begins to set up its equipment in places where people have never had the opportunity to view a movie, particularly in their own language.

Sometimes the film team members operate at great personal risk to present the film. They have been attacked, robbed, imprisoned, poisoned, even burned with firebrands. But they count sacrifice and persecution for our Lord Jesus Christ as worth the cost.

What the Lord does through their availability is thrilling. At the height of civil war in El Salvador, *JESUS* was shown in Santa Telca during one week of fierce fighting. Half the city of 52,000 saw the film with 5,600 indicating salvation decisions. By the end of that year, more than 250,000 people in El Salvador had received Jesus.

In Burma (Myanmar), the remote people of Hsanguang asked a Campus Crusade film team to show *JESUS* during their harvest festival. The primary way to travel into this remote area was by helicopter, and the expense was more than the film team could afford.

But the villagers did not give up. Soon projectors, a generator, kerosene, the screen, electrical cords, follow-up materials, and the team members were loaded onto elephants, which carried them over the mountains. During the two nights of the harvest festival, 6,500 people saw the film and 141 people professed faith in Christ.

Film teams and their impact continue to multiply. Through the efforts of 2,150 full-time Campus Crusade film teams, over 2 billion had viewed the *JESUS* film as of May 1, 1999. As the number of teams increases, we trust that everyone in the world will have at least one chance to encounter Christ's life and message by the end of the year 2000.

From the beginning, we have viewed the *JESUS* film as a tool for the whole body of Christ. More than 815 denominations and organizations use the film as part of their outreach. An increasing number of organizations now partner with us to field their own film teams.

God Is Working

Team leader Vishal Nath coordinates fourteen film teams in the Western Uttar Pradesh region of India. The teams use various language versions of *JESUS*. He recalls the reaction of one religious society which is described as "vehemently against all things Christian." Nath recalls, "When we went to speak with them and they learned that we had made a film in their own language, they were really excited. They arranged for the auditorium and paid the rent and everything, and some 750 came."

Nath also tells of 150 or more new believers attending Bible study groups in the Mathura area. A few months before, however, the reception was far from friendly. Local religious militants had tried to force the team to leave, but local viewers defended the team so strongly that the militants eventually came and apologized. In subsequent follow-up meetings, 150 people told of trusting Christ; a nearby church baptized one-third of them.

Add to that the creative uses of the film by volunteers. A scientist took the *JESUS* video to Antarctica and placed it in a video lending library there. Sunday school classes and others reaching out to international students in America invite them to special showings of *JESUS* in their own languages. Men and women have donated *JESUS* to their public libraries and video stores, where records show the videos are usually checked out.

Among Islamic peoples, we find a continued, if discreet, interest in the person of Christ. Even though governments often place many obstacles in the way, *JESUS* film team workers report tremendous openness, even eagerness, to know more about Jesus.

Our *JESUS* film team director in Jordan courageously placed an ad in the nation's top newspaper, offering an audio-cassette of the *JESUS* film soundtrack, a New Testament, and the *Four Spiritual Laws* booklet—all in Arabic. Within days, letters began pouring in for the gift packet. By January 1, 1999, responses from throughout this predominantly Muslim nation surpassed 40,000.

In countries that are hostile to Christ, the *JESUS* film makes it easier for people to learn about God's love. Wherever possible, film teams continue to show the 16mm film to large groups. But in many areas of the world, open showings are not possible. In those countries, distribution of the audiocassette recording of the *JESUS* film works well, often coupled with international radio broadcasts.

Other Uses of the *JESUS* Film

The annual Love Southern Africa training conference has incorporated the *JESUS* film into its evangelism strategy. In 1996, forty-two outreach teams fanned out into fifteen neighboring countries to show the *JESUS* film. After days of driving, one team showed the film on eight consecutive nights to 12,000 Chichewa people. Another team showed the *JESUS* film next door to a mosque, while a Muslim teacher helped distribute the more than 1,000 pieces of evangelistic materials given out that evening.

In Romania, since the country's release from Communist dictatorship, the *JESUS* film has helped launch a remarkable discipleship and evangelism strategy called The Romania Project. This cooperative effort involves many Romanian churches and our national staff. Within the first four-and-a-half years of the effort, 6,524 trained volunteers showed the *JESUS* film. The 16,076 showings drew more than one million viewers, and nearly one-third of those indicated salvation decisions. The volunteers, working with their own churches, then met for additional spiritual nurture with 30,344 new believers, all of whom completed a series of discipleship lessons. At least 185 churches have been started.

I am often astounded at what God is doing in areas once inaccessible to the gospel. Until 1992, Albania was both the world's only official atheist nation and one of Europe's poorest countries, ruled by one of Eastern Europe's most repressive dictators. Today, hundreds of thousands in the remotest villages have seen the *JESUS* film, and newly planted churches exist in areas that had no witness of the Savior for decades.

Through those efforts and TV as well as theatrical showings, half of the country has had the opportunity to encounter the life and message of the Savior. Teams composed of Albanians and volunteer workers from Western Europe and North America have faced steep mountain trails, illness, gangs, robbers, even death threats to show *JESUS* in the nation's hundreds of remote villages. A 15-minute helicopter ride provided by the Europeans saves the teams days of travel by rural bus or on foot. Many organizations recruit volunteer film team workers and disciplers who afterwards nurture the new believers and plant churches.

CoMission

In the years since the *JESUS* film was released, the most amazing story may be what has happened since 1990 in the former Soviet Union and the Eastern bloc countries. After decades of enforced atheism and hostility toward Christianity, walls that had seemed impenetrable began to crack in the 1980s. Committed believers were already discreetly using the *JESUS* film in some areas, but the risks were high. Many believers met secretly, and contact with outside Christians could mean arrest and imprisonment. God's people in the mighty Soviet bloc often paid a high price during those years of oppression.

Then God's time for those nations arrived, and the walls came down. The Georgian Republic, known for its independent thinking, hosted the first *JESUS* film premiere in 1989. Within a year, the Russian translation of *JESUS* premiered to an overflow crowd of invited officials in the primary movie houses in Moscow, Leningrad, and the Ukraine. Within the next few years, twenty language versions of *JESUS* premiered before top secular and religious officials of the republics and nations of the former Soviet Union. Distributors reported that 7.7 million viewers saw the film in public cinemas and about 100 million watched nationwide telecasts of *JESUS*.

Volunteers were recruited and trained to take the 16mm *JESUS* film to their own people. As the stories trickled back, it became clear that they had done exactly that, going to the farthest corners of their nation.

These events in the former Soviet Union meant more to me than you can imagine. Years ago in 1947, I heard Dr. Oswald J. Smith, the famous Canadian evangelist and missionary statesman, challenge a thousand college students and singles at a Forest Home Conference to commit their lives to helping fulfill the Great Commission. He asked each of us to place our name on a country and claim it for the Lord through prayer and finances as God led—if necessary, even to give our lives to help reach that country for Christ. I put my name on the Soviet Union and began praying for its people.

Since our marriage, Vonette has joined me in continuing to pray for the Russian people. We were thrilled when the doors opened for the gospel to be openly preached throughout the Soviet bloc countries. Campus Crusade staff and volunteers were on the front lines of spreading the good news. Yet the Lord had in mind a most unusual distribution channel for the *JESUS* film—the very school systems of the former Soviet Union.

After each premiere of the *JESUS* film, Paul and his team invited leaders to a reception. At one such gathering attended by Russia's minister of education, the idea was discussed of training the teachers to show the *JESUS* film to their classes as part of an ethics curriculum. The minister of education responded warmly to the offer to help lay a moral and ethical foundation in a nation that had suffered under enforced atheistic philosophy for so many years.

If ever an idea was by faith, this was. No curriculum for such an effort existed at the time. Back in the U.S., Paul assembled a team of individuals to develop both an elementary and a secondary curriculum that teachers could use to help lay a moral foundation in the lives of their students. The first educators were invited to the "trial run" convocations—and the Spirit of God expanded this simple plan beyond all expectations.

Within six months, the first teacher training convocations took place in Moscow, Vologda, and St. Petersburg. In the years to come, more than 41,000 educators would attend, view the *JESUS* film, and learn about the God who loves them personally. By the end of the five-year effort, convocations had been held in more than 140 cities of the former Soviet Union.

The Lord had an unusual distribution channel for the *JESUS* film—school systems of the former Soviet Union.

At convocation after convocation, educators and others from North America, Asia, and Europe saw the Lord change hearts toward Himself and His Word. The vast majority of the educators pledged to show the *JESUS* video they received to their students. More than half told of plans to use the morals and ethics curriculum with their students. Person after person asked for more information to help them better know this God who loved them.

Within a few months, however, it was obvious that no one organization, even Campus Crusade for Christ with its thousands of staff members, could handle such an overwhelming response. Through a wonderful chain of relationships, the Lord provided the follow-up care through an effort called the CoMission. Eighty agencies, denominations, and Christian organizations formed a five-year alliance to contribute resources, personnel, or finances for sending one-year teams of volunteers to the cities that had hosted convocations.

Since the CoMission's launch in 1991, more than 1,600

volunteers have served in 55 cities. CoMission II has continued to seek individuals to go for two weeks or longer to cities that did not receive the one-year teams. Character Development Seminars (CDSs) serve to encourage educators in those cities, while training them to better understand and study the Bible. The CDS teams, composed largely of volunteers who develop their own funds to go, also help the educators see how they can continue to influence their students and communities to follow God's values.

Reaching the Unreached Areas

Weekly I hear thrilling stories of how the *JESUS* film is helping to reach areas of the world that have previously been resistant to the gospel. Japan, for example, has never embraced Christianity like other Asian nations such as South Korea. Despite decades of missionary work, approximately one percent of the Japanese people are believers.

Recently, Campus Crusade for Christ leaders in Japan requested that a special version of the *JESUS* film be produced which would have a greater appeal to Japanese unfamiliar with Christ and His message. We decided to use professional actors and retranslate portions of the script to avoid words confusing to non-Christians. Film stars immediately recognizable by Japanese television and movie viewers provided voices for the main characters in the film.

The Japanese marketing company we consulted told us that a smaller, more exclusive premiere, rather than a huge crowd, would attract greater interest among Japanese media executives. Our staff in Japan agreed. A newspaper article announced the availability of a few complimentary tickets for an advanced screening of a new film on the life of Jesus. Requests poured in for 8,000 tickets!

In all, 350 tickets were issued, including fifty given to a select group of business and entertainment industry leaders. On the evening of September 30, 1998, 350 Japanese arrived at the Tokyo Westin Hotel where a room was specially prepared for the showing. Although relatively small, this was the largest audience ever gathered in Japan to see a film about Jesus. A nationally recognized TV announcer served as emcee. She greeted the audience and introduced Paul Eshleman, director of the JESUS Film Project, who is responsible for the film's international distribution, translation, and funding efforts. Paul presented the background of the film, mentioning its release by Warner Brothers in 2,000 theaters in North America in the early 1980s. After its release, he said, it was shown on cable television where it was aired by HBO, Showtime, and The Movie Channel. A Warner Brothers executive had described the film as "two hours of peace in a world of chaos."

After Eshleman spoke, two powerful video projectors beamed a 40-minute selection of key scenes from the film. While the audience enjoyed a buffet dinner following the showing, Paul met with a select group in another room. One of Japan's top three media critics gave a twenty-minute analysis of the film in which he said, "This film can be understood by the Japanese, even though they have not had much background in Christianity...I recommend it highly." Listening were representatives from the local television station, newspapers, and magazines. Each guest received a video copy of the movie as a gift.

The response to the showing was very positive. A typical comment was: "My family is not Christian. This film helped me understand who Jesus is." One person commented that the film must be a faithful version of the Bible story. He thought the film helped to explain why there are so many followers of Jesus around the world. The president of the marketing company said with tears in her eyes, "I'll remember this evening for the rest of my life." We see this as a giant step for Christianity in Japan, one that we trust our Lord will use to help accelerate the spread of the gospel of Jesus Christ all over Japan. Please pray with us to this end.

The JESUS Video Project

In Canada and the United States, a different strategy developed for using the *JESUS* film. The question we asked ourselves was: How can we saturate every home with the gospel of Jesus Christ? The answer: By using the *JESUS* film in video format. Studies show that at least 80 percent of American homes have VCRs. This was our inroad to the American audience.

The JESUS Video Project seeks to offer *JESUS* to every home in the United States. As part of the *JESUS* video strategy, a city task force is formed to pray for wisdom, unity, and a spirit of belief. Then Christian leaders identify and target certain communities and set a specific distribution period. A holiday such as Easter, for example, is a good time to offer *JESUS* videos because people are more open to considering the claims of Christ. Participating churches decide which areas their members can reach, then train those who will be giving the *JESUS* video as a gift. Church members canvass homes in their own neighborhoods and offer a *JESUS* video to people who agree to answer survey questions about what they watched. Two weeks later, church members return to each home that accepted a video to do the survey and provide follow-up information for those who indicate they have received Christ.

Results show that as many as 75 percent of the people are home when the videos are distributed, more than 44 percent of those accept the video, and more than 16 percent of those who watch the video indicate that they have prayed to receive Christ at the end of the film!

As you can see, God provided the *JESUS* film at the most appropriate moment. Who could have foreseen the fall of the Berlin wall and the opening of the former Soviet bloc countries to the gospel? Who could have predicted the invention and widespread use of VCRs and other technological advances that have proven so advantageous in presenting the message of our Lord Jesus Christ through the medium of film? Only God could. As I look back over 33 years of waiting on God to provide a film on the life of Jesus, I recall the heartfelt prayers of thousands that have allowed us to saturate the world with the gospel through this film. This has been one way of helping to fulfill the Great Commission. Praise our almighty, wise, and loving God for what He has done—in His way and in His time!

Today, the *JESUS* film and video continue to transform the ways we can reach people with the gospel. In our technologically wise but confused world, God so often moves in directions we never expect. But what blessings we experience as we allow Him to guide us!

As of Easter Sunday 1998, Dr. Bob Cosby, Director of the JESUS Video Project for Alabama, and his team had placed a copy of the *JESUS* video in approximately 1.7 million homes in Alabama. Tapes were distributed to 758 post offices across the state. Some 9,300 churches have received letters asking for their participation in follow-up ministry. Based on prior responses to the video showings, hundreds of thousands of people in Alabama will receive Christ as Savior. We are praying that our Lord will raise up dedicated, generous servants in every city and state to place the *JESUS* video in each of the 120 million homes in America.

The *JESUS* film and video are only one new direction for ministry in Campus Crusade during the last ten years. In the next chapter, I want to share with you about other exciting events and plans for the future. Truly, this is the time to come aboard and join us in helping to change the world! If the *JESUS* film and video projects appeal to you, or if you would like to help saturate your city, state, entire country, or some other part of the world with the gospel, we would like to hear from you.

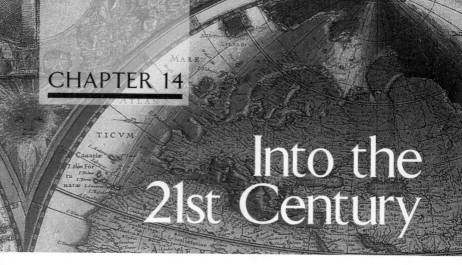

CHAPTER 14

Into the 21st Century

OUR GREAT GOD, creator of over one hundred billion galaxies, is an awesome, supernatural God. Yet, amazingly, He chooses to work through humans. As His people, we are called to help fulfill Christ's Great Commission. I trust that by now you have observed that this has been the single focus of Campus Crusade from day one—and is still our only reason for existence. Only God can fulfill the Great Commission, but miracle of miracles, He does it through the yielded lives of His children.

Our part in God's eternal plan will require supernatural faith, supernatural effort, supernatural resources, supernatural favor, and many open doors that God supernaturally provides. Can we do it? Of course, our success depends on how much we are in tune with God's will as we serve in the power of the Holy Spirit.

We must always remember that the Great Commission is God's idea. It is not a human plan. Therefore, no one wants it completed more than He does. We are merely His servants. When we pray for His leading to know our part in fulfilling God's will and work toward it in the power of the Holy Spirit, we shall live supernatural lives endued with supernatural power.

As staff of Campus Crusade, we always keep in mind that we are only one of many Christian organizations working together toward the same goal. Millions of believers in hundreds of mission groups and thousands of churches are involved. As you read in the previous chapter, many godly groups are working in cooperation with us and many use our resources such as the *JESUS* film and various discipleship materials.

God deserves all the glory for what has been accomplished already and for what He will accomplish in the future. The possibilities for worldwide ministry are mushrooming everywhere. I am absolutely confident of the promise God gave us through Paul: "God, who began the good work within you, will continue His work until it is finally finished on that day when Christ Jesus comes back again" (Philippians 1:6, NLT).

Although I am now in my seventies and have served our Lord for over fifty years, I have never been more excited about the unprecedented worldwide spiritual harvest that is taking place today. As part of this revolutionary move of God, I have seen God expand the ministry of Campus Crusade for Christ to every major country representing 99.7 percent of the world's population. The late '80s and the '90s saw our ministry change in so many ways.

As you journey with me through this chapter and read of the more recent events in this movement, it is my prayer that you too will catch the excitement and spirit of renewal that God is sending those who desire to serve and follow Him.

Move to Orlando

One of the most exciting recent events was that our headquarters outgrew our beautiful facilities at Arrowhead Springs, California, and we moved to Orlando, Florida. It was during the early 1980s that the Lord began to impress on me the need for us to relocate our international headquarters to another major city in the U.S. We had maximized the Arrowhead Springs campus and even constructed seven buildings off campus about five miles away. Yet our facilities were stretched to the limit. It became clear that the Lord was leading us to move from San Bernardino.

Do not misunderstand—Vonette and I love the people of San Bernardino. Arrowhead Springs had been our home since 1962. We raised our sons there. Every blade of grass, flower, and fountain on those beautiful grounds is familiar and loved. But we were no longer operating efficiently. As leadership staff, we faced the reality that we would have to undergo a major building effort if we stayed. What would be the best alternative—to move or to stay? What did God want us to do?

First, our worldwide staff and I began to pray for God's leading. Then I assigned a committee of staff members to evaluate more than three dozen cities using 56 criteria. Eventually, we narrowed our choices to five cities.

I traveled to those five cities looking them over as part of a careful feasibility study. To help evaluate our possibilities, I met with various governors, mayors, educators, and Christian leaders. In each location, I received a warm reception. On a visit to Colorado Springs, we were offered a great facility—the prestigious Tiffany Square. This fine property and other financial incentives totaled in the millions of dollars.

But when I arrived in Orlando, Florida, a group of about 500 business and professional men and women of that city gathered to meet me at a luncheon. Pat Williams, Senior Executive Vice-President of the Orlando Magic basketball team and a leader in the local community, assured me, "Whatever offers any other cities have made, we will more than match." Over and over again, I heard leading laymen and women, the mayor, and other prominent officials say, "Please come to Orlando." I was awed at their well-organized reception and their commitment to helping us move to Orlando.

While still in Orlando, I arranged a telephone board meeting to discuss our possibilities in light of what I had learned. By this time, some problems developed with the facility we were considering in Colorado Springs. As the board members and I discussed our options—and more importantly what God was leading us to do—we agreed that we should accept Orlando's invitation and move our international headquarters to Florida.

When I announced the board's decision to our headquarters staff leaders, I was shocked to receive an almost unanimous objection to the board's decision. "We don't want to go to Orlando. It's too humid. There are too many alligators and bugs. That's the last place in the world I would like to go!"

At that moment, the Lord gave me a strong impression that I should say to them, "Whatever you want to do is fine with me. Vonette and I are willing to live anywhere God wants us to go. We don't expect to be around as long as the rest of you who are younger than we are. Let's go back to prayer and study and decide if God really wants us to move to Orlando. You are godly, intelligent leaders and I trust your judgment. I am more concerned with what you want than anyone else."

Our staff leaders did just that. They prayed and thoroughly evaluated the various cities and the many factors that would help determine where we should move. To their credit, they did not leave any stone unturned in prayer and evaluation. After thirty days, they announced, "We believe we should move to Orlando."

One of the reasons we chose Orlando is its excellent transportation system, including one of the best airports in the world. Other reasons included the pleasant climate, the almost 40 million international tourists who visit the area every year, and the low cost of living for our staff. For our international staff members, the location is more centrally situated. In the meantime, the costs of living and doing ministry in Southern California had skyrocketed.

Once the decision had been made, we began planning the thousands of details that would make the move more efficient. For the most part, all went according to plan. Our donors and friends of the ministry hardly noticed our move. Our computer connections and mail delivery were smoothly transitioned. Hundreds of staff made the long move with household goods, children, and office equipment to begin their lives in Orlando. I praise God for the good spirit of our staff and for God's hand of blessing in what could have been a difficult transition for our many ministries, offices, and families.

Lake Hart Campus

With great excitement, we moved to Orlando in 1991 with the understanding that we would move into an intermediate location until we could build our new campus on the Lake Hart property donated by a Christian businessman. We purchased a large warehouse in the Sunport Industrial Park and converted it into staff offices. Within a short time, however, we outgrew this location and expanded various ministry offices into nearby facilities.

Meanwhile, an excellent team of architects, builders, and contractors began erecting our new Lake Hart Campus. The Lord worked in miraculous ways to provide the necessary permits and approvals. In just two months, the project passed through the building-approval process without a single dissenting vote. The gift of the Lake Hart land plus local and state grants provided $14 million to defray our overall project costs!

From the beginning, we made a commitment that raising funds for the new headquarters would not detract from our commitment to help fulfill the Great Commission worldwide. Yet the staff and I realized the importance of building the new center as quickly as possible. We had discovered when our headquarters was located at Arrowhead Springs that a "home base" facility drew many thousands into our movement, built them up in God's Word, and challenged them to give, go, and pray to help fulfill the Great Commission. I like the way Bailey Marks, our International Executive Vice President, described the mission of our new headquarters: "Our MPTA (Million Population Target Areas) strategy to saturate the world with the gospel will be clearly seen and fully understood by tens of thousands in the Christian community as they visit our new international headquarters. The global telecommunications capacity it will offer will be invaluable in linking our dedicated staff around the world with their leadership, supporters, and one another."

To effectively accomplish these purposes, the Campus Crusade for Christ Lake Hart Campus will include the following buildings:

- Operations and Administration Support Center, which will house the world headquarters offices
- Chapel to help us constantly seek God's face
- Vision Center in which friends and visitors to our headquarters will observe, through the most advanced technology available, what God is doing around the world
- Retreat Center
- Training and Conference Center

Here they will discover how they can become part of a mighty movement of God

When completed, the new headquarters will have room for more than 1,000 staff and will attract tens of thousands of visitors each year from around the world—many of whom will be exposed to the gospel for the first time. A large conference center with athletic facilities and the finest accommodations will host world leaders, world-famous personalities, and people from all walks of life. Here they will discover how they can become part of a mighty movement of God in linking arms with others to take the message of God's love and forgiveness to generation after generation and to the ends of the earth.

The latest technology at the facilities will allow us to push a button and get an up-to-date report on what God is doing in every part of our planet. We will have several theaters where people who do not know Christ will hear the gospel and many will be brought into the kingdom. Through displays, tours, and personal contact, uninvolved Christians will be challenged to surrender their lives to the Lord and be filled with the Holy Spirit. We are praying that our Lake Hart Campus will be one of the most attractive places to visit in America, including Disney World, Sea World, and Universal Studios.

On October 18–20, 1996, we held a ground breaking celebration on the 285-acre Lake Hart property. That weekend was a time of glorious celebration. It also marked the forty-fifth anniversary of Campus Crusade for Christ. Many friends, both local and from around the nation, came to hear about our plans for the new facilities.

One of the highlights of the weekend was the surprise seventy-fifth birthday celebration given for me by the Campus Crusade for Christ staff. I was thrilled! Former President George Bush spoke at the banquet and Jeb Bush, his son and now governor of Florida, gave the invocation. A choir of staff members sang praises to our magnificent God. Many old friends of the ministry and new staff were present to make the evening complete.

On the 19th, we held the site dedication. The fall weather was gorgeous. Nine hundred people attended, including Orlando Mayor Glenda Hood and Orange County Commissioner Chairman Linda Chapin. Charlie Bradshaw, who donated the Lake Hart property to Campus Crusade for Christ, received a standing ovation.

Although plans to build the Lake Hart facilities exceed any single investment in buildings this ministry has ever made, we believe that with these facilities God will enable us to accomplish a greatly accelerated strategy to present the gospel continually to the entire world. As in our purchase of Arrowhead Springs, we have once again stepped out in faith, trusting our great God and Savior to provide and leaving the results to Him.

In April 1999, the Operations and Administration Support

Center was completed, and we began moving various ministries into the new facilities.

Fasting and Prayer Movement

As you will remember, one of the first ministries we began at Campus Crusade was a 24-hour Prayer Ministry. That is because we believe prayer is the foundation for our work and lives. This emphasis has become an increasing priority each year since we began in 1951.

For many years, I have been deeply concerned with the moral and spiritual decadence of America. We as a society have lost our way. We once held sacred the biblical foundations on which our country was founded. Over the last few decades, our principles have been discarded one by one. The Supreme Court removed prayer and the Bible, including the Ten Commandments, from our schools. Premarital sex and abortion-on-demand led to plunging morals. Increased crime, divorce, drug use, and suicide rates all indicate that our nation is in a life-and-death struggle because we have abandoned God.

On July 5, 1994, God led me to begin a forty-day fast for a mighty revival among believers and a great spiritual awakening among nonbelievers. I was also fasting and praying for the fulfillment of the Great Commission throughout the world. On my twenty-ninth day of fasting, I was reading 2 Chronicles, chapters 20 through 30, when God's holy Word spoke to my heart in a most unusual way. Previously He had clearly impressed on me that He was going to send a great spiritual awakening to America, but that revival would be preceded by a time of spiritual preparation through repentance, with a special emphasis on fasting and prayer.

I also felt impressed by the Lord to invite several hundred of the most influential Christians in the country, including heads of denominations and parachurch movements, to gather in Orlando as guests of Campus Crusade for a time of fasting and prayer. This would be strictly a time for seeking God's direction on how we, His servants, could be instruments of revival and awakening for our nation and the world.

I was hoping for at least a Gideon's three hundred to respond. Instead, more than six hundred came. God met with us in a supernatural way! Most of us agreed that it was truly a life-changing experience for each of us.

During my forty-day fast, God led me to pray that at least two million North Americans will fast and pray for forty days for revival in America and throughout the world. We are also praying for the fulfillment of the Great Commission in our generation. I believe that as millions of Christians discover the biblical power of fasting as it relates to a holy life, prayer, witnessing, and the Great Commission, they will be reawakened spiritually. And out of this great move of the Spirit of God will come the revival for which so many have prayed so long, resulting in the fulfillment of the Great Commission.

I have fasted for forty days every year since 1994. I am confident that millions of believers have joined me for the same reasons—some for forty days, some for shorter periods. The Fasting and Prayer Gathering first held in Orlando has now become an annual event. Each November, thousands of believers meet in a selected city to fast and pray. In addition, many hundreds of thousands, if not millions, join us through satellite hook-ups all across the country and in many other countries around the world.

World Changers Radio

Since 1951, I have had a growing conviction that there is a critical need for Christians to be trained and prepared to share their faith as a way of life where they live and work. Tragically, all our surveys show that fewer than 2 percent of Christians in America regularly share their faith in Christ with others.

That is the reason we launched World Changers Radio. It is the only national radio program today that specifically trains and challenges Christians to introduce others to Christ and to help fulfill the Great Commission. Steve Douglass, our Executive Vice President and Director of U.S. Ministries, and I engage in a rapid-fire dialogue during a daily fifteen-minute program. We lace our comments with powerful testimonies and live interviews of everyday people who are changing the world through their witnessing. We also emphasize fasting and prayer for revival and give reports of Campus Crusade activities around the world.

I truly believe that this program offers "Fifteen Minutes that Matter Daily," which is the subtitle of the World Changers Radio program. It draws from the fifty years of leadership and experience which Campus Crusade staff have accumulated while working with millions in all walks of life throughout the world.

International Leadership University

Did you know that godly followers of our Lord Jesus Christ founded the first 119 colleges and universities in America? For example, the Puritans established Harvard College in 1636 to train leaders for the church. Harvard alumni were originally called the Sons of the Prophets. Princeton was started by a group of Presbyterian evangelists as the result of a great awakening. How sad that most, if not all, of these institutions have abandoned their Christian heritage.

Today, the world has many excellent Christian colleges and universities, but they educate less than 2 percent of the tens of millions of world leaders. That is one of the reasons we have set our sights on a "university without walls" that can help train tens of millions of believers all over the world. Called the International Leadership University, it is one of the tools we will use to reach the next generation of young people for Christ. In the early '70s, God gave me a vision to start this worldwide university for evangelism and discipleship, but I needed a president who shared my faith and vision.

One day, Stan Oakes walked into my office. He is a staff

member and valued friend of over thirty years who became a believer through the ministry. He has had phenomenal leadership experience in directing our ministry to over 14,000 college and university professors. Suddenly, the Holy Spirit impressed upon me that Stan was the person to assume the role as president. I turned to him and said, "Stan, the Lord has impressed me that you are to be the first president of the International Leadership University."

He was taken by surprise, but after prayerful consideration, agreed to accept the challenge. Several years have passed since that day, and I am even more excited about his leadership today. He has demonstrated remarkable skills for which I give thanks to our great Lord and Savior. Miracles of God have confirmed the leadership of Stan and Ginger Oakes.

Did you know that Christians founded the first 119 colleges and universities in America?

The mission of the International Leadership University is to educate and equip millions of Christians from America and around the world to reach their countries with the gospel and influence their national institutions, the media, courts, businesses, governments, schools, and churches. The University development involves four phases:

- Phase 1: Acquire The King's College in New York. This institution, which had closed due to financial difficulties, is a liberal arts college with a sixty-year tradition of academic excellence and commitment to the mission of Christianity. This phase has been accomplished.

- Phase 2: Establish the first campus of the new university— a non-residential campus in the Empire State building to educate and equip leaders from New York City. The plan is to take education back into the city. Then other urban campuses will be opened in the great cities of the world. The first classes begin in the fall of 1999.

- Phase 3: Build the flagship campus—an elite residential campus on beautiful Blue Lake, sixty miles from New York City. The University will invite the best and brightest young leaders from every country in the world for study and leadership development at The King's College.

- Phase 4: Develop Internet classrooms. Technological advances such as the Internet, CD-ROMs, DVDs, and satellites have made it possible to develop an entire university curriculum that students can access from anywhere in the world. This phase will give tens of millions of students worldwide access to the finest Christian training and resources provided by scholars from Christian and secular campuses who are devout followers of Christ.

The International Leadership University will work in cooperation with the six Campus Crusade seminaries on five continents: International School of Theologies in San Bernardino, Kenya, the Philippines, and Latin America; the East Asia School of Theology in Singapore; and the Jordan Evangelical Theology School in Amman, Jordan. The possibilities for training literally millions of dynamic leaders are phenomenal! We anticipate at least 10,000 ILU centers around the world by the year 2010.

Into the New Millenium

As the new millennium approaches, we as an organization are planning a massive worldwide celebration honoring our Lord Jesus Christ and our fifty years of helping to fulfill the Great Commission. The celebration, which will include thousands of our leaders from most nations of the world, will take place at our Lake Hart Campus in Orlando from December 31, 2000, through January 4, 2001. Many millions are expected to join in the celebration via satellite. The purpose of this celebration is to praise God and give glory to our great Savior, the

Lord Jesus Christ.

Beginning with the year 2001, our goal in the new millennium will be to continue our emphasis on evangelism. However, we will also give more attention to training disciples who can in turn, as Paul explains to Timothy in 2 Timothy 2:2, train others who will in turn train others to be faithful witnesses of Christ in the power of the Holy Spirit. We are truly committed to helping change our world for Christ, generation after generation!

I urge you to join us in our vision to help change the world for Christ. Over the years, the Lord has enabled us to expand our U.S. base to include more than fifty ministries. In addition to students in high schools and on college and university campuses, our staff reach out to people as varied as children, junior high students, executives, diplomats, athletes, musicians, military personnel, prisoners, minorities, and others. We have developed very effective tools that are friendly to the people to whom we minister.

Beginning in the next chapter, I want to share with you a brief description of some of the more than fifty ministries in Campus Crusade. I pray that God will lead you to work with one or more of them as a full-time staff member or volunteer. The first and greatest need we have is for prayer. For which group of people has God burdened your heart? We have many opportunities for those who are called by God to work, whether for a few months or a few years, in the United States or internationally. Ministry opportunities are available all over the world for dedicated Christian warriors who want to bring their talents and gifts to help us in our goal of serving Christ on a full-time basis.

I encourage you to prayerfully review the ministry areas that interest you. I have included the five main Campus Crusade for Christ ministries in the next chapter. In addition, there are many others that are very important and equally committed to helping fulfill the Great Commission.

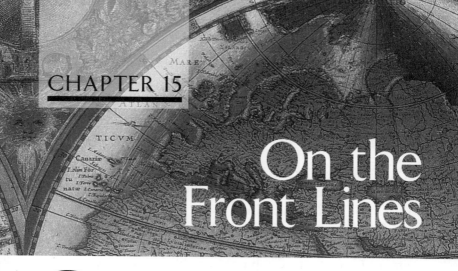

CHAPTER 15

On the Front Lines

GOD HAS BLESSED Campus Crusade for Christ with some of the most creative, talented staff members in the United States. Each of them has a vision for fulfilling the Great Commission, but through many different types of ministry. One of the distinctives of our organization is that we have given our staff the freedom to do what God has led them to do within the parameters of our focus and purpose.

For this reason, Campus Crusade has branched out from the college campus to many other areas of ministry. Even within ministries that have existed for decades, God is leading in new and strategic ways. It amazes me what God has done through these dedicated staff men and women.

In this chapter, I want to give you a taste of our dynamic ministries and strategies in the U.S. We have five basic ministries: the U.S. Campus Ministries; the Josh McDowell Ministry; Athletes in Action; Student Venture; and FamilyLife. Together, these ministries reach out to millions of Americans each year.

We have another category of ministries that we call the Group Ministries. These are presented in Appendix A. Each of these plays a vital role in our overall strategy to win our country for Christ.

I encourage you to read this chapter to get a flavor of the many things Campus Crusade is doing throughout our country. Then browse through the appendix to find additional areas that may fit in with your ministry abilities and interests. I urge you to come alongside us and be our partner in spreading the gospel and training believers to grow in their faith.

U.S. Campus Ministries

Any organization is only as good as its leaders. I am so blessed to have godly men and women who have taken God's call to help fulfill the Great Commission as the purpose for their lives. This is true in both the international and U.S. areas of Campus Crusade. In Chapter 17, I will introduce you to the leadership of our International Ministries, but in this chapter I would like to help you get to know those who direct our U.S. staff.

Dr. Steve Douglass, Executive Vice President and U.S. Field Director for Campus Crusade for Christ, serves the leaders of approximately fifty ministries in the U.S. Ministries division. Since 1967, Steve has played a marvelous role in helping to keep this ministry focused on the fulfillment of the Great Commission, and he and his wife, Judy, have been a special blessing and encouragement to Vonette and me.

Steve is assisted through the able help of Chuck Price, Associate National Director, and group directors Ed Maggard, Pam Davis, Sherry Fields, Donna Wright, Lillie Nye, and Bill Baumann. Crawford Lorritz is responsible for special projects. These dedicated men and women serve the many divisions and ministry leaders in most communities across America.

Ken Heckmann, Vice President for Administration, is responsible for giving leadership to approximately 800 staff serving our Lord at our headquarters. The Lake Hart campus is the nerve center and heartbeat of our worldwide ministry and is always in need of people knowledgeable in administration, computer operations, finance, and management. You can help change the world from the Lake Hart campus.

The mission statement of the U.S. Campus Ministry, under

the able direction of Steve Sellers, is to "turn lost students into Christ-centered laborers." The majority of leaders in every segment of culture come from the university campus. Change the campus and we can change the world for Christ. Therefore, to see this mission become a reality, our campus leadership staff have developed a ministry grid which we believe will enable us to help reach students worldwide. It is called the "Four Lanes."

The Four Lanes are Staffed Campuses, Catalytic Ministries, InterCultural Resources, and the Worldwide Student Network. Each lane targets a segment of the population of college students, and the four cover the scope of the 60 million college students around the world.

Staffed Campuses

Staffed Campuses refers to the traditional placement of a staff team on one campus. When Vonette and I set foot on the UCLA campus in 1951, we began the first Staffed Campus ministry. Today, we have staff teams on more than 200 campuses across the United States. These teams do a tremendous job introducing students to Christ, training believers, and sending them into the harvest. Their efforts are a good example of implementing our strategy to "win, build, train, and send."

Staff teams are most often placed on the larger universities. Through the teams, students see the body of Christ in action. Yet, with more than 3,600 colleges and universities in the U.S., there are simply too many campuses for us to provide staff. Therefore, the Campus Ministry devised a new strategy to reach students without physically placing staff on every campus. It is another lane in the Four Lane strategy.

Catalytic Ministries

New campus ministries are being opened through an innovative Catalytic strategy called Student LINC (Leaders In New Campuses). Working from our headquarters in Orlando, Florida, and other locations around the country, experienced campus workers communicate regularly with five to ten key volunteers or students on a non-staffed campus. Using phones, E-mail, and the Internet, staff members train volunteers and students to develop ministries on their campuses. With Catalytic Ministries presently operating on about 500 campuses, we are trusting God to raise up students and volunteers to start, lead, and develop an additional 2,500 new campus ministries in the near future.

We believe the resources exist within five miles of every campus to reach these students for Christ. Therefore, we build partnerships with local churches and individuals who share the same heart for reaching college students. We offer training,

materials, and conferences on how they can effectively reach students in their area with the gospel. Local churches provide laborers, a meeting place, and a stable environment where students can connect with a loving community of believers.

Another Catalytic strategy is a Metro Team—staff members and volunteers (students, laypeople, and church leaders) who form a team to reach specific campuses in a major city. Resources from our staff, church partnerships, and key students are pooled to reach the students of an entire city. This creates more momentum than what can be accomplished by any one group.

One student who received Christ through the Boston Metro strategy was Steve Sawyer, a student at Curry College. A hemophiliac who contracted HIV through tainted blood when he was young, he was confronted with the reality that his life on earth would be short.

Steve wanted to spend the rest of his days on earth telling

everyone how God had changed his life and given him hope. Before his death in 1999, Steve spoke to more than 100,000 college students around the world. It is estimated that more than 10,000 indicated salvation decisions for Christ during Steve's brief years as a student evangelist.

InterCultural Resources

The mission of InterCultural Resources is to reach, disciple, and mobilize the 3.2 million ethnic minority students in the U.S. for the cause of Christ. We desire to see God give people the ability to effectively engage ethnic communities with the truth of the gospel, then disciple and develop leaders.

Impact is the U.S. Ministries' national strategy to reach African-American students. We sponsor the Impact Conference, a bi-annual winter event for African-Americans. The conference has grown from 550 in 1991 to 2,450 in 1998, and has helped launch African-American ministries on numerous campuses. Summer Projects to countries such as Ghana, Kenya, Nigeria, South Africa, and Zambia are also a part of our Impact strategy.

Destino focuses on reaching Hispanics, the fastest growing ethnic minority in the United States. Destino Conferences and the El Paso Juarez Summer Project play a key role in this student strategy.

We recently launched a national strategy called EPIC to reach Asian-American students. Through Asian-American Student Leadership Conferences and a Summer Project in Los Angeles, we develop student leaders committed to evangelism and discipleship.

Worldwide Student Network

In 1986, several leaders in the Campus Ministry met to challenge students to crisscross the globe, offering a network of resources and laborers to reach students and expose every person on our planet to the love of Christ. This web of students reaching students is called the Worldwide Student Network (WSN).

In 1992 the Campus Ministry made a formal commitment to open new campuses around the world through the WSN. Teams of students from the Campus Ministry have been trained and sent as laborers to unreached university campuses on every continent. National students are being trained and equipped to reach the people of their own countries and beyond. To date, more than 10,200 people have gone overseas through the efforts of WSN and more than 1,000 have completed year-long STINT projects.

Dina is a Kazakh Campus Ministry staff member who came to know Christ as a student through a Campus Ministry team sent to her city. She says, "One summer, God laid it on my heart to reach people of my nationality in nearby East Asia. The Lord brought resources together for six of us to go from our country [Kazakhstan] to nearby East Asia on a summer project!"

While studying in St. Petersburg, Russia, during the Communist regime, Andre Furminov heard the gospel through students making covert trips into his country. Later, after meeting with students on an international summer project, he trusted Christ. That fall, a team of American students moved to St. Petersburg and discipled Andre. He is now the senior pastor of one of the fastest growing, most dynamic churches in the former Soviet Union.

WSN has pioneered new ministries on 172 campuses in 42 countries. Nationals now lead many of these campus ministries. We believe God will use these pioneering efforts to establish movements for Christ on every campus in the world.

Josh McDowell Ministry

It is always a tremendous privilege for Vonette and me to join Josh and his team, whether it is on a project in Russia or at a student conference in America. We look forward to his thrilling reports and exciting stories about changed lives.

Since 1965, the Josh McDowell Ministry has been telling the world the truth about Jesus Christ. I can still see Josh as a talented young man who joined our staff in 1964. He lectured on the university campus as a traveling representative of Campus Crusade for Christ. Josh always carried an overloaded briefcase of notes and papers wherever he went! His zeal for truth was contagious.

By the late 1970s, requests for Josh to speak increased. He began publishing books and recording his talks on tape. Today, Josh McDowell is known as one of the most articulate and popular youth speakers, having spoken to more than 7 million young people in at least 84 countries, including 700 university and college campuses.

Josh still speaks about two areas: relationships and apologetics. But he adapts the issues and his communication styles to keep pace with changing times. Josh has always talked to young people, targeting contemporary sexual attitudes. For example, in his talk on relationships, Josh became more frank as he discussed sexual purity through the "Why Wait?" campaign. Now, through his "Right From Wrong" campaign, he talks about making right choices based on the nature and character of God.

As he discovered that junior high and high school students were grappling with issues that once faced high school and college students, Josh shifted his target audience to include younger teens. He has also broadened his ministry strategy to include equipping church staff, parents, and other significant adults.

The Josh McDowell Ministry (JMM) provides resources through a variety of communication mediums, from worldwide distribution of Josh's bestseller, *More Than a Carpenter*, to a site on the worldwide web. To date, Josh is the author or co-author of 52 books. He has developed nine workbook studies and has been featured in twelve video series and numerous television and film specials. In the last decade, more than 14 million of Josh's books in Russian have been placed into the hands of men and women throughout the former Soviet Union.

In Romania, approximately fifteen minutes before Josh was to speak at the University of Bucharest, he was approached by a young lady. She shared that three years ago, when Josh had last been in Romania, her brother had gone to hear Josh speak. Her brother asked Jesus Christ to come into his life that night. At the close of the meeting, each person was given a copy of *More Than a Carpenter* in Romanian. Her brother brought one home. Later, he shared the same gospel message with his family. His father, mother, and sister trusted Jesus Christ as their Savior. The young lady handed Josh a bouquet of flowers to say thank-you for helping her be introduced to Jesus Christ.

Meeting Physical Needs

Twice a year, Josh and thousands of men and women take food, medicine, gifts, and the love of Christ to those in Russia who have so little. Meeting physical needs often allows the ministry to address spiritual needs and lends credibility to local churches and missionary efforts. This year, 360 American Christians participated in Operation Carelift, a humanitarian aid mission trip to Russia, Belarus, and Ukraine. One story in particular captures what God is doing.

Operation Carelift bus captain Ward Coleman was scheduled to take his bus to a boarding school in the town of Tuchkovo, outside of Moscow. The school was for disabled children and had 154 students. Along the way, Ward saw a public school, mistook it for the boarding school, and stopped. He soon discovered he was in the wrong place, but one of the teachers there had heard about Carelift and invited the group to come in anyway. Ward and the other participants were able to share the gospel with the 800 students at this public school, and many prayed to receive Christ. Afterward, the bus group found the boarding school and shared the plan of salvation with the children there. Where man had planned for this bus group to visit one school and tell 154 kids about Christ, God planned for them to visit two schools and tell 954 students about Christ!

The major departments in JMM include the International Team; National "Right From Wrong" Team; Communications (Marketing, Radio, Writing, and Graphics); Operations (Data Entry, Finance, Computer Services); International Resources; and Development. JMM affiliate staff also represent JMM in their respective communities, from Pennsylvania to California.

As we enter the new millennium, JMM may be one of the few Campus Crusade ministries with no numerical goals or well-defined strategies. By continuing to offer projects, media resources, and issues-based campaigns, their objective is to assist others in the body of Christ to reach their own ministry goals and objectives.

For example, the Josh McDow-ell Ministry recently took a small group of volunteers to Cuba to deliver humanitarian aid and Christian literature. Josh's son, Sean, met a young Cuban who had read *Evidence That Demands a Verdict*. Sean asked him where he got a copy. The young man's answer caught him by surprise. "My church has only one copy but I wanted a copy too. So I bor-

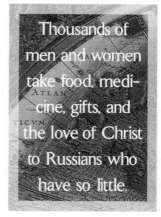

Thousands of men and women take food, medicine, gifts, and the love of Christ to Russians who have so little.

rowed the church's copy and made a copy for myself." Sean thought he must have misunderstood the young man's answer and asked if he could see the book. The Cuban went home and returned with a two-inch-thick, handwritten copy of *Evidence*. Sean asked how long it had taken him to copy the entire book. The young man's mother quickly replied, *"Dia por dia por dia por dia!"* Day after day after day after day.

Athletes in Action

As a young seminary student, I saw athletes respond to the gospel. In 1955, Vonette and I were meeting with ten starters on the UCLA national championship football team. Then in the early 1960s, Dave Hannah, a Campus Crusade for Christ staff member and former collegiate football player, caught a vision for how to use sports to reach athletes for Christ. Dave shared his vision with me in 1966, and out of that meeting we launched the sports ministry of Campus Crusade, Athletes in Action (AIA).

Today, under the direction of Wendel Deyo, hundreds of full-time staff serve AIA worldwide to help reach others for Jesus Christ through the influence of sports. Ministry results are multiplied by evangelizing and discipling college and professional athletes and coaches.

Global Media Strategy

AIA launched a global media strategy in January 1998, an initiative designed to help expose half a billion people to the gospel by the end of 2000 through thirteen media projects. Famous athletes speak candidly about their faith through videos and "Heart of a Champion" radio spots. Estimates report that 40 million people heard testimonies or the message of Christ in the first six months of the campaign.

A Super Bowl Outreach video, featuring well-known quarterbacks, was viewed by more than 350,000 people in January 1999. AIA's videos *Give Me the Rock* (NBA) and *Unfading Glory*, a new video featuring Olympic wrestlers, have both been translated into a number of foreign languages.

AIA's national office, located near Cincinnati, Ohio, is home to their World Training and Resource Center. Through AIA internships and a month-long summer project, many college-student athletes are discipled at AIA's headquarters each year. Project participants receive training in ministry and in turn co-direct sports camps for hundreds of youth each summer.

The property also serves as an ideal camp and conference center. Besides being a respite for staff on the front lines, AIA's facilities allow the ministry to host and minister to sports teams from around the world.

AIA staff and key volunteers, located in approximately 20 cities with professional teams, are involved in the direct discipleship of more than 6,000 student-athletes, coaches, and administrators. Besides having staff on 83 university campuses, AIA staff serve as chaplains with 35 professional teams.

Staff and volunteers develop spiritual multipliers as they speak to sports teams, lead Bible studies, and address spiritual needs. They also help train influential athletes to talk about the Lord with the media and in other public forums. Key volunteers have established ministries on more than 25 of the more than 1,200 campuses without full-time staff. AIA staff also serve as LINC consultants, training volunteers through phone calls, E-mail, and personal visits.

Equipping the World for Outreach

AIA-USA joins with nationals in approximately 40 countries on six continents by praying, providing financial resources and materials, and by traveling to minister personally. More than 25 AIA sports teams, involving nearly 400 amateur athletes and coaches, travel internationally each year.

Through sponsoring high-profile evangelistic breakfasts, competing in many of the world's elite collegiate gymnasiums, and conducting large-scale outreaches, AIA takes aggressive steps to saturate the world with the gospel through athletes. AIA basketball teams playing each fall in the nation's Division I schools have provided high visibility for the sports ministry over its three-plus decades of existence.

The Olympic Games and the World Cup tournament have more recently proven ideal for ministry. At the 1996 Olympics in Atlanta, about 110 athletes from around the world participated in the AIA-sponsored project, "More than Gold." Staff and participants conducted thirty evangelistic clinics in partnership with Atlanta churches. AIA staff also helped distribute 3,500 copies of the *JESUS* film in 52 languages to Olympic athletes.

AIA Communications helps link resources to the ministry with brochures, media guides, player testimony cards, Bible studies, press releases, and a quarterly publication. The primary focus is on developing the Internet in the next millennium.

While approximately 60 percent of athletes are African-American, minorities have long-represented a very small percentage of AIA staff. A scholarship fund was recently established to allow collegiate minority athletes to take advantage of summer opportunities, conferences, and retreats.

Student Venture

Since its beginning in 1966, the high school ministry of Campus Crusade has focused on reaching teenagers with the life-changing message of Jesus Christ. Junior and senior high schools are the two doors through which virtually every individual passes. Who will reach today's generation? Student Venture, our high school and junior high outreach, is a ministry to tens of thousands of students conducted by 900 full-time staff, volunteers, and VITAL LINC Affiliates throughout the world.

VITAL LINC is a program where full-time staff train, advise, encourage, and provide materials for VITAL LINC Affiliates who volunteer 8 to 10 hours per week to minister to teenagers in their local communities.

Leaders from more than fifty denominations and Christian youth organizations are combining their efforts and resources in Challenge 2000 Alliance. This is a cooperative effort to reach *every* student at *each* of the 56,000 junior and senior high schools in the U.S.

God is blessing in each ministry area of Student Venture,

from incredible increases at FastBreak, Getaway, and Something's Happening USA conferences to new highs in the number of VITAL LINC Affiliates. The InterCultural Resources department accelerates reaching ethnic, urban, and inner-city students. As they target local campuses, staff help involve the entire community. The VITAL LINC team provides top-notch coaching and training for more than 115 Affiliates across the nation—from small towns in rural states to the booming metropolis of New York City.

Randy, a VITAL LINC Affiliate in Alabama, says, "The decision that only students can now lead [religious] activities makes high school campus ministry an explosive Christian weapon. Student-led activities will work."

For years Student Venture, under the capable direction of Chuck Klein, has been a leader in developing relevant messages for kids. Now Student Venture staff also develop, package, and distribute resources to help students, staff, youth pastors, and concerned adults reach their campuses. Venture Media provides tools and strategies for starting new campus ministries through a church or community group. This includes an evangelism and resource center on the Internet, Campus Starter resource kits, and Character Development resources for use in either public or private schools.

Student Venture is also experiencing growth around the globe as nationals ask for the resources to help them win their youth for Jesus. In addition to partnerships and staffed outposts, Student Venture continues its successful spring and summer international projects.

FamilyLife

In the mid '70s, when few people talked about the family, we held a conference for engaged Campus Crusade staff members. Our vision for strengthening families crystallized when those couples, now married, wanted further guidelines. Soon our FamilyLife conference speakers began training more people to speak at conferences.

Today FamilyLife, launched in 1976, and directed by a very gifted and godly Dennis Rainey, is one of the fastest growing Campus Crusade ministries. Through conferences, home Bible studies, a nationwide daily broadcast, and publications and materials, staff reach out to families to point them to Christ. Strengthening families and returning people to the Scriptures —God's blueprints for marriage and family—have been the goals of the ministry for more than twenty years. The core messages FamilyLife teaches on marriage and the family are:

- Repentance and purity: Encouraging people to establish a relationship with God and walk closely with Him
- Marriage: Helping people honor the marriage covenant
- Roles: Equipping husbands and wives to fulfill biblical roles
- Parenting: Encouraging dads and moms to raise godly children

FamilyLife utilizes four outreach channels: events, materials, broadcasts, and publications. These are strategically integrated so that each outreach promotes, extends, and reinforces the others.

Events and Materials

In the 1998–1999 conference season, more than 90,000 people attended FamilyLife Marriage Conferences in 116 cities. In addition, FamilyLife launched a FamilyLife Parenting Conference and also helped sponsor Urban Family Conferences. The staff also cooperate with our Hispanic Ministry, offering Family Conferences for Spanish-speaking communities.

FamilyLife created the HomeBuilders Couples Series™, widely used each year in Sunday schools and home Bible studies. One couple, for example, began a HomeBuilders group in their neighborhood in Marietta, Georgia. For some time, they had been troubled by the needs of their neighbors. They passed out nearly three hundred flyers inviting neighbors to their home for a dessert and to hear about the study. Ten of the fourteen couples who showed up decided to participate. While participating in the HomeBuilders study, at least half of them started attending church with this couple. Their pastor was so impressed that he asked the husband to help the church assemble a small-group plan for the entire church.

"FamilyLife Today"

In November 1992, FamilyLife launched "FamilyLife Today," a half-hour daily radio show featuring Dennis Rainey and co-host Bob Lepine. By 1999 the program was heard by an estimated 1.5 million weekly listeners on 234 radio stations in almost 450 communities. One woman wrote, "I really enjoy your program. It has a been a great benefit to my husband and me. It is better than going to a counselor." Another person stated, "I was out jogging with my radio on, heard your program, and started crying so hard I had to run home and call. I'll be 'running' with you daily!"

Resources for Evangelism, Marriage Enrichment, and Parenting

From unique products such as Resurrection Eggs™, to books and audiocassette series, to diagnostic tools for churches, FamilyLife offers biblically based resources that make a difference in building godly families.

The Resurrection Eggs includes a dozen colorful eggs, each containing a miniature object that illustrates a key event in the death, burial, or resurrection of Jesus Christ. In 1998, nearly 170,000 sets of Resurrection Eggs were distributed; 44,000 of these were given to 176 inner-city ministries in 45 states through the FamilyLife's Jesus Loves Me Project. One mission director said Resurrection Eggs were "the best evangelistic outreach we've ever used. The women at the mission loved it more than the kids. We told the story over and over!"

Real Family Life is a recent monthly publication communicating God's truth on marriage and family. It is a communiqué for the ministry's key events and materials.

Since 1993, FamilyLife has been networking with the international ministries of Campus Crusade. Starting with 24 marriage conferences in twelve countries, expansion continues. To date, representatives from 72 countries have received training. Translating existing materials and making them culturally relevant are ongoing strategies. Another strategy includes providing countries with resources that integrate FamilyLife materials into existing ministries of evangelism and discipleship.

A Mighty Work of God

As you can see, the variety of outreach occurring through these five ministries is astounding. Each area is strategic to our nation and to the Church. We cannot take the credit for what God is doing. His Spirit is working in hearts all over our country.

God is also doing a mighty work through our International Ministries. In the next chapter, you will discover the amazing things happening in places you may never have dreamed were being touched by the gospel. In all this, we constantly praise God for His love toward us and for allowing us this part in His eternal plan to bring men and women to Him.

CHAPTER 16

World Impact

B
Y HIS SPIRIT, our wonderful God is making an impact on every continent with the glorious message of His love and forgiveness. Campus Crusade for Christ is now ministering in 181 countries, and since 1951 we have seen approximately 3.5 billion people exposed to the gospel as of June 1, 1999. In this chapter, I want to give you a sample of some of the developments on the various continents. For a closer look at the countries in which our staff serve and their activities, see Chapter 17 on the individual ministry areas.

Africa

The people of Africa are undergoing dramatic change due to the collapse of the traditional family, and they are searching for purpose. Our staff is finding ripe harvest fields as they present the gospel. For example, in a large Muslim city a movie about Mohammed was shown for three weeks in every part of the city. Muslim leaders assumed people would choose Mohammed over Jesus and allowed only limited showings of the *JESUS* film. However, the Muslims responded to the *JESUS* film in a way totally unexpected by their Muslim leaders. The people said, "Oh, at last we understand! Mohammed was only a prophet. It's Jesus who is the Savior! We must follow Jesus!"

As an example of the varied and creative ways our nationals communicate the gospel, the staff in Kenya developed what they call a SEND strategy. They organized a three-week mission with 28 volunteers and were able to expose 15,000 people to the gospel through the *JESUS* film. In addition, through open-air meetings, hospital visitations, and personal conversations, they were able to share Christ individually with many of those same people. More than 1,000 indicated decisions for Christ during the ministry outreach. Thousands of such efforts have taken place across Africa.

Asia

The power of the gospel is also being felt throughout Asia. For example, South Korea has been incredibly responsive and is now a missionary-sending nation, sending its own missionaries to other nations. An estimated 100,000 Korean missionaries are serving Christ in other countries. In Australia, 80,000 nonbelievers per month are watching *JESUS* videos in their homes. Japanese students are awakening to the gospel and being trained to spread Christ's message abroad.

Astounding spiritual multiplication continues to take place in the small Buddhist country of Thailand. Since 1980, more than 5 million gospel presentations have resulted in an indicated 1.3 million decisions for Christ. In one year alone, the number of new churches that Campus Crusade for Christ helped denominations establish increased from 2,900 to more than 7,200.

In one Nepalese village, Nepal Campus New Life Training Center team shared Christ with the people. New believers brought their former idols and discarded them in the center of the village for all to see! Staff members then began discipling the new believers, and more and more villagers came to the church. The believers in Nepal now number 2.5 million according to government statistics.

In India during one ten-day period, the *JESUS* film was shown on nationwide television to an estimated 127 million people, or about ten percent of the population. The audience was given an opportunity to receive Christ. In Singapore, a country with only 3 million people, our ministry on four university campuses has raised up over 150 full-time staff, 27 of which are currently serving in other countries, with 40 more in training.

Europe

The political changes in Eastern Europe continue to provide unprecedented opportunities for ministry. At the request of government officials in the Commonwealth of Independent States (CIS—the former Soviet Union), Campus Crusade has taken the *JESUS* film and a course on "Christian Ethics and Morality" into thousands of public schools. The students responded with so many questions that education officials requested additional information for their teachers. The result is that thousands of Russian teachers have attended and will attend special convocations where they are trained to use these tools. In the process, a high percentage of teachers and students are coming to Christ.

Another example is Hungary where we have trained hundreds of teachers to present the story of Christianity. The curriculum, titled *Take Jesus to the School*, will reach 5,000 public schools consisting of one million students.

Latin America

An incredible move of God's Spirit is taking place in Latin America. Karl Marx's ideas are losing power, no longer gripping the minds of faculty and students on college campuses throughout the area. Young people and their professors are finding freedom in the person of Jesus Christ. In a unique and effective strategy on college campuses, staff are boldly walking into classrooms and asking professors for permission to share Christ with the students present. The response is overwhelmingly positive. Doors are opening to classroom evangelism throughout Latin America.

As elsewhere, Campus Crusade is cooperating with other Christian movements to help fulfill the Great Commission in Latin America. I was privileged to speak at the *Latin America 2000* conference in Panama, along with Luis Bush, international director of the AD2000 and Beyond movement, and Loren Cunningham, founder and president of Youth With a Mission (YWAM). Our cumulative goal is to help fulfill the Great Commission by the end of the year 2000.

When he spoke to the conferees, Luis Bush exclaimed, *"Ya es la hora!"* (Now is the time!) We all agreed. I challenged the audience that to accomplish our goal, "We must all think, pray, plan, and walk supernaturally in love and faith."

Middle East

In spite of what you hear and see daily in news reports about the people of the Middle East, many of them are searching for the truth. The youth of the region make up 50 percent of the total population, and many are looking for answers. Our staff throughout the area are sharing the good news of our Lord in many ways:

- One-on-one presentations
- The *JESUS* film
- Evangelistic and discipleship radio programs broadcast from many stations in the three major languages of the area
- Direct mail and Bible correspondence courses
- Professionally produced, dramatic evangelistic TV programs

As a result of these and other outreaches even in the face of opposition and in hostile environments, many are turning to Christ.

In Jordan, the king's declaration of democracy opened doors for new avenues of evangelism. The day after the declaration, our national director placed an advertisement in two prominent newspapers offering a free copy of the *JESUS* film and other Christian literature. Since then, more than 64,000 people have requested the materials and more than 4,000 have written back that they have accepted Christ as their Savior.

A Mighty Army

The greatest asset the Lord has given Campus Crusade for Christ in our world outreach is not our strategy. It is not our organization. It is the people. It is the mighty army that God Himself has called, and is continuing to call, including many who are reading these words at this moment. I am confident that many of these will contact us. My heart sings with praise every time I think of all the tens of thousands of staff, associate staff, and volunteers from many nations, cultures, and languages, proclaiming the good news of our Lord Jesus Christ all over the world. I am reminded of the praise song to the Lamb of God in Revelation 5:9:

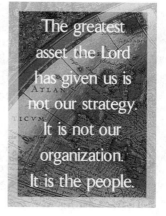

The greatest asset the Lord has given us is not our strategy. It is not our organization. It is the people.

> They sang a new song: "You are worthy to take the scroll and to open its seals, because you were slain, and with your blood you purchased men for God from every tribe and language and people and nation."

Every tribe, language, people, and nation! Our Lord Jesus, the perfect Lamb, has purchased them with His blood, but He has commissioned us to go and tell them. To do so, He has called many people from these same nations and languages to be a part of this wonderful, mighty army.

Many of these staff members work at great personal sacrifice. Most are not from the U.S., but are from every continent, many from developing nations. Some are in constant physical danger; others have lost their lives. Inspiring stories of bravery and commitment abound. I would like to share two of these stories with you.

Miracle in Cambodia

I think of Vek Huong Taing, his wife, Sameoun, and their son. Vek Huong Taing was our National Director in Cambodia when the Khmer Rouge Marxist revolutionaries took over Cambodia on April 17, 1975. This action began one of the worst bloodbaths the world has ever known. The Khmer Rouge brought an earthly hell to the people of Cambodia. Some 3 million people, about 38 percent of the country's population, were slaughtered like animals by their vicious captors or died from hardship. Vek Huong Taing and his family managed to escape, fleeing as refugees. God miraculously spared their lives. They later discovered that Huong's mother and sister starved to death, as did the mother, father, and three sisters of his wife, Sameoun. He had two brothers who were executed. Sameoun also had a brother who was executed.

Because of their association with a U.S. organization, Huong and his family were prime targets for execution, but God miraculously spared them and did one miracle after another in protecting them. Four years later, they escaped to a United Nations refugee camp in Thailand. After a few days they were discovered by an international journalist, who mentioned them in a story. A Campus Crusade staff member in Guam read the story and relayed the news to Campus Crusade headquarters. Within a few days, swift diplomatic action won their release to the U.S., where they stayed until the political situation in Cambodia changed. Then they chose to obey God's call and return to Cambodia to serve Him and their people, even in the face of continuing danger—even if it costs them their lives.

"I feel scared to escape what God called me to do," Huong adds. "We cannot escape from death. In America, people die too. I believe that my future is in God's hand, so I have peace."

"The Bible says a lot," Sameoun says, "about how people obeyed God, and God blessed them."

The Taings are but a sample of the tens of thousands of

totally committed people all over the world—servants of the
living God— with whom we are so blessed to be associated.

God often uses evil to accomplish His purposes. The people of Cambodia tasted death in a way few cultures have.
Because of that they are now open to the good news of Jesus
Christ. Before the Communist takeover in 1975 there were
only approximately 1,000 believers in the entire country. Now
out of the refugee camps of Thailand alone, where Campus
Crusade has ministered, there are more than 15,000 Cambo-
dians involved in ministry, many going through our New Life
Training Center training, preparing themselves for "spiritual
multiplication" and sharing their faith and discipling others.

Miracle in Nepal

I fondly think of Adon Rongong and his wife from the distant
and isolated nation of Nepal. We had the opportunity to work
with him in 1975, and we started challenging him to come on
staff. At that time there were approximately 500 known believers in the entire country of Nepal with its 14 million people.

When we first started talking to Adon about reaching Nepal
for Christ, he looked at us like we were crazy. Here he was
going to this one little church, and we were talking to him
about seeing his whole country reached for Christ.

Adon really wanted to believe God for reaching his country, but at that point he did not think it could happen. He
wanted it so badly, however, that he was willing to join our
staff. He went to Manila for three months of Campus Crusade training, leaving behind his wife and three daughters.
Before he left the Philippines to return to Nepal, Bailey Marks,
at that time our Asian director, spoke with him: "Well, I
know you are glad to go back, and are looking forward to
being with your family tomorrow."

"Oh, yes," he replied. "But I'm concerned."

"About what?" Bailey asked.

Adon replied, "Concerned about what will happen to me

if I go home and do what I've been trained to do here."

Although Bailey knew what Adon meant, he asked, "What do you mean? I know you could experience persecution."

Adon replied, "Persecution? I could be killed!"

Bailey told him about the only thing he could say, "Adon, all I can tell you is that I won't ever put any pressure on you to put your life in jeopardy. And if you do place your own life in jeopardy, it's going to be between you and God, not between you and me."

Adon did return to Nepal, and since that day he has voluntarily put his life in jeopardy thousands of times. But now for the rest of the story...

Nepal's 5,000-fold increase in believers began with the faith and obedience of one man.

Adon now relates that for the first three to four months after arriving back in Nepal, he didn't do anything about evangelism. He just sat at home and translated materials all day long, a safe alternative. Finally one day, at lunch, he told his wife, Mannu, "I'm miserable."

She asked, "I know you are, but why?"

Adon replied, "Because I'm being disobedient. I'm not doing what God has told me to do and what I've been trained to do, and that's to be a witness for Christ. After lunch, I'm going to get up, and I am going to walk down those steps, and I'm going to stop the first person I see and talk to them about Jesus."

It is significant that he planned to stop the first person because I believe that if he had walked past that first person— whom God had prepared as an object of Adon's faith and obedience—what happened later might not have happened.

Immediately after lunch and with a new determination, Adon walked right out his door and down his steps. He, indeed, stopped the very first person he saw. In God's sovereignty, this first person was a young Hindu university student. After Adon shared Christ with him, the student opened up his heart to the Lord. I do not know how many other people Adon talked to that afternoon, but he led three people to the Lord. All three were university students. He invited them all to come to his house for lunch the next day. They came and he began to disciple them. Adon, greatly encouraged, also continued to share his faith.

Here are the results of Adon's obedience that day. The number of known believers in Nepal has grown from 500 in late 1975 to an estimated 2.5 million believers today! This miracle began with the faith and obedience of one man, even though other organizations have since come in and many people are working there now. This 5,000-fold increase in approximately twenty years is all to the glory of our mighty God and Savior!

Repeated Stories

Stories similar to that of Vek Huong Taing in Cambodia and Adon Rongong in Nepal can be repeated in nation after nation, wherever we have gone in the power of the Holy Spirit. These stories are not unique.

Another example is Henri Aoun, our Director of Affairs for North Africa and the Middle East. Henri once prayed, "Lord, I want to be used." He received a dramatic reply. Dr. Bailey Marks, our International Vice President, says of him, "I do not know of a man alive who has demonstrated greater faith and boldness in reaching the militant Islamic world, a most difficult assignment. Henri prays more and works harder than anyone I have ever known."

God has blessed Campus Crusade for Christ with wonderful, committed, and talented staff. In obedience to the Holy Spirit, and with His fellowship and help, we are helping to fulfill the Great Commission—the task to which we were called.

In the next chapter, I will introduce you to key international areas and the Directors of Affairs of the thirteen areas that comprise the International Ministry. As you read about the work taking place throughout the world, pray for each director and for those who have yet to hear about our great God and Savior, Jesus Christ.

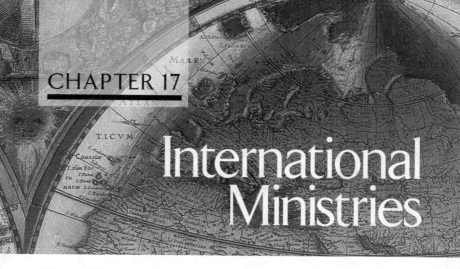

CHAPTER 17

International Ministries

MOSES HAD AN overwhelming responsibility given to him by God—leading millions of his people across a wilderness to the Promised Land. Moses soon learned the importance of organization. His father-in-law, Jethro, observed Moses trying to do everything himself and realized that his one-man strategy was impossible. With godly wisdom, Jethro exhorted Moses:

> Select capable men from all the people—men who fear God, trustworthy men who hate dishonest gain—and appoint them as officials over thousands, hundreds, fifties and tens (Exodus 18:21).

Thus, about 3,500 years ago was born the modern management principle of "delegation of authority." You might say that Jethro was the first recorded management consultant! No one person can have an accurate picture of what God wants to do. Nor can one man or woman handle the entire task alone.

An organization the size of Campus Crusade for Christ needs strong, dedicated, godly leadership and must be efficiently organized in order to effectively use the resources God has given us. It takes a multitude of godly men and women working together. Without such wisdom from above and the people God sends, we could not survive. Surely the *NewLife 2000* plan could not have progressed as far as it has without the creative dedication of our international leadership.

As you have seen, the U.S. Ministries side of Campus Crusade has a wealth of talented and godly leadership. I also constantly thank and praise God for the wonderful and capable International Ministries leaders He has provided for us to help fulfill His glorious Great Commission.

In addition to the North American ministries of the United States and Canada, the worldwide ministry of Campus Crusade for Christ is divided into twelve geographical areas, which we call Areas of Affairs. All nations fall within these areas and are grouped as best as possible with similar geographical, political, and cultural backgrounds in mind. Each Area of Affairs is headed by a Director of Affairs. I would love for you to meet these remarkable individuals. The testimony of God in their lives and ministries is truly inspiring. My hope is that as you read through this section, you will be able to marvel, as I do, at God's ability to provide "faithful men." Invite God to speak to you. He may want you to join with us.

Dr. Bailey Marks, Executive Vice President of International Ministries, gives leadership through the International Vice Presidents. They are Dr. Thomas Abraham, Vice President of Asia, Oceania, and Latin America; Roger Randall, Vice President of Europe and Eurasia; and Dr. Dela Adadevoh, Vice President of Africa, Middle East, and Central Asia Republics.

Supporting the work of these men and their staff is a wonderful team of men and women based at the Lake Hart campus. This Orlando-based team's many functions include strategic planning of campus and community evangelism and discipleship, coordination and sending of U.S. International Representatives, crisis management, financial management, financial development, ministry tracking and information systems, technology development and implementation, leadership development and academies, and mobilization of prayer through the Great Commission Prayer Movement. Without this team of committed men and women, we could not serve our extremely large worldwide outreach staff.

Dr. Bailey Marks – Executive Vice President of International Ministries

Dr. Bailey Marks has played a major role in helping to introduce tens of millions of people to our dear Lord and Savior. For many years I traveled the world day and night helping to establish and direct ministries in various countries on every continent. But God was preparing a man to lift my arms in the international ministries battle as Joshua and Hur did for Moses.

Coming from a successful career in the furniture business, Bailey demonstrated remarkable leadership and communication skills. He served as my personal associate for eighteen months and as our Asia director for thirteen years. So, when I reached my saturation point, I knew Bailey was the logical person to help carry the load. Since 1981, he has done a phenomenal job. He and his wife, Elizabeth, are a great encouragement and help to Vonette and me.

Dr. Thomas Abraham – Vice President of Asia, Oceania, and Latin America

Although he was raised in a Christian family in India, Thomas Abraham did not care about nor follow God. In fact, he had become a Communist student leader. One day in 1957, his mother asked him to take her to an evangelistic meeting. Wanting to follow the custom of pleasing one's parents, he complied. That night he heard an evangelist explain what Christ had done for him. Thomas accepted Jesus as His personal Savior and began to follow Him as his Lord.

Thomas and his wife, Molly, also from South India, lived in the United States while Thomas attended seminary. When I met them in 1967, I was impressed with their heart to serve the Lord and challenged them to begin a Campus Crusade ministry back in their home country. With definite leading from the Lord, they accepted his challenge and committed their lives to helping reach India for Christ.

The following year, Thomas and Molly moved to their

home state of Kerala, India, where they began a ministry on one college campus. They soon had ten disciples, most of whom are leaders in the India ministry today. God continued to use Thomas and Molly, and the ministry spread throughout southern India and into other parts of the country.

In 1975 Thomas felt led to ask the Lord for an opportunity for every single person in the state of Kerala to say yes to Christ by the end of 1976. Circumstances suggested this was an impossible dream. But the Here's Life "I found it!" campaign was just the answer to get started on that goal.

With confidence in the Lord's power, the staff and disciples trained 30,000 laymen and students between January and July and challenged them to reach their own areas for the Lord. Helping to accelerate the saturation project were 900 village evangelists, volunteers who had received Campus Crusade training in evangelism and discipleship and were committed to saturating their own communities or villages with the gospel. During one sharing session with only 69 of the village evangelists, the staff discovered that through their ministry alone 6,160 individuals had heard the gospel and 1,439 of these had received Christ. More than 10,000 people had heard a gospel presentation in group meetings.

As the months passed, more and more stories and statistics poured in from various parts of the state, and district after district was being completely saturated with the claims of Christ. At the end of 1976, all the staff, trained workers, and village evangelists converged in the center of the state to celebrate the amazing answer to their prayer: Kerala had been completely saturated for Christ during 1976!

Having seen what God did in Kerala, they were ready to trust God to use them to help reach India, the second most populous country in the world, with the gospel. They continued to believe God for miracles. The *JESUS* film had just been introduced in the United States, and the idea was planted into the hearts of Thomas and his staff to expose all of India to

Christ through the film. In a record time of six months, the film was scripted, translated, and recorded into the first ten Indian languages. Next, the staff was faced with the question of how to distribute the film. They literally drew 31,200 nine-kilometer squares across the map of India. Through this God-given plan, 200 *JESUS* film teams systematically covered one square per day, and were able to show the film to 120 million people in six months! Today 1,200 film teams sacrificially travel throughout India, contributing to the goal that everyone will have a chance to say yes to Christ.

Seeing God's power to reach a country prepared Thomas and Molly for the challenge of trusting God to reach entire continents. Bailey Marks, who had just been named Executive Vice President of the International Ministries, challenged Thomas to take over part of his continental responsibilities. Thomas and Molly knew that they should accept Bailey's challenge. In 1981, they moved with their three children to Baguio, Philippines, to direct the Central Asia and Pacific ministry and serve as Provost of the International School of Theology–Asia. They watched God do amazing things in reaching Buddhists, Hindus, and Muslims throughout their new area, home to two-thirds of the world's population.

Sadly, the Lord took Molly home in January 1995, less than five months after being diagnosed with cancer. But as we expected, Thomas continued to faithfully follow His Lord. After mentoring his successors, Thomas passed on his Asia directorship responsibilities in 1997 to Ivan and Felicita Sikha and George and Annie Ninan.

Once again a new challenge was given, and Thomas became the first Vice President of Campus Crusade to come from outside of North America. His faith to see God reach one state in India laid the foundation for him to trust God to reach all of India, then Central Asia and the Pacific, and now his present region, which encompasses the bulk of the world's population and every major religion. Thomas currently serves as Vice President of Asia, Oceania, and Latin America.

Thomas also gives direction to Oceania, an area comprising Australia, New Zealand, and the Pacific Region. In all, there are fourteen countries and island areas, including National Offices in Australia, New Zealand, Chuuk, Fiji, Micronesia, Papua New Guinea, the Solomon Islands, Tonga, and Vanuatu, along with the Pacific Regional Office. The Oceania area has active ministries on fifteen campuses, in two communities, and in 31 MPTAs.

Australia's ministry commitment is to evangelize the lost through *JESUS: Gift to the Nation*, the vision of placing a *JESUS* video in every home in Australia. This effort has produced much fruit and partnerships among believers in Australia. I praise God for the many who have come to Christ through this strategy. This strategy began in Australia, spread to Canada, then to the United States, and now (with many cultural modifications) is being used in hundreds of major urban centers throughout the world.

East Asia Area of Affairs

This area includes eight countries with National Offices in Hong Kong, Japan, Korea, Macau, Mongolia, Singapore, and Taiwan, as well as the U.S.-based Chinese Ministries Office. Special ministries in this area include Asia Impact, East Asia School of Theology, and Silk Road Ministry. God has opened the door for establishing ministries on 171 campuses, within 30 communities, and in 110 MPTAs in East Asia.

The East Asia area is under the committed leadership of Dr. Victor Koh and his wife, Kah Kiat (KK), Chinese born and raised in Singapore. Dedicated at birth to the crocodile god for protection against evil sprits, Victor's family were devout Buddhists. After his family came to know the Lord through his sister, they burned all their idols and took a public stand in their faith. Shortly thereafter, when Victor was a young lad, an automobile struck him. With her young son lying in a hospital bed not expected to live, his dear mother, a new Christian at that time, asked God to allow Victor to live so that he might serve him. The Lord honored his mother's request.

Victor and KK joined the staff of Campus Crusade in 1972. After serving as National Director of Singapore and in many other leadership roles in Asia, Victor was named Director of Affairs for East Asia in 1990. The ministry there has grown significantly under his charge. With his many years of experience in leading a continental ministry, expanding the ministry into new arenas within East Asia, and his academic credentials (Master of Divinity and Ph.D. in International Business), Victor is well-suited for the responsibilities as Vice President of the International Leadership University based in New York City. His new role will give him the opportunity to use his experiences in Asia to help train future Christian leaders for the world.

In keeping with Campus Crusade's philosophy of developing younger leaders within the movement, Victor and KK are in the process of mentoring and handing over their responsibilities to a Korean staff couple, Insoo and Eunsook Jeong. Continental leaders have increasingly moved on to higher levels of responsibility, making way for younger leaders to assume more responsibility. Insoo and Eunsook have moved from Korea to Singapore to fulfill their new roles.

Born into a strong Confucian family in South Korea, Insoo's grandfather named him according to the Confucian philosophy before he was born. But God had a special plan for Insoo's life. He came to know Christ in college through the ministry of Korea Campus Crusade for Christ (KCCC). As a student leader on his campus, he mobilized one-tenth of the student population to be involved with KCCC under his able leadership. As the first Christian in his family, he led his five brothers and sisters, his parents, and other relatives to Christ. His father and mother became leaders in their church.

During his eight years as an associate staff member, Insoo

was a high school math teacher. His position gave him the opportunity to share Christ with all the students in his school. Seventy percent of them received Christ. He also mobilized more than 700 area people to attend EXPLO '74, a Christian training conference that drew more than 300,000 delegates.

Personally challenged by KCCC Director Dr. Joon Gon Kim, Insoo and Eunsook became full-time staff members in 1981. Serving in many different capacities within KCCC, Insoo eventually was asked to assist Dr. Kim before assuming his new responsibilities as Director of Affairs for East Asia.

God has been doing some unprecedented harvesting in East Asia. Last year more than 2.7 million people were exposed to the gospel, and more than 1.2 million received Christ. Out of this number, more than 467,000 people were discipled in New Life Groups, while more than 40,000 believers were trained to share their faith and disciple others.

Many countries within this region serve as a model to the body of Christ. Specifically, I think of the Korean ministry led by national director Dr. Joon Gon Kim, who has an unlimited vision for Korea as a sending nation to the world. That ministry alone has trained 10,000 laymen to serve as missionaries in other parts of the world, a great majority of whom are already in place outside of Korea.

In fulfillment of their vision and dream to help reach every major campus in the world, Korean Campus Crusade is preparing for Student Mobilization 2002 (SM 2002) in Korea in the summer of 2002. This gathering will help equip campus leaders to reach their own campuses as well as mobilize and train professors, pastors, and volunteers to help reach campuses worldwide. That conference will also afford an opportunity for 80,000 Korean students to be exposed to the needs and opportunities around the world.

Southeast Asia Area of Affairs

The Southeast Asia Area of Affairs oversees the ministry in six countries: Cambodia, Indonesia, Malaysia, Pakistan, the Philippines, and Thailand, along with the International School of Theology–Asia. Ministries have been established on 109 campuses, within 48 communities, and in 304 MPTAs.

As I mentioned earlier, Thomas Abraham passed on part of his responsibilities as Director of Affairs of Asia to a former Indian disciple and long-time India staff member, Ivan Sikha. Ivan and his wife, Felicita, and their two college-age sons moved to Baguio, Philippines, to fulfill their new role in overseeing the Southeast Asia Area of Affairs.

Ivan became a Christian as a student in 1969. At the time of graduation, he was pondering how to make an impact for Christ. Campus Crusade had just started a ministry in his city, and the director gave him a copy of *Come Help Change the World*, and challenged him to consider joining the ministry. After reading the first edition of this book, he decided to join our staff in 1974. He served as campus staff in Madras City and Vellore, and later became Campus Coordinator for the state of Tamil Nadu. During the Here's Life campaign, he helped train hundreds of church leaders. He was also involved in the JESUS Film Project as a Great Commission Training Center trainer. He also found time to complete his Master's degree with Campus Crusade's International School of Theology in Asia. In 1988, Ivan and Felicita moved their family to Delhi to begin the regional ministry in northern India.

The ministry experiences the Lord has given Ivan uniquely prepared him to lead this Area of Affairs. This is a very difficult area for which much prayer is needed. According to government statistics, only 1 percent of Thailand's population is Christian. In Malaysia, sharing the gospel with the Malay population is banned. There are many unreached people in this area, and restricted areas pose much danger. However, Ivan and his staff are using many creative strategies to help reach people of all religions and help them know the truth of Christ.

One amazing transformation has been seen in the country

of Cambodia, the site of the killing fields. But today new life, not death, is the event of the day. Looking at the vast untouched field for harvest among executives and government leaders, the ministry held its first Phnom Penh Executive Luncheon. This first ministry event brought 135 executives to a prestigious hotel in town. After hearing the gospel presented in a relevant way, 69 indicated on their comment card that they had prayed to receive Christ. Through follow-up meetings where recent believers and new people gathered, 255 more were exposed to the gospel and 188 received Christ. This was just the beginning of the ministry into the community where the fields are definitely ripe for harvest.

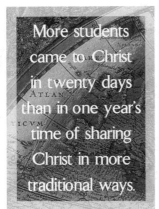

More students came to Christ in twenty days than in one year's time of sharing Christ in more traditional ways.

South Asia Area of Affairs

The ministry is flourishing in nine locations in South Asia, including seven regional ministries in India. In addition to the staff in the vast land of India, national staff are serving in the countries of Bangladesh, Myanmar, Nepal, and Sri Lanka. Active ministries have been established on 150 campuses, within 51 communities, and in 744 MPTAs.

The Director of Affairs for this area, George Ninan and his wife, Annie, accepted their responsibility in 1997 after quite a process of commitment. George came from a Syrian Orthodox family in Kerala, South India. As a young man he rejected God and began working with the Communist Party of India. In 1969 after growing disillusioned with the Party, George came in contact with the ministry of Campus Crusade. Through the influence of the staff, he committed his life to Christ and became a student evangelist on his campus.

Becoming convinced that God was calling him to full-time service, George joined the campus ministry at the University

of Kerala, South India, in 1971. He served under the leader-
ship of Thomas and Molly Abraham, who started the Campus
Crusade ministry in India beginning with campuses in Kerala.
After serving in several positions, including assistant to the
National Director, George became the National Director of
India. In 1997 he accepted his present responsibilities as Di-
rector of Affairs for all of South Asia, having been groomed
for greater responsibility by Thomas Abraham.

South Asia includes some 1.2 billion people, most of whom
are Hindu, Buddhist, or Muslim. With these numerous religious challenges, as well as political and social turmoil through
the area, the staff is seeing the Lord do mighty things.

Amazing spiritual breakthroughs are occurring among India's
Hindu and Muslim students through the use of new creative
campus evangelism strategies. Capitalizing on Indian students'
love of movies—especially the *Titanic*—one campus team in
West India decided to use that movie as a platform for sharing
Christ. Out of that idea was born the *Titanic and Beyond* package, which presents the gospel in a very relevant way.

West India staff and their disciples watched in awe as 1,500
students, normally resistant to the gospel, eagerly accepted the
packages. High caste Hindu and Muslim students began making commitments to Christ, and even elite and future leaders
of the business and governmental sectors of India have received Christ. Professors began catching on to the strategy and
opened the way for Christian students to share Christ with entire classrooms. As the creative *Titanic and Beyond* folder was
used on campus, more students came to Christ in twenty days
than in one year's time of sharing Christ in more traditional
ways. Initial responses indicate that 60 percent of the recipients
of the folders have responded to the message of the gospel and
received Christ. God's Holy Spirit is at work!

Latin America Area of Affairs
The Latin America Area of Affairs encompasses 28 identifi-

able countries as well as some confidential countries. God has raised up 570 staff members who faithfully minister in Argentina, Bolivia, Brazil, Chile, Colombia, Costa Rica, the Dominican Republic, Ecuador, El Salvador, Guatemala, Guyana, Haiti, Honduras, Jamaica, Mexico, Nicaragua, Panama, Paraguay, Peru, Puerto Rico, Surinam, Trinidad & Tobago, Uruguay, and Venezuela. Under the leadership of Rolando and Carmela Justiniano, the ministry in Latin America has expanded to 65 campuses, 39 communities, and 323 MPTAs.

Reaching the university student has personal significance for Rolando. On the morning of June 14, 1969, Rolando prayed that something would forever change him and the plan he had for his own life. Rolando, a Marxist university student in Bolivia, said, "God, I do not believe in You, but if You really exist, come into my life and change me. You have 15 days to change me!" After receiving the Lord as his Savior, he began to share Christ with his friends at the university. Before his very eyes, Rolando saw his life being transformed. Nine months later, the Lord convinced Rolando that the best place to invest his life was through the ministry of Campus Crusade. In this way he could be used to help others experience the change of life that comes only through Jesus Christ.

Rolando assisted in starting the Campus Crusade ministry in Bolivia. In 1973 he ministered in the country of Colombia, before serving as National Director of Peru from 1978–1980. He later served in Mexico, then in 1988 assumed his present responsibilities as Director of Affairs for all of Latin America. Rolando and Carmela are committed to helping to reach this entire continent for Christ.

Latin America is experiencing a time of great harvest and increased unity among believers, with the church growing at an annual rate of 8 percent. Millions are being reached with the *JESUS* film and other strategies.

One major challenge the ministry faces is reaching the 500 MPTAs in Latin America for Christ by the end of the year

2000. Knowing that it had been taking them three years to reach one MPTA, Rolando and two men from his staff met with a staff member from the Canadian ministry in 1997 to consider how they could accelerate the ministry. Out of their meeting came the idea of MIAMI (Million in a Month International), which utilizes 29 different evangelism approaches to reach the goal of exposing one million people to Christ within each MPTA during a month's time.

The pilot project took place in Managua, Nicaragua, where they tested the reality of reaching such a lofty goal. One of the strategies was the *JESUS* film strategy. Sixty *JESUS* film sets were distributed to partner churches that conducted mass evangelism in the streets. Another strategy centered around a traditional holiday called the Day of the Dead "celebration" on November 1–2, when people gather in cemeteries to pay respect to their dead. The staff team mobilized 10,000 Christians, and on those two days alone, they exposed 900,000 people to the gospel. The MIAMI strategy is now being used throughout Latin America as well as other parts of the world.

Roger Randall – Vice President of Europe and Eurasia

It was not until Roger was a sophomore at Oregon State University that he ever recalls hearing the gospel. In his years growing up in a small town in Oregon, he had no religious upbringing. A Campus Crusade for Christ staff member shared the gospel with Roger at a meeting in his college dorm. Several days later during a personal follow-up appointment, Roger placed his faith in Christ. Later he moved into a fraternity house and continued steadily receiving Campus Crusade for Christ training and was growing in his faith. Burdened to share with his fellow fraternity brothers, Roger saw more than half the men in his house come to faith in Christ.

Roger joined Campus Crusade in 1968, and with his wife, Sara, began a ministry at Auburn University. From there they served on the executive team of EXPLO '72, directed the Southeast Region for the U.S. Campus Ministry, and served as National Director and Women's Coordinator of Student Venture. Roger also served as National Director of the U.S. Campus Ministry before moving full-time into the international arena in 1985. Roger has directed the campus ministry for all of Africa and coordinated campus ministries worldwide. Before becoming the Vice President for Europe and Eurasia, he served as director of the International Strategy Resource Group, which provides resources for our global ministry with strategic planning, training, and creative ministry applications.

Eurasia Area of Affairs

Operating as an undercover ministry during most of the Cold War and Communist Era, this area includes Armenia, Belarus, Estonia, Georgia, Latvia, Lithuania, Moldova, Russia, Ukraine, and seven other countries. This area has active ministries on 20 campuses, within nine communities, and in 158 MPTAs.

Until 1998, Dan and Babs Peterson gave leadership to this area before accepting the responsibility to direct the Great Commission Prayer Movement based at the Lake Hart campus. Dan joined the U.S. Campus Crusade staff in 1972. In 1977 he and Babs joined the Soviet team and two years later moved to Russia. The only way they could serve in the country was for Dan to become a teacher with the international school. During this time, Dan met many God-fearing Russian pastors and learned the Russian language fluently. They began to realize that Russia could be changed only through prayer.

Instrumental in the planning, Campus Crusade and other evangelicals set forth the call for one month of concentrated prayer in 1989. Who could have believed that seeking God's face for the nation of Russia would have such dramatic results? Within months, the Communist powers started to lose their grip and the walls of Communism fell, enabling millions to finally have the opportunity to pursue God freely. Already in place, Campus Crusade ex-patriots and nationals were able to show *JESUS* and talk openly about their faith. Along with the wave of evangelistic activity, Dan and his team were instrumental in starting the "Heal Our Land" prayer movements, bringing together believers from various denominational backgrounds to pray and seek God's face for the healing of their nation. Pastors and their congregations who for so many years had been denied public gathering came to the training sessions and learned how to pray with power and authority.

Great social and political problems face Eurasia, perhaps unprecedented in their scope. Also unprecedented are the open doors and opportunities for the gospel brought about by the prayers of many, including the "Heal Our Land" prayer movement and conciliatory meetings with Christian leaders. These meetings have produced a historic decision to work together to see the Great Commission fulfilled in Eurasia.

Today the fruits of these prayer efforts are still developing. A presidential mandate by Russian President Boris Yeltsin declared that all sectors of government should plan to celebrate the new millennium and 2000 years of Christianity. Roger Randall, who served for a time as Director of Affairs for Russia, and his team initiated with the Russian Ministry of Education to bring an evangelistic education strategy to Russia's 67,000 schools. Building from the *JESUS* film, Russian staff made an audio drama of *JESUS* and combined it with a Christian morals curriculum. I praise God for the 21 million students who will have a chance to know Christ through this project.

Eastern Europe Area of Affairs

As with Russia, when countries emerged from their Communist bondage, a great openness and responsiveness to the gospel resulted. Virtually overnight our American and national staff, who had been quietly working to advance the gospel, had full license to share the good news. Seventeen countries are included in this area with national ministries in Albania, Bosnia-Herzegovina, Bulgaria, Croatia, Czech Republic, Hungary, Macedonia, Poland, Romania, Slovakia, Slovenia, and Yugoslavia. To date, the area includes ministries on 85 campuses, in 11 communities, and in 238 MPTAs. Larry Thompson, one of our last remaining American Directors, is steadily building movements with his staff team in these post-Communist countries. And now more than 600 East European nationals are on the staff of Campus Crusade for Christ.

Larry came to know the Lord when he was a senior in high school. Having been raised in a Christian home, he was familiar with the stories of Jesus, but still wondered about the real meaning and purpose of life. After meeting a group of committed young people who showed Larry a new kind of love, acceptance, and relationship with the Lord, he fully committed his life to Christ. Larry's involvement with Campus Crusade in college gave him the desire to dedicate his life to helping fulfill the Great Commission.

Larry has been on staff with U.S. Campus Crusade since 1975 and his wife, Debbie, since 1972. They served in the Campus Ministry. In 1978, during the height of the Cold War with the Soviet Union, Larry and Debbie were challenged to believe God for the impossible and move with their new baby to Poland. This made them the first American missionaries to live permanently behind the Iron Curtain. They have lived continuously in Europe since that time. Larry served as Country Director for Poland and Regional Director to Eastern European Countries before assuming his present Area of Affairs responsibilities for Eastern Europe in 1992.

Partnerships with other Christian organizations highlight some of what is happening in this region. In Romania, our Campus Crusade staff have linked arms with the Romanian Evangelical Alliance to give the entire country a chance to see the *JESUS* film. Particular emphasis has been placed on reaching the nation's fathers, and as their lives are changed, the entire family will change also.

Because a partnership with the Albanian Evangelical Alliance was formed more than five years ago, Christians from across Albania were ready to provide help for the Kosovo refugees that started pouring across the borders. What makes it so amazing is that just nine years ago, only twelve believers were known to exist in all of Albania. Through the partnership to take the gospel into every Albanian village via helicopter or Landrover, thousands heard and responded to God's call. Today they unite to help others find hope in Him.

In Hungary, the "Take Jesus to the Schools" campaign is helping to fulfill the government's mandate that all students, by the age of 16, know at least two Bible stories and the meaning of words like Redeemer, Savior, and Christ. National staff took the initiative to develop evangelistic education curriculum to change the lives of entire generations in Eastern Europe. So far more than 3,400 of Hungary's 5,000 schools are using the curriculum to teach their students.

Western Europe Area of Affairs (Agape Europe)

With a heart to see revival spread into all of the countries in this area, Rev. Markku and Aulikki Happonen give leadership to 25 countries with National Offices in Austria, Belgium, Estonia, Finland, France, Germany, Greece, Ireland, Italy, Latvia, Lithuania, the Netherlands, Norway, Portugal, Spain, Sweden, Switzerland, and the United Kingdom. Special Ministries include AIT Base, England; Christian Embassy (Leadership Encounter); Regional Director for S. Europe; and Crescendo-Music Ministry. This area has ministries on 50 campuses, within 20 communities, and in 79 MPTAs.

Markku and Aulikki, both from Finland, joined Campus Crusade staff in 1972. Markku, born and raised in a Christian home, gave his life to Christ at a youth rally in the early '60s. His future wife, Aulikki, also gave her heart to Christ that same night. They first became involved with the ministry at Helsinki University. As students, they helped launch ministries on five new campuses. Markku served for many years as

Campus Director and National Director of the university ministry in Finland. From 1978–1981, they both coordinated the "Here's Life" campaigns in more than 80 cities in Finland. They later served in Germany and helped with evangelism outreaches in Russia. With Finnish evangelist Kalevi Lehtinen, Markku developed the strategy and the implementation of Mission Volga and later the development of Mission Urals.

Mission Volga set new standards for evangelistic missions in Russia. Boarding a cruise ship, Campus Crusade staff and partnering missionaries sailed for 42 days, stopping to proclaim the gospel in thirteen cities along the way. In 1996, Markku was appointed the Director of Affairs for Western Europe.

Although agnosticism is still prevalent in Europe, signs of revival are beginning to stir. Spiritual openness toward religion is increasing. People are seeking religious fulfillment, not only in Christianity, but also in every religious phenomenon, good or bad. This means, however, that there is a great opportunity, an open door for the gospel to change lives, which is far greater than any in the past. The Western European team is continually faced with the challenge of communicating the gospel in relevant and contemporary ways. We can rely on the power of the Holy Spirit to help us.

Athletes in Action has had a big influence in this part of the world through their athletic teams. Throughout the year, foreign and national teams conduct soccer and basketball sports camps for students and are involved in competitive matches with amateur and professional leagues.

In addition to their regular ministry activities, our European staff took on the huge task of turning a sporting event into a platform for the gospel. As soccer teams and fans from many nations descended on Paris in 1998, Campus Crusade made a special adaptation of the *JESUS* film for the soccer event. Featuring testimonies of previous World Cup Soccer winners, more than 70,000 copies of the video were distributed throughout France. Scores of staff and volunteers from churches and Christian organizations handed out the video, gave away *Four Spiritual Laws* booklets, and talked with interested seekers. This was the largest evangelistic event ever seen in France. Many of our national ministries around the world translated the soccer testimonies into their languages and showed it on national television to millions of soccer fans.

In the post-modern climate of Western Europe, connecting with the lost can sometimes be a challenge. New ways of thinking about evangelism, such as the production of an evangelistic music CD for youth in the Netherlands, are unfolding new opportunities to present the ageless message of God's love. We know that, like all people, Europeans have a heart-shaped vacuum that only Christ can fill. Western Europe is one of the world's greatest challenges. More new staff and resources are urgently needed to reach this difficult area.

Dr. Dela Adadevoh – Vice President of Africa, Middle East, and Central Asia Republics

As a freshman student at a prominent university in Kumasi, Ghana, Dela was constantly interested in spiritual issues. He had been introduced to Christianity as a young boy, but considered it to be superficial. As a college student, he tried to find holes in the faith he had rejected. While attending a special campus evangelistic outreach out of curiosity to prove his point, Dela heard and understood that he could have a personal relationship with Jesus and invited Him into his life. He immediately began to invest as much energy and time in understanding his newfound faith as he had in pursuing other religions. The hunger for truth and spiritual reality that he had so earnestly sought was fully released in Jesus. Dela began to seek ways to express his new faith, and the Lord lead him to an American staff couple on his campus.

Dela and his good friend, Ben Ecklu (now Director of Affairs for Nigeria/West Africa), joined several other students to equip themselves and their peers with skills and tools in effectively sharing the gospel with other students. Dela's leadership gifts were evident to all with whom he came in contact. Those gifts were exercised sacrificially as he gave much of his discretionary time to helping reach his campus for Christ.

But Dela's vision extended far beyond the campus. As a sophomore, he once asked his campus ministry leader to describe what sort of plan he had for all of Ghana. At the end of that discussion, Dela made it known that if Ghana Campus Crusade for Christ had no Ghanaians on staff by the time he graduated, he would be the first. Although Dela was not the first, because he was continually exhorting those who graduated before him to join staff, Dela kept his word and the following year, in 1980, Dela and Betty joined the movement. Dela's first assignment was as a Great Commission Training Center trainer in Nigeria from 1980 to 1981. He then served in the campus ministry in Ghana, and was later appointed as the first Ghanaian National Director. Soon the scope of his responsibilities included other West African countries.

When an organizational restructuring occurred in 1989, Dela and Betty moved across the continent with their three children, and as cross-cultural missionaries, took the reins of leadership to become the Director of Affairs for Eastern Africa. Today, as Vice President of Africa, the Middle East, and Central Asia, Dela carries the same passion for reaching the lost that first ignited his heart as a student in Kumasi.

North Africa, Middle East, and Central Asian Republics Area of Affairs

Although few details can be given for reasons of security, every day people in this area are coming to know Jesus Christ as their Lord and Savior through the vision and leadership of Henri and Ruth Aoun. The Aouns have seen God's hand at work through a variety of creative evangelism strategies in these limited- or closed-access countries.

Henri was born and raised in Lebanon and Ruth in the

Philippines. Growing up in a nation with both Christian and Muslim populations, Henri had the opportunity to receive Jesus as his Savior at an early age. Consistently wanting to know and understand God's Word, Henri was invited to attend Campus Crusade's Institute of Biblical Studies while a college student in Colorado. It was there that Henri decided to serve the Lord in full-time ministry.

Henri and Ruth have been on Campus Crusade staff for more than twenty years and have served in Jordan and in Northern Africa. Before his present responsibilities, Henri was the director of the Paris Project and the Paris Training Center.

Henri and his staff desire to see that everyone has the opportunity to hear about God's love—a big task for people you cannot usually approach directly. Yet God has sovereignly honored their faith. Every single hour of the day, a resident within this area can encounter a radio or television program created by Campus Crusade national staff partners and hear that Jesus is the Son of God. One such drama, called "Thirsty Hearts," a professionally produced evangelistic drama series, is distributed via satellite. It is seen by tens of millions across North Africa and the Middle East.

Also helping to advance the gospel are literature distributions at key locations in Western Europe. Packages of Christian material and New Testament Bibles capture the attention of Arab travelers anxious to know about the man named Jesus. Correspondence Bible Studies that protect a seeker's or new convert's identity are operated through eight Communication Centers across the region. Bags of letters come from people wanting to know more about Jesus and salvation.

In countries that are difficult to reach, God has provided a crack in the wall. These countries are predominantly Muslim, but several have growing Christian communities. Although Islam continues to be dominant in the lives of the people and many pursue a path of fanaticism, many young people are beginning to search for the truth about God.

Francophone Africa Area of Affairs

This unique region of Africa commonly united by the French language covers ministry in seventeen countries, including National Offices in Angola, Benin, Burkina Faso, Burundi, Cameroon, the Central African Republic, Chad, Congo, Cote d'Ivoire, Gabon, Guinea, Mali, Niger, Rwanda, Senegal, Togo, and Zaire. Dr. Kassoum and Koutan Keita have developed a ministry team that has active groups on 25 campuses, within 32 communities, and in 119 MPTAs.

Dr. and Mrs. Keita are both from the country of Mali and have been on staff since 1975. As a well-known and respected Christian leader throughout Africa, Kassoum's experiences have been used by the Lord to minister across Africa. In addition to his Campus Crusade responsibilities, he serves as the president for the Association of Evangelicals in Africa and the president of the Evangelical Churches and Missions in Mali. He is also the representative to the government for all Protestant churches and missions in Mali and is often consulted by the Head of State in times of national crisis.

Kassoum grew up in a Muslim and animist home. He first heard about Christ when he was twelve years old, but at that time he had little more than an intellectual belief. Five years later, his faith was tested for the first time after hearing a Muslim priest's sermon on God's judgment. Kassoum began to question if he was truly saved. His local pastor assured him of the Bible's promise of salvation and said that if he had asked Christ to be his Savior and Lord, he could be sure of his eternal security. Later he became pastor of a church in Mali.

Since joining Campus Crusade staff, Kassoum has also continued as a full-time pastor. His desire to be a part of Campus Crusade grew out of his frustration at not seeing growth in his congregation. One of his church members had come back from EXPLO '72 enthusiastic about the training in evangelism he had received. Though skeptical at first about the effectiveness of such evangelism in a Muslim context, the ministry of his young member soon convinced him to try it for himself. After attending pastors' training in Liberia sponsored by Campus Crusade, he put into practice what he had learned. The transformation of his small church into a large congregation gave birth to the idea that he should offer this training to other churches. This led to his decision to join the staff of Campus Crusade for Christ so he would be able to share these principles with other churches.

In addition to the outstanding work in training church leaders, the Francophone staff team is also involved in the CrossRoads strategy. Working with leading doctors and educators, they were able to begin placing this morals-based education curriculum into the hands of teachers. They were the first area to try the new curriculum and the first to develop their own local trainers. After launching the strategy in Gabon, the trainers have taken CrossRoads into the Democratic Republic of Congo (formerly known as Zaire), Burkina Faso, and Cote d'Ivoire. This strategy is very timely and valuable for Africa because the spread of sexually transmitted diseases and AIDS kills many thousands of Africans each year.

Southern and Eastern Africa Area of Affairs

Africa, the land of the rising sun, has consistently seen the development of a solid movement and strong leadership. Recognizing the emergence of new leaders and moving into another leadership position himself, Dela Adadevoh challenged Bekele Shanko to take over the guidance for this area. The Southern and Eastern Africa Area of Affairs comprises eighteen countries, including National Offices in Botswana, Eritrea, Ethiopia, Kenya, Lesotho, Madagascar, Malawi, Mozambique, Namibia, South Africa, Swaziland, Tanzania, Uganda, Zambia, and Zimbabwe, plus three unnamed locations. Special ministries include Kampala GCTC (Great Commission Training Center); Nairobi GCTC; Nairobi International School of Theology; and TIME (Training Intracultural

Missions Evangelism) Ministries, which are active on 13 campuses, within 34 communities, and in 104 MPTAs.

Bekele Shanko came from a farming community in rural Southern Ethiopia. He received Christ at the age of five along with the rest of his family. He felt the Lord calling him into full-time ministry, but received a full scholarship to Emory University in Georgia for a Master's Degree. After a short time in the U.S., he again felt God's call on his life and quickly returned to Ethiopia. Soon after arriving back in Ethiopia, he

The spiritual climate for evangelism is very good but challenging because some countries are Islamic.

applied to join Campus Crusade for full-time ministry work. He and his fiancée, Shewaye, were soon married and together attended training with Campus Crusade in Uganda.

Due to the sudden death of the National Director, Bekele was appointed national coordinator of the rural ministry team. Under his leadership, the ministry grew to about twenty full-time supported staff and ten *JESUS* film teams.

The spiritual climate for evangelism is very good but challenging because some countries are Islamic. In nations like Kenya and Uganda, more than 70 percent claim to be Christian; however, discipleship is greatly needed. In places like Ethiopia, the number of Christians is growing rapidly.

In 1998 the Ethiopian national staff team decided to saturate the capital city of Addis Ababa with the claims of Christ. In a 52-day project called Operation Philip, they mobilized thousands of believers and used more than thirty types of evangelism strategies to accomplish the task. From training taxi drivers to play the *Four Spiritual Laws* audiocassette for passengers to encouraging artists to paint biblical scenes as part of a competition, more than 1.5 million people were exposed to the gospel. Of those, at least 50,000 received Christ.

Nigeria and West Africa Area of Affairs

In the heart of Africa lies the populous region of Nigeria and West Africa. Covering six countries with National Offices in Ghana, Liberia, Sierra Leone, Nigeria, Gambia, and Guinea-Bissau, Drs. Tim and Elizabeth Gyuse have given leadership to this area. Ministries are active on 19 campuses, within 17 communities, and in 163 MPTAs.

The son of a head schoolmaster, Tim grew up in a Christian home. However, no one had explained to him how he could know God personally. While attending a boy's camp as a high school junior, Tim heard a Christian give an invitation to receive Christ. On that day in March 1963, Tim did so. He and Elizabeth met while they were both in Canada for part of their university education. It was there that they became acquainted with this ministry. Their parents did not approve of the match because they were of different tribes in Nigeria, but God had plans to use this couple to influence thousands.

Upon their return to Africa, Tim became a lecturer with the University of Jos. He also joined an executive ministry Bible study lead by a Campus Crusade staff member. Tim's involvement in the Bible study grew, as did his hunger to become more involved in evangelism and discipleship. Tim and his wife became associate staff, but were soon challenged to become full-time staff. Their careers (Elizabeth was also a university lecturer) turned from being teachers of men to fishers of men. They have been with Campus Crusade since 1981.

After his first year of intensive training, Tim became the Nigerian National Director. In 1989, when West Africa became a separate Area of Affairs, Tim became its first director.

The Gyuses have been used by the Lord to bring their ministry to the point where they are able to turn over the leadership to another. Because of their educational background, they are moving to the International Leadership University in New York to become Vice President of Academic Affairs. They will once again be teaching men and women, but this time they have a wealth of fishing experiences to use as they share how the Lord can build movements of evangelism and discipleship through their students.

Rising to the challenge that the Gyuses leave behind, Ben and Charlotte Eckule of Ghana have accepted the Director of Affairs leadership role for Nigeria and West Africa. The University of Science and Technology in Kumasi, Ghana, has been the seedbed for spiritual blessing to countless people in Ghana and the whole world.

Ben became a Christian while reading a *Transferable Concept* in his dormitory room at the university. He then joined the student movement on his campus. Ben worked closely with Dela Adadevoh, a fellow student, introducing students to Jesus and helping many to grow in their faith.

Ben was the first Ghanaian from the university ministry to respond to God's calling in 1979 and join the ministry of Campus Crusade. After completing new staff training in Nigeria, he returned to Kumasi with his wife to help give direction to the same campus ministry where he had grown so much spiritually as a student.

Ben's gentle spirit and servant heart have equipped him to serve in a variety of critical support roles, both in the Ghana national ministry and for the past ten years in the Nigeria/West Africa regional office assisting Tim. As the Gyuses move on to New York, the Eckules take over the responsibilities as Director of Affairs for West Africa, coordinating efforts to reach Africa's most populous country, a region complicated by political turmoil, language differences, and Islamic extremism, yet characterized by great spiritual hunger.

Today in this area, there is encouraging evidence that the church is awakening. In Ghana for instance, national staff have been asked to train local pastors and leaders in evangelism strategies so churches can be more effective in reaching their communities. The "Pass It On" campaign led by national staff is helping to mobilize church leaders and give them skills they need for effective prayer movements and developing multiplying disciples. After these training sessions, pastors comment that the effectiveness in witnessing and passion for the lost has steadily increased among their church leaders. As evidence, the churches in this area of the world continue to grow.

In 1997, under the direction of Tim Gyuse, Nigeria and West African staff trusted God to use them to multiply the number of university ministries in the region. Announcing plans for the Destiny conferences, students from each of the top fifty universities were invited to come and learn how God could use them to radically change their campuses for Christ. The first year after being challenged to go and start new ministries, students from 32 campuses came forward. They shared amazing testimonies that the conference had challenged their perspectives and taught them to grow in their faith. Greater still, the students captured a vision for reaching the lost, their families, and friends with the message of God's love and forgiveness. Today movements of evangelism and discipleship are still growing from the seeds planted by these faithful students.

Campus Crusade for Christ, Canada

Marvin Kehler and his wife, Katherine, provide leadership to our Canadian ministry and its 306 full-time and associate Canadian staff who serve virtually every segment of Canadian society and evangelistic thrusts around the world.

Marvin Kehler was born into a Christian family living in a small village in the prairie province of Manitoba. He began his business career by buying his father's egg-producing operation, which he expanded into other areas. But he took the challenge to spread God's message in a full-time capacity. In 1972, he and his wife joined the staff of Campus Crusade and then became the Canadian director in 1974. Since then, God has used them and their godly team to help bring the good news of God's love and forgiveness to more than 100 countries.

The Canadian staff members and volunteers are well-known for their innovative ministry, which has expanded far beyond the borders of their country. In 1976, the "I Found It!" campaign resulted in one of the largest evangelistic thrusts in Canadian history. Thousands called in to find new life in Christ. In 1992, the Canadian ministry launched a pilot project in Surrey, British Columbia, called the JESUS Video Strategy. In 1995, a five-year vision was launched to reach 500 million people by the end of 2000 in nearly 120 countries. Today, the JESUS Video Strategy is being used all over the United States.

Some of the ministries in which the Canadian staff are involved include: KIDSTREET; Athletes in Action; Campus Ministry; Christian Embassy; Executive Leadership Ministry; Christian Business and Professional Association; women's ministries such as Women Today, Women Today OnLine, and Mothers Who Care; Church Resources; FamilyLife Conferences; and the JESUS Video Strategy. Overseas, the Canadian ministry is involved in the JESUS Film Project, *JESUS* film translation, Global Aid International Network, Filipino International Network, and International School Projects in many countries. As the end of this millennium draws closer, Campus Crusade for Christ, Canada is trusting God for an unprecedented spiritual harvest in Canada and around the world.

As you have read this chapter about our international leadership, you have no doubt observed that God has graciously supplied some of the most qualified people in the world to be a part of this movement. However, with a movement that is growing and expanding as fast as Campus Crusade for Christ, there is always a need for more and more qualified staff. Please ask the Lord of the harvest if He wants you to join us.

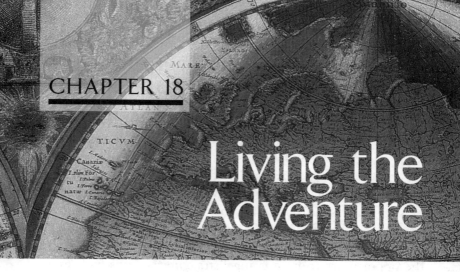

CHAPTER 18

Living the Adventure

I N THE FOLLOWING pages, I want to introduce you to people who have taken to heart my challenge to come help change the world. Each of them is a beloved colleague and a faithful worker for their Lord. Their excitement comes through in their stories. They truly are living the adventure that results from a full-time commitment to God's service.

God continues to call ordinary but faithful people to Himself and to this movement. I have asked these few to reflect on how God led them to join staff and to share some of their exciting experiences. I encourage you to read their accounts with a heart that is open to God's leading.

Fresh Impressions

Staff life is new to Gorden Fleming. He has worked with the U.S. Campus Ministry for six months. But working with Campus Crusade staff is not new to him.

"I was very involved in Campus Crusade as a student at Ole Miss," he said. "My campus director, Isaac Jenkins, had the most to do with my coming on staff. He showed me how God can use just one man to influence many college students."

This passion for student ministry is being passed on from Isaac to Gorden and now to Greek students at Auburn University. It has been an exciting semester.

"When I first reported to Auburn I really wanted to be able

to work in the Sigma Nu fraternity house," said Gorden, "because I was a Sigma Nu at Ole Miss." God marvelously intervened and this desire quickly became a reality. His campus director got a call from an Auburn Sigma Nu alumnus who explained that this year's house chaplain wanted to start a Bible study but was frustrated and not getting any response from the guys. Gorden started a weekly Bible study, a weekly prayer breakfast involving another fraternity and two sororities, and a Bible study involving four fraternities.

One night Gorden was praying that God would give him the opportunity to have evangelistic conversations with more people. The next morning, a student from another fraternity called and said he wanted to do something to spiritually benefit his fraternity brothers.

"Since then we have started a study involving about twenty guys. We're doing *The Quest for Authentic Manhood*, which has been a real blessing and is meeting real needs."

Mid-Course Correction

Randall and Mary Gayle Kennedy serve as Field Directors for the Dallas Metro Christian Leadership Ministries. They came on staff a year ago after Randy left his position as sales manager with Netscape Communications in Dallas. "To my surprise," admits Randy, "much of what I learned in the high-tech business world applies to this ministry. Many of the interpersonal skills, work ethics, and balance needed to succeed in business apply to my new role."

Not long before, a good friend, Mike, had asked, "Randy, why don't you quit your job and come join us full-time at Christian Leadership Ministries?"

This question did not come out of the blue. Randy explains, "God had been tugging at my heart for several years to make a stronger commitment to Him. And I had responded in a number of faith-stretching ways, at church and in the community. But I was still frustrated. At 37, I thought I was going through a mid-life crisis. It seemed I was giving only the extra hours in the day—my tired hours—to ministry. After some honest self-examination, it became clear that I was being called to serve as a full-time missionary."

Mary Gayle had no hesitations. "Because of some things that had led up to this, I was on board in a minute." Randy finally decided to apply for a staff position to see if God confirmed what they thought was His leading. The Kennedys saw God's hand in the sale of their house and the purchase of their new home. Many other direct events over the next six months confirmed their call, including raising their entire financial support base just six months after Randy left his job.

Randy has seen God do incredible things at the University of Texas in Arlington. "Even though this is a city-college commuter campus, it is strategic. With 20,000 students, it's the fourth largest campus in Texas. I saw the potential of ministering to professors as a vehicle to reach the students. But a faculty ministry was virtually non-existent when I showed up last fall. There were only five professors meeting weekly." In less than a year, Randy had the privilege of mobilizing seventy Christian professors who are drawing up a two-year plan to evangelize their campus.

Even with a major lifestyle change, the Kennedys are content. "I truly feel I have already contributed in a significant way to the work of Campus Crusade," says Randy, "and to the work of the kingdom." Mary Gayle agrees, "We have never been happier or more fulfilled."

Family Matters

By helping churches build healthy families, Jared and Marisa Elmquist have been helping to change the world through FamilyLife Ministries for two-and-a-half years.

They have a definite reason for choosing FamilyLife Ministry. "My wife's childhood memories are painful," explains Jared. "She married me for my family. When Marisa met them for the first time, she was dumbfounded. She had no idea something like this exists."

"This was definitely what I wanted in my marriage and family," adds Marisa. "I got to watch Christianity lived out in real life. This was a great starting point for our life together."

Some friends invited the Elmquists to go with them to a FamilyLife Marriage Conference. Despite their earlier concerns about its effectiveness, less than an hour into the conference they both knew it was going to be an incredible weekend They received information on the practical, everyday stuff that life brings to marriage and how to handle it God's way.

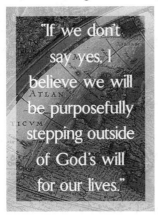

"If we don't say yes, I believe we will be purposefully stepping outside of God's will for our lives."

Jared explains what happened next: "After the conference, as we were waiting in line to get out of the parking garage, we made a commitment right then and there that this would be our annual checkup for our marriage. Whatever it took, we needed to be here to make sure we were staying on course."

During the next year's conference, they attended the Staff Opportunities meeting. In the final session, they decided to fill out a response card and were later contacted by FamilyLife Ministries.

"Raising our own support was the big issue for Marisa," said Jared, "so I prayed that God would make it clear to her whether or not He wanted us here."

They went to Little Rock, Arkansas, for their preview, and in their motel room on the last night, Marisa said, "Honey, if they offer us a staff position and we don't say yes, I believe we will be purposefully stepping outside of God's will for our lives."

They got a call the next week, asking if they would accept the challenge of coming on staff. They said yes.

Now the Elmquists minister to many couples who are hurting and searching for answers to struggles similar to those Marisa has experienced. In their ministry they see families beginning to experience the healing and hope that come through a relationship with Christ.

"We feel so privileged to be on staff," Jared says. "Together we're helping other couples develop a legacy of strong, godly marriages."

From the Campus to the Ends of the Earth

A campus ministry began for Lynn Henry when she was a charter member of her college sorority. Eager for her friends to know Jesus, she volunteered to be chaplain. "But as I look back at my own college experiences and witnessing efforts," Lynn says, "I was pretty pitiful at expressing my faith and the gospel, even though I think I shared with all of them."

After graduate school, Lynn got a job as a speech pathologist in a public school in Atlanta. She became active in a new church there. "A group of us started meeting with a missions pastor, a former Campus Crusade staff member in Africa," she said. "We used Campus Crusade training materials. One thing led to another and I signed up for a Crusade summer project in Poland with a group from church."

This trip helped her gain a heart for missions and see the need for training in how to effectively share the gospel. The next summer she traveled to Poland and joined another group from her church on a project in Czechoslovakia.

After that overseas ministry opportunity, Lynn felt God calling her to go on STINT to Eastern Europe. She feels it was an incredible time ('89–'90) to be ministering in Eastern Europe.

"It was not uncommon," she explains, "to meet people who had never been to church or read the Bible. When one girl was asked what she knew about God she responded, 'It is like a blank page.' Another was asked, 'Do you know anything about Jesus?' She responded, 'I know baby Jesus who brings gifts at Christmas, but I don't know this Jesus you speak of.'"

Following her assignment with STINT, Lynn joined the staff of Campus Crusade. "Of course," she says, "I had to work through the usual objections. After all, I was already 30-something. Would this be good stewardship of my education? Another job change. What would this look like on my résumé? But I really wanted to be trained to be able to share my faith more effectively. And I really appreciated Crusade's commitment to working on teams."

Of her eight years on staff so far, Lynn spent the first five in the Northeast, on a campus ministry team at the University of Massachusetts and Smith College. Then she was assigned to the Metro Catalytic team in Atlanta.

Atlanta Metro established a partnership with Croatia. Now Lynn finds herself back in Eastern Europe with another STINT team. She recently E-mailed this report: "A Croatian girl befriended someone on our team here. She just took a job as a nanny in the same city back in America where one of my friends from Smith College lives. So I put them in touch with each other and the girl I discipled years ago at Smith College had the privilege of sharing Christ with this young Croatian and getting her involved in a local church in America."

A Credible Witness in the Workplace

Dr. Yang Chen finds that a credible witness for Christ is often missing in a place where life and death issues are common— the medical field. "In recent years," he says, "numerous peer reviewed studies have confirmed the value of spiritual intervention in medicine. We work to equip health professionals to integrate their faith and practice for the advancement of the kingdom and the good of the patient."

As an undergraduate student, Dr. Chen was discipled by Campus Crusade staff member J. Kent Hutcheson. Dr. Chen was so transformed by this that he wanted his life to be a "bright light for God." At the University of the Philippines College of Medicine, Yang shared Christ with nearly every student in his class, but response was minimal. He has since refined his approach to gain and hold his colleagues' attention. The Medical Strategic Network was born. Today, Medical Strategic Network, headed by Yang, is designed to teach medical professionals to share their faith in the workplace.

Dr. Chen recalls one exciting story in his ministry. One day, a newly released felon stormed into the emergency room where he worked. "I just got out of prison after serving time for murder! Where is Dr. Chen?" the man insisted. Hearing these words, the emergency room staff came to a halt.

Months earlier, two armed marshals were transporting Jim, a muscular 250-pound felon, to Folsom Prison when he began to complain of chest pains. After Jim's arrival at the hospital, Dr. Chen stabilized this convicted murderer and admitted him to the intensive care unit. Over the next few days, Dr. Chen felt impressed by God to go and talk with this prisoner about Jesus Christ. Each time, Dr. Chen promptly dismissed it. "God, I'll talk to anyone in this hospital, but I really don't think Jim will be interested." Truthfully, Yang was scared.

A couple of nights later, Dr. Chen had a chance to catch some sleep during a lull at work. Yet sleep would not come. He kept thinking of the prisoner somewhere in the hospital. Would he be willing to consider the claims of Christ?

Dr. Chen pulled himself out of the bed and made his way to the prisoner's bedside. To his surprise, Jim was open to hearing about God's love and forgiveness. As Dr. Chen talked, this 250-pound man, with one wrist chained to the bedrail, began to openly cry. The two armed guards became embarrassed and decided to wait out in the hall. Minutes later, Jim invited Christ into his life. He told his new friend, "Dr. Chen, I know you are here tonight because my grandmother has been praying for me for over fifteen years."

Months later, Jim was pardoned and released from Folsom

Prison. He headed straight to the emergency room where he had first met Dr. Chen. The staff informed Jim that Dr. Chen was not working that night. Jim smiled and explained, "Several months ago I was admitted to this hospital. Late one night Dr. Chen took the time to visit with me. Now that I am out of prison, I wanted to come back and personally thank him for what he shared with me. Please tell him I was here."

Dr. Chen has been on our staff for fourteen years. He has been used by God to disciple many other doctors and medical

"Everything we do is carried out in the context of faith. Leaders are being produced here."

personnel who have in turn won and discipled others, generation after generation. His influence is far-reaching in many cities and nations.

Pioneering and Pressing On

Thomas G. Fritz has been on staff for twenty-six years and is director of the U.S. InterCultural Resources. "What I like about Campus Crusade," says Tom, "is that we are a movement. It's a significant place for ministry—still relevant, not stagnant. Campus Crusade is constantly focused on personal growth and development and training. Everything we do is carried out in the context of faith. Leaders are being produced here."

The road to full-time ministry for this African-American collegian began in Philadelphia in the '70s. Although there were no staff on his campus at Temple University, he had a heart for evangelism. "With Crusade's campus director from nearby Penn State, I put together an outreach event," he explains. "Then I went to one of his evangelistic events and saw some diversity there. He talked me into attending EXPLO '72, the gathering of some 85,000 collegians in Dallas, Texas."

While in Dallas, Thomas's life was changed. The Great Commission moved from the pages of Scripture to become a reality in his life. He learned how to share his faith and saw two people come to Christ. That week he also heard Dr. E. V. Hill from Los Angeles and the music of Andre Crouch, both African-American Christians. But he was most impressed with a group of African-Americans who were full-time staff.

From the time he joined Campus Crusade, he encountered struggles and challenges as an African-American in full-time ministry. "But my colleague, Dan Hayes, provided an environment of creativity," says Tom. "As our director back then, Hayes just turned us loose on the freeway of ministry. And we thrived. When things didn't work, he encouraged our team to keep going. He shared the vision, and we expanded to Jackson State and Howard University with the goal to reach at least seven of the 100 'Historical Black Campuses' nationwide.

"What touched my life the most was a ministry trip I took to Africa with Hayes. We were out in a remote area and this African singled me out to talk with me because he realized I was from the U.S. He made me promise that I would try to see more African-Americans get to Africa."

Thomas believes that African-Americans have a vital mission in reaching the world because of their color. "We are not limited to our campuses and our communities," he says. "We are liberated to go to the world."

Experiments in the Laboratory of Life

In addition to the "open classroom" in his faculty-student chat room on the Internet, Dr. Walter Bradley and his wife, Anne, open their home for ongoing dialogue with students. They have been on staff for thirty-one years and serve as Faculty Partners with Christian Leadership Ministries.

The Bradleys met as college students at the University of Texas where they were involved in Campus Crusade activities. After Anne received her education degree, Walter earned his Ph.D. in Materials Science and Engineering in 1968. During their seven years at UT, they never had a professor who was openly identified as a Christian. And professors who were not Christians seemed to enjoy ridiculing their Christian faith. This influenced them to join the newly formed Christian Faculty Ministry as associate staff.

Their vision has been to model the significant spiritual impact that a faculty couple can have by allowing God to direct and empower them. "We find that our involvement with Campus Crusade has been crucial to keeping fresh our vision. It provides a platform for translating what we are doing locally into a much bigger venue," Walter says. "We receive great ideas for ministry from around the country and can see our best ideas being replicated elsewhere."

This fall the Bradleys invited ninety students from his two classes to their home for pizza and a video. Movies were selected with the intent to raise important questions about God and life. A total of 45 students came to the three open houses. In the spring Dr. Bradley started a seeker study of the Gospel of John with fourteen students, most of them non-Christians.

Dr. Bradley will take early retirement this year to work full-time with Christian Leadership Ministries, a ministry to almost 15,000 mostly secular university professors. "We hope to find other couples our age who God will call to join us in taking early retirement to give some of their best years to serving God full-time in the ministries of Campus Crusade."

I am sure you can see how each one of these staff members were led by God into the very place He had prepared for them. He gave them their talents and abilities and placed burdens on their hearts for their ministry.

Perhaps you are at a crossroads in your life right now. Maybe you are wondering if there is a place of ministry for someone like you in Campus Crusade. God may be preparing a place for you in Campus Crusade for Christ. I urge you to read the next chapter with an open heart, asking God to show you how He would have you serve in His kingdom.

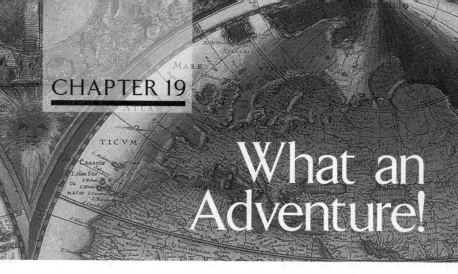

CHAPTER 19

What an Adventure!

I TRUST THAT WE have communicated some of the miraculous workings of the Holy Spirit through this ministry. Our Lord has raised up this great work through the partnership of hundreds of thousands of staff, volunteers, and supporters; millions of believers; tens of thousands of churches; and hundreds of Christian organizations. I feel so privileged to be part of this vast movement of God's Spirit. Since 1951, when God gave me the vision for Campus Crusade for Christ, I have experienced the most liberating, life-changing adventure anyone can know. It is a life full of miraculous events, dynamic challenges, and intimate fellowship with others and our great God and Savior. I also have the incredible knowledge that I am a part of helping to consummate what God has begun and is bringing to pass—the fulfillment of the Great Commission.

Whatever the cost, I am committed to winning and discipling millions more people whom the Lord of the harvest will call. My prayer is that the example of our generation, and the effectiveness of saturating the world with the gospel in the past few years, will motivate the generations to come to directly or indirectly help fulfill the Great Commission.

Imagine how privileged we are to spend our time on earth helping to change the lives of people for eternity! What investment could be greater? Where could we better spend our time, talents, treasure, and influence to bring greater glory to God?

I encourage you to be a part of this world-changing movement. Do not be satisfied with a life of mediocrity. You may be just starting your career or have reached the top of success and fulfillment. But let me challenge you to move from your present success and accomplishments to a far greater life of significance. God has something better for all of us when we live moment by moment doing His work for His glory and praise.

The national media will not likely report on the magnificent things that are happening all over the world—including in your hometown. You will not read about changed lives in the newspaper or in secular, best-selling books. But as you have seen through reading this book, God *is* doing an extraordinary and unprecedented work around the world. Whatever your gifts, your training, or your situation, you have the ability to become a world-changer for Him. You will be completely amazed at what God will do through you when your life is surrendered and available to Him.

Let me tell you about a dear friend who made himself available for God's leading. Don Preston was a small businessman in Greenville, South Carolina, when he decided to become a world-changer. He had worked for eleven years as a butcher in a supermarket when he started a small business packaging meat for restaurants. He hoped that his new business would at least provide him with a decent income for his family.

At the same time, he increased his giving to the Lord's work from 10 percent to 15 percent of his income, even though the financial demands of his new business drained his cash flow. But God began to bless Don's business.

Don also became involved in evangelistic outreaches during those years. The Lord used him to reach executives in his community for Christ and support an evangelistic campaign in his hometown with a $36,000 gift. Meanwhile, retirement plans forced Don to consider his future. That was when the idea came to mind to give a $1 million pledge to Campus Crusade for Christ to help fulfill the Great Commission. He thought, *I am not a rich person, but I could go back to work and surely I could make $50,000 a year, which I could give for the next twenty years to reach my $1 million pledge.*

With his wife's complete support, Don planned to earn and donate this amount in twenty years—a goal that was totally beyond his human ability to achieve. After he retired at the age of 44, he continued working in another job and began giving away 50 percent of his income. God honored Don's faith and enabled him to meet his commitment to give $1 million dollars in just ten years rather than twenty!

Don and his wife then began traveling to various continents giving their testimonies of God's faithfulness and looking for opportunities to help finance missionary ministries. They visited Africa, Hong Kong, and Singapore. Even after his wife's death from cancer, Don continued serving others with the gifts God had given him. He is now well on his way to giving his second million dollars and has dedicated his life full-time to serving various ministries of Campus Crusade.

I could relate hundreds of other dramatic stories of faithful men and women of God who were inspired and enabled by the Holy Spirit to do the impossible. Hundreds of thousands have volunteered many hours in the various ministries of Campus Crusade and seen their communities and neighborhoods change as a result. Thousands more have joined our ministry as full-time staff who now serve God in the fifty-plus U.S. Ministries and all over the world in our International Ministries. There are also thousands of committed believers who respond to God's leading to go on a summer project, a year-long STINT, or other short-term mission opportunities. In addition, our work is blessed to have hundreds of thousands of prayer and financial supporters who faithfully undergird each facet of Campus Crusade for Christ.

I thank God for each person who has yielded to His call and become a partner with us in His work of helping to fulfill the Great Commission. Working together with over a thousand national and international mission groups and tens of thousands of churches of all denominations, we have helped to present the gospel to 3.4 billion people since 1951.

Willing and Available

We know that anything we have accomplished for God is "not by might nor by power, but by My Spirit" (Zechariah 4:6). All glory and praise belong to our great God and Savior!

I urge you to make your commitment to help fulfill the Great Commission, which is the biblical privilege and responsibility of every believer. Ask yourself these questions as you pray and wait upon God to direct you:

Am I willing and available to do God's will no matter where He leads me? This is the most important question you can consider. Through the years I have observed that God is more concerned by our availability than our ability. God does not need people with extraordinary talents or money; He is looking for those who will surrender their life into His hands. If you can answer this question with a "Yes!" then God can use you no matter how little you think you have to offer Him. He is in the business of enabling us by His Holy Spirit to accomplish miracles with what we surrender to Him. Many mid-career believers are moving from success in their businesses and professions to greater significance in their ministry for Christ. You may want to join them.

How much time am I spending in prayer for the salvation of others and for organizations like Campus Crusade that are taking God's Word to people throughout the world? Prayer is our greatest need, both in our own lives and for this ministry around the world. Without prayer, we will not be effective. My associates and I need your prayer support. Join with us as we pray to the Lord of the harvest to bring forth laborers into the field and for a great spiritual harvest of at least one billion souls.

Has the Lord laid on my heart a deep desire to spread His message to others? If Christ came "to seek and to save the lost," how much more should we as His followers carry on His mission of seeking and saving the lost in the power of the Holy Spirit. Ask God to give you a heart for others. Make a list of ten nonbelievers, and in your daily devotional time claim them for our Lord. Also pray for organizations that are involved in discipleship and evangelism and are committed to carrying out Christ's Great Commission.

Has God given me a burden for a group of people or another country? Sometimes God lays certain areas of the world on our hearts. Other times, He leads us into a ministry that opens up new areas to us. Be assured that God will direct your life into the very place He wants you to serve if you will genuinely invite Him to do so.

Is there a particular group—executives, students, athletes, foreign visitors—for which God has given me gifts to minister effectively? Sometimes our life situation is the training God has given us to reach a particular group. If you have been involved in business for several years, that may be just the "school of experience" God intends for you to use to help reach other business professionals. If you are an educator, you may want to volunteer your services on the university campus, or you may wish to join our university staff full-time. As you seek God's will, list all the areas in which you are interested or involved and ask Him if these are where He wants you to serve.

Do I have talents or gifts that I want to use for God's glory? God has made each of us different, with various abilities and spiritual gifts. As we use them, we feel a greater joy in His service. With more than fifty different ministries under our umbrella, Campus Crusade offers a variety of ministries—one that can fit your personality and gifts. Please review the list of opportunities in Appendices A and B.

Do I have work skills that God can use to build up the Body of Christ? In recent years, many laypeople have taken mission trips to the former Soviet Union to train school teachers how to reach students with the gospel. Many of those who have gone are gifted with a teaching ability. That does not necessarily mean that they have a degree as an educator, but that God has given them the ability to explain truth to others. Many staff and volunteers who have joined us through the years have brought business skills, knowledge in computers, administrative gifts, training in music, and countless other talents. The skills you have developed in your life are very likely a part of God's plan to enhance your ministry through full-time or volunteer service with Campus Crusade.

Do I need training in evangelism and discipleship? Campus Crusade offers years of experience in training that really works! We have special training for our full-time staff and volunteers. The training, based on God's Word, can change your life and ministry. You will work with experienced staff who will in field-based demonstrations lead someone to Christ or disciple a new believer.

Am I looking for dynamic resources I can use for ministry? Since 1951, we have developed resources and ministry strategies that are very effective on the college campus and in every segment of our society, as well as in our more than fifty ministries. These books, booklets, videos, audiocassettes, CDs, DVDs, and other materials can transform the way you do outreach in your church, witness to your neighbor, or live as a lighthouse in your home or workplace. Along with the resources, we offer training on how to implement many of them, such as using the *Four Spiritual Laws* for sharing your faith. Over 2.5 billion copies of this tract have been distributed in more than 200 languages. Another booklet, *Have You Made the Wonderful Discovery of the Spirit-Filled Life?,* helps believers appropriate the power of the Holy Spirit for holy living and fruitful witnessing. Millions of Christians have used these resources with amazing results. (See the Resources at the back of the book for more information on these and other materials available from Campus Crusade for Christ.)

Am I involved with a mission board, church committee, or

other group that desires to reach the world for Christ? Tens of thousands of churches of all major denominations have teamed up with Campus Crusade to have a more effective outreach in their community and local church body. I encourage you to purchase a copy of this book for each member of your board, then pray that God will lead you as a group to deepen your involvement in helping to reach the world for Christ with a greater sense of urgency.

Is the Lord calling me to give above what I am already giving? The Lord owns all that we have. He wants us to place it all in His hands and use it as He directs. Perhaps you have never given sacrificially before. Stretching your faith to give above what you believe you can give is one of the greatest joys of the Christian life. Turn your finances over to God—and you will rejoice over what He will do with them. Remember, "It is more blessed to give than to receive" (Acts 20:35), and "whoever sows sparingly will also reap sparingly, and whoever sows generously will also reap generously" (2 Corinthians 9:6).

Is the Lord leading me into a full-time commitment of a summer, a year, or longer? For some of you, God may be asking you to take a completely new turn in your life. The harvest time has already begun. I am confident that as we obey Christ's mandate to help reach the world with the gospel, we will see at least a billion people come to know Christ through the staff and associates of this ministry alone. But we need your help.

It Is in Your Hands

As I look back on my life, I have no regrets, only great joy, gratitude, and excitement. I am heading toward the eighty-year mark, yet at times I still feel thirty. My surrender to Jesus Christ has not only given me far greater joy and accomplishment than I could ever have known otherwise, I have also developed the dearest friends, seen the most amazing miracles, and walked closer to my Lord and Savior with each passing year. Today, I sense that the best years of my life are before me. I have known the thrill of being a slave of Jesus Christ since 1951. What could be better?

I encourage you to join Vonette and me and our wonderful, dedicated staff and volunteers in this great adventure of following Christ. Commit yourself to being His slave no matter what it costs and no matter where He leads. There is no greater privilege, no higher calling than this.

If you are unsure about your decision, Appendix C will help you discern God's will for your life, according to the "Sound Mind" principle of Scripture. When you feel the leading of the Lord to join us in some way, the back page of this book has a Response Form that can get you started in your great adventure. The human resource professionals on our staff can help find just the right place for you as you partner with us. We want to come alongside you to encourage you in your decision-making, support raising, placement, and training.

I urge you to prayerfully consider God's exciting role for you in this great drama for the souls of men, women, boys, and girls. The decision is in your hands. Come join us and help *change the world for Christ!*

> *Whether or not we are believers, we are going to have problems in this life. Believers or not, we will one day die. If I am going to be a follower of Christ, I want all that God has for me and I want to be all that He wants me to be. If I am to suffer at all, and one day die, why not suffer and die for the highest and best, for the Lord Jesus Christ and His gospel!*

Though we have tried to present Campus Crusade for Christ in a dynamic, exciting way, we readily admit that we are only a part of the vast body of Christ. We see ourselves as only a leaf from a twig of a branch of the vine. We salute all those who are preaching that Jesus Christ is Lord and are helping to fulfill the Great Commission.

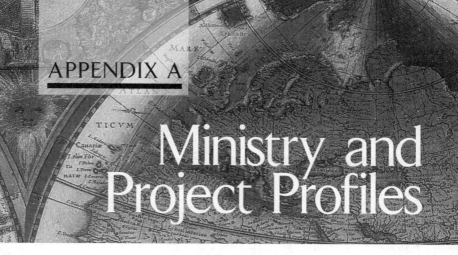

APPENDIX A

Ministry and Project Profiles

M inistries are listed in alphabetical order. Ministries that were presented in Chapters 9, 13, 14, 15, and 17 are not repeated here.

Agape International Training
Founded 1973

In 1998, *Agape* International celebrated its 25th anniversary of providing cross-cultural training for international staff and other missions agencies. More than 2,000 interns have completed the *Agape* International Training (AIT) program. In addition to Campus Crusade U.S. staff, AIT instructors have helped train missionaries from the Presbyterian Church in America, Frontiers, Greater Europe Missions, Grace Brethren Foreign Missions, and Korean Campus Crusade for Christ staff.

Initially, AIT was conceived for vocational staff going overseas with the *Agape* Movement. Today, its internship program is designed for those desiring to serve overseas long-term. In 1988, the AIT Training Center relocated to Bakersfield, California, to work in the culturally diverse Black and Hispanic communities.

AIT's mission is to equip the whole person for living and ministering cross-culturally as servant-leaders. Its vision is that through the lives and work of AIT trainees, people of all cultures will experience a life-changing relationship with Jesus

Christ. Missionary interns are placed in ethnic host homes, churches, and communities so they can experience living in a culture different from their own. Interns attend classes to undergird their daily experiences.

AIT also offers cross-cultural material to groups who may not need the full internship, provides in-service follow-up for missionaries on the field, and assists in the development of AIT-type programs worldwide.

Alumni Relations
Founded February 1980
The Alumni Relations office was established in 1980 to thank and honor former staff members, to let them know they are still considered part of the Campus Crusade for Christ family, and to inform them of what is happening with other alumni. Alumni Relations staff also seek to involve alumni in the broader ministry of Campus Crusade in ways that fit the ministry they have assumed since leaving staff.

To accomplish these goals, the Alumni Relations office keeps track of the alumni as they leave staff, ministers to them so they can minister to others, and helps create a network between alumni and the Campus Crusade movement. The Alumni Relations office also tries to reconnect with alumni who have lost contact with the ministry through change of address or other reasons. An alumni newsletter, *Keep In Touch*, helps keep alumni informed with what is going on within the ministry and reports alumni news items. Alumni Relations serves about 5,500 former staff.

Arrowhead Conferences and Events
Founded 1987
Arrowhead Conferences & Events (ACE) is a non-profit subsidiary of Campus Crusade for Christ and is the largest, full-service meeting planning company in North America. Over the last decade, ACE has served a wide variety of Christian min-

istries including Campus Crusade for Christ, Promise Keepers, Presbyterian Church in America, Christian Management Association, California Southern Baptists, Teen Mania Ministries, Christian Church of North America, Lutheran Church Missouri Synod, C. S. Lewis Foundation, and National Network of Youth Ministries. In an average year, ACE secures more than 150 conferences and books more than 75,000 room nights!

Serving the religious market, ACE's professional expertise covers conference site selection, negotiation, and Internet event registration and housing reservation. ACE creates a bridge between Christian ministries and commercial enterprises, such as hotels and venues in a city.

Arrowhead Productions International
Founded early 1980s

Arrowhead Productions International (API) motivates and trains Christians to help fulfill the Great Commission by producing documentary, promotional, and inspirational videos, radio and television programs, web sites, and interactive multimedia. API offers full video and studio production services, including scriptwriting, location shooting, final editing, audio sweetening, and duplication.

API personnel include producers, writers, videographers, artists, audio engineers, and administrators. The media ministry is dedicated to serving the ministries of Campus Crusade for Christ, churches, and other Christian ministries by producing media that accelerate, enhance, and expand their work.

Key events from recent years include:

- Production of three nationally aired, daily radio shows for Campus Crusade: *World Changers Radio* featuring Dr. Bill Bright and Steve Douglass in cooperation with Mission America; *The World Changer*; and *Women Today With Vonette Bright*. The latter two are one-minute programs.

- Over a five-year period, one-third of the participants in Josh

McDowell's Operation Carelift said that the primary influence in their decision to join the Carelift ministry was the promo/documentary videos produced by API.

■ An API video, *Touching the Heart of the Dragon*, helped recruit more missionaries to an East Asian country than had been recruited in the previous ten years.

■ A fictional news broadcast video shown to CCC's first all-international leadership conference in thirty years set the stage for strategic discussions about fulfilling the Great Commission in each country when it simulated the CCC headquarters under terrorist attack.

■ A crisis-training video is being used by mission organizations to train their leaders how to properly respond should a disaster strike any of the missionaries in foreign countries.

■ Promotional radio and television spots called thousands to participate in Fasting and Prayer conferences.

Award Recognition
Founded 1984

As a ministry, we feel it is important to acknowledge the people who have contributed so much to evangelism and discipleship within Campus Crusade. Therefore, the purpose of the Award Recognition project is to express this recognition and appreciation to full-time supported and paid Campus Crusade staff and associate staff for their years of service.

How I enjoy greeting staff members who have served fifteen-plus years in our ministry! I feel greatly privileged to present these dear, committed men and women with their appropriate gift and hear of their joys in ministry. The fellowship we enjoy is truly blessed.

During Campus Crusade's bi-annual staff training, awards are given out to hundreds of staff members who have served for 15, 20, 25, 30, 35, 40, and 45 years! In 1997, Vonette and I had the privilege of receiving an award for 46-plus years of ministry along with two other dear friends, Roe Brooks and Gordon Klenck, who were honored for 45 years of ministry with Campus Crusade.

As our ministry continues to grow and many more staff make ministry a lifetime involvement, the number of awards we give out each year has mushroomed. Vonette and I feel our hearts swell with pride and deep gratitude to the great Lord of the harvest as we shake hands with men and women who have given so much of their time, talents, and influence to building Christ's kingdom.

Children of the World
Founded 1992

The purpose of this ministry is to win children to Christ and develop their conscience and character toward God. Children of the World began as a way to reach children whose parents watched the *JESUS* film. Initially the ministry focused on training international film teams to work with children in small groups at *JESUS* film showings. Using still shots from the *JESUS* film, *The Greatest Promise* booklet was developed to show children the story of God's love and to guide them to invite Jesus to live in their heart.

When the Soviet Union opened its doors to the *JESUS* film in 1990, founders of Children of the World helped to design a character development program and curriculum for elementary school children. In four-day convocations, teachers were trained to use this curriculum. In cooperation with other organizations and volunteers, the training and materials used so successfully internationally were adapted for North American schools, churches, and homes. Children of the World teams facilitate six 90-minute Character Education sessions for parents, teachers, and other significant adults.

In a partnership project, Children of the World and The JESUS Film Project are producing a children's version of the *JESUS* video. The video is the first step for the Safe Place strategy, which challenges ordinary people to do the extraordinary to mentor children for Jesus.

Christian Embassy, Washington, D.C.
Founded 1975
With the White House, Capitol Hill, the Pentagon, and 168 foreign embassies, no city in the world represents political, military, and economic power more than Washington, D.C. Christian Embassy staff bring the message of Christ to these strategic men and women, helping them discover the relevance of God's truth in their personal and professional lives.

Christian Embassy is a nonpolitical, nonpartisan outreach that Vonette and I established in 1975. For several years we spent approximately one week per month launching this ministry to the leaders of our country in Washington. Our vision was to focus on government leaders not only because of their personal needs, but also because of their position as decision-makers influencing the families and freedoms of every person in America. The response was encouraging as government and business leaders joined us to help begin this strategic witness for Christ.

Through personal appointments, special seminars, and creative outreach events, Christian Embassy staff seek to give every leader in our government the opportunity to understand the gospel. Special speakers such as Dr. Billy Graham, former Redskins football coach Joe Gibbs, author Chuck Swindoll, and members of Congress challenge their contemporaries to follow Christ.

An annual Thanksgiving outreach has proven to be the most fruitful outreach among foreign diplomats. After a dinner of traditional Thanksgiving dishes, staff dress in authentic Pilgrim costumes, presenting the Christian background of the first American Thanksgiving through a historical drama. In the following weeks, staff visit each guest to offer them a copy of the *JESUS* video in their own language and share the gospel with them.

Some forty weekly Bible studies, discipleship groups, and prayer breakfasts throughout Washington help fortify Christians to stand strong amidst the demands and pressures of public life.

Christian Leadership Ministries
Founded 1980

There are about 540,000 professors in the United States who influence our culture through their ideas, research, advice, and teaching. They also touch the lives of more than 14 million students each year. Christian Leadership Ministries' mission is to boldly proclaim Jesus Christ and His life-changing love and truth to every person in the college and university world, and mobilize professors as co-laborers in the global harvest. The professors multiply themselves through personal interaction, unifying Christian faculty, and providing spiritual resources for the campus.

"Favorite Faculty Banquets" are one effective strategy. Students invite non-Christian professors to a banquet in which they are given awards for teaching and other honors. A keynote speaker communicates the relevancy of Jesus Christ to the academic world.

Today, about 15,000 professors are actively expressing their faith on campus. In the next decade, Christian Leadership Ministries wants to recruit 3,000 faculty as Faculty Affiliates, organize faculty fellowships for ministry outreach at 300 major American university campuses, and accelerate the growth of organized ministries among professors on major university campuses worldwide.

Christmas Gatherings
Founded 1981

In 1981, Joyce Bademan spoke at two Christmas gatherings attended by forty guests. In response to her gospel presentation at these parties, more than half of the participants joined home Bible studies. This strategy continued to expand as six women hosted five gatherings the next year.

A Christmas Gathering is a casual or informal party for friends and neighbors in a private home. It features holiday food, spontaneous sharing of Christmas traditions, a brief and non-threatening talk about the meaning of Christmas, and an opportunity to receive Christ. Often after a party, Bible studies are started to provide an ongoing ministry in a neighborhood or workplace. Christmas Gatherings staff provide a training manual and seminars in how to organize a Christmas Gathering and how to start a four- to six-week Bible study.

This ministry began as an outreach for women, but over the years changes in our culture led to hosting parties mostly at night for couples, co-workers, sports groups, teens, as well as the original strategy of parties for neighborhood women. Today, more than fifty denominations, many churches, and scores of individuals are experiencing tremendous results from the Christmas Gatherings.

Church Dynamics International
Founded 1982

Church Dynamics International was established to serve pastors and church leaders by helping them develop healthy and dynamic churches and as a result see society reached and transformed by Jesus Christ. To do this, the staff come alongside the pastor and leaders of a church to help them evaluate the ministry of their church, develop a strategy for making disciples, develop a climate for growth, and recruit and train leaders to implement the church's ministry strategy.

In the United States, about 95 percent of the churches have reached a plateau in their growth or have become dormant. The Church Dynamics team of church-growth experts specializes in helping pastors equip their people for more effective ministry. This training has resulted in significant church growth in 97 percent of the participating churches.

To date, Church Dynamics has helped more than 2,000 churches in the United States. In a continued effort to develop specialized ministries, the staff have also developed materials, such as a one-to-one discipleship strategy to better equip the people to minister in the churches served.

ChurchLIFE
Founded 1992

Today in America, we find that 60 percent of church members do not have assurance that their sins are forgiven and that they have eternal life; 90 percent do not understand how to live the Christian life in the power of the Holy Spirit; and 98 percent have never shared their faith with another person. Yet ChurchLIFE trainees who share their faith with their neighbors, friends, associates, or even strangers consistently see from 21 to 38 percent of those with whom they share the gospel openly respond. ChurchLIFE addresses these problems and helps people learn how to share their faith as a way of life through these services:

- *The Joy of Hospitality:* Based on *The Joy of Hospitality*, co-authored by Vonette Bright and Barbara Ball, this is an effective method of practicing hospitality as an outreach lifestyle.

- The JESUS Video Strategies: Independent research reveals that from 16 to 43 percent of the viewers commit their lives to Christ. The strategy helps churches use the *JESUS* video for evangelism leading to discipleship.

- Prayer Workshops: Combines Biblical teaching with practical application.

- Evangelistic Speaking and Training: Staff speak at outreach events and train church members to do the same.

- Lifestyle Institute For Evangelism (LIFE): Staff provide training in how to witness in the Spirit, which involves combining an effective personal testimony with a gospel presentation.

- Sharpening the Focus of Our Faith: This helps believers prepare for the coming revival through a special worship-service message that speaks to the four most common needs of people.

- How to Build Your Church's Vision for the Great Commission: This program helps leaders build a vision for prayer, evangelism, and discipleship by preparing "new wine skins" of leadership for the "new wine" of awakening laity.

- The Way of Life Plan: This is a flexible plan for discipleship, evangelism, and assimilation using small groups to make the Great Commission vision a growing one.

Communication Center
Founded 1983

The purpose of the Communication Center is to further the Great Commission by helping Christians become skilled, accurate, relevant, creative, and confident communicators of biblical truth. The strategy is to train Christians in communication skills by modeling excellent communication and inventing and pioneering new approaches to communication in ministry.

For example, in February 1996, the Communication Center staff designed, wrote, and produced "The Greek Classic," a conference geared toward non-Christians. More than eight hundred students attended the three-day conference in Nashville, Tennessee. Many of these students received Christ.

This ministry has also written and produced a series of tools called LifeSkills. They are small-group materials on topics relevant to college students which introduce them to biblical content in a non-threatening way and allow relationships to be formed within small groups.

Disciplemakers International
Founded 1992

Disciplemakers International was started for the purpose of helping fulfill the Great Commission by producing practical discipleship and leadership training materials and strategies. These materials offer a long-term, systematic approach to disciple making and to training pastors and lay leaders in their use. The main resource of Disciplemakers International is the book, *Personal Disciple Making*.

Beginning in 1999, Disciplemakers International will offer a video training series on disciple making, produced in partnership with Western Theological Seminary in Portland, Oregon. The series consists of 24 thirty-minute videos designed to teach lay Christians how to disciple one-to-one or in small groups. Student notes and a discussion leader's guide are included.

The ministry action plan has three stages: 1) Develop spiritually mature assessment tools. This phase has been completed. 2) Develop a primary resource, *The Disciplemakers' Encyclopedia*. This is in the planning and implementing stage. 3) Implement three thrusts: U.S. training seminars; establish computer versions of the Resource Network; and adapt all materials for international and inter-organizational use.

When the *Disciplemakers' Encyclopedia* is completed, staff will be sent nationwide to train pastors and laypeople in its use. At the same time, computer versions will be distributed as a resource to pastors, missionaries, and counselors.

Executive Ministries
Founded 1976

For more than two decades, Executive Ministries has been effective in witnessing changed lives among outstanding business and social leaders across America who have received Jesus Christ as their Savior and Lord. The purpose is to help fulfill the Great Commission in this generation by reaching the executive, professional, and leadership community. For example, the ministry's Outreach Dinner Party strategy has proven to be effective in reaching this "forgotten minority" for Christ. It helps build leaders in their faith, equipping them to use their positions of influence to make a difference in their particular sphere of influence. They in turn help change the world with the positive impact they have on people in diverse sectors of society: business, politics, culture, law, medicine, education, media, arts, literature, and more.

Executive Ministries has two strategies to *win* others to Christ: the Outreach Dinner Party and the Small Dinner Party. They use follow-up and Bible studies as components of their *build* strategies, and discipleship and international trips as their *send* action plans.

The Outreach Dinner Party is an elegant social gathering in a non-threatening environment such as a spacious home, country club, or hotel. A formal invitation encourages invitees to enjoy a lovely evening with a spiritual emphasis. After the speaker's relevant talk, which includes a presentation of the gospel, guests are given an opportunity to receive Christ. Comment cards filled out at the end of the evening show that 30 to 65 percent of the guests have received Christ at that meeting or want more information about how to know Him personally. A similar strategy, the Small Dinner Party, is set in a more intimate environment.

Recently a "Fall Kickoff" Luncheon was held in Greenville, South Carolina, attended by almost 350 women. After the gospel presentation, 53 guests indicated their decisions to receive Christ. That evening, a Coffee and Dessert was attended by 110 women, of whom 33 trusted Christ as their Savior. Currently, 175 women participate in the large group Bible study held each week. Women at different levels of discipleship training break into smaller, intimate groups for study and prayer.

Grad Resources
Founded 1990

In 1990, Barna Research of Glendale, California, conducted a survey to determine the needs, pressures, and values of graduate students in the United States. It revealed that they often are stressed, driven, high-achievers who suffer loneliness, isolation, and skepticism.

Grad Resources began reaching out to these students. The staff participate in student orientation and offer resources such as investigative Bible studies and articles on topics related to stress, fatigue, and professor/graduate student relationships. Campuses at Seattle, Washington, and the University of Texas at Austin are staffed, with several others connected through the Internet.

The purpose of Grad Resources is to address the personal and spiritual needs of the 2.5 million grad students. One outreach is through E-mail. A student is sent a brief message stating the ministry's desire to serve students. Grads who respond are sent a Grad Student article by George Barna and are given an opportunity to receive additional assistance.

This is an example of a response: "I would love to receive the article on fatigue and stress in grad students' lives. It is great to see people actually studying lifestyles of grad students and addressing their problems. Sometimes one feels very alone being a grad, especially with the funding problems getting worse every year. I'm looking forward to hearing more from Grad Resources."

Great Commission Prayer Movement
Founded 1972

Campus Crusade for Christ was founded with a 24-hour prayer chain led by myself and Vonette. We believe that much of our amazing growth and results can be attributed directly to prayer. Vonette saw a need to expand the ministry of prayer in 1972, and founded the Great Commission Prayer Crusade.

The name was later changed to The Great Commission Prayer Movement.

The purpose of the Great Commission Prayer Movement is to assist prayer saturation of territorial, ministry, and administrative goals of Campus Crusade for Christ. This work is done under three divisions: National Movements of Prayer, Global Adoptive Prayer, and the Great Commission Prayer Center. These divisions, in turn, carry out their functions by seeking to:

1. Maintain a 24-hour daily Chain of Prayer

2. Assist the equipping of National Prayer Coordinators in every country and community

3. Enlist and inform international Adoptive Intercessors—people who accept prayer responsibility, as the Lord leads, for a Million Population Target Area, a major university, or a major city in the world

4. Operate high-speed global communications between field operations and Intercessors

5. Implement two annual World Wide Days of Prayer for our staff

6. Encourage Intercessors to take a Prayer Journey to countries with limited access

7. Network efforts with other prayer movements

Results of prayer in Campus Crusade for Christ are inspiring. In 1975, Christians in the Hindu kingdom of Nepal numbered about 500. Punishment for conversion to Christianity was a year in jail, six years for leading a person to Christ. One newly trained Christian leader in Nepal devoted two months to prayer. His wife started seventy women's prayer groups. Today, restrictive religious laws have been repealed, and followers of our Lord now number 500,000! They now serve as Campus Crusade Director for Nepal and Northeastern India.

Here's Life Inner City
Founded 1983

In the inner city, if you can't touch it, if you can't use it, if it doesn't help you survive, then it isn't real. Don't talk about "hope" unless you can demonstrate it. Here's Life Inner City has accepted that challenge.

Here's Life was launched by a Campus Crusade staff team working in New York City. They realized that you cannot talk about reaching a city for Christ without dealing with the very core of that city—the urban poor. There are dedicated and enthusiastic Christians in poor communities who know the culture, speak the language, and have a dream of making a difference in their corner of the world. But their churches are usually small and lack resources.

Here's Life's mission is to serve the people of the inner city by assisting the urban church. This service includes three broad areas: *connecting, empowering,* and *developing.*

To make the first *connection* with the poor, Here's Life Inner City provides resources that can be used by the local church to meet a felt need in the community. Boxes of Love, complete holiday meals for a family of six, enable churches to offer gifts of food to people in need. Homeless Care Kits give a warm blanket, a hat, scarf, gloves, socks, and toiletries to people living on the street. Easter Bags, new shoes, and school supplies are other ways we seek to demonstrate care. These compassionate evangelistic efforts help establish relationships by meeting the crisis needs of the poor and drawing them to Christ.

Here's Life *empowers* inner-city churches through training in evangelism and prayer and conferences on the urban family. Here's Life also provides the enthusiastic manpower of committed college students during Urban Immersion (spring break) and Summer in the City (summer break).

To see long-term change, *developmental* resources are also necessary. Through S.A.Y. Yes! Centers for Youth Development, Here's Life provides curriculum and training so that a church can offer a quality after-school program for kids. This biblically-based values curriculum gives children the moral and academic compass needed to navigate through the challenges they face in their young lives.

Hispanic Ministry
Founded 1985

It is estimated that by the year 2000, Hispanics will be the largest minority in the United States with a population of more than 40 million people. The Hispanic Ministry is committed to acknowledging the varied cultural aspects of Hispanics through a threefold strategy: first, to cooperate with existing churches to train pastors and laymen on how to live victorious lives and win others to Christ; second, to organize small and large events for evangelism; and third, to produce and distribute literature and win and affirm new and more mature believers in their faith.

To accomplish these goals, the Hispanic Ministry translates, publishes, and markets basic Campus Crusade for Christ materials. They also offer Spanish-language Christian Management and FamilyLife seminars through interested groups and churches. The staff networks with other ministries, denominations, and groups that work with Hispanics. Recently, they helped organize and participate in the South Texas Billy Graham Crusade in San Antonio, Texas, which has a high Hispanic population. More than 22,000 people indicated they made a decision to receive Christ. One staff member is now discipling fifty college students who came forward during the Crusade.

History's Handful
Founded 1991

History's Handful is dedicated to helping provide resources for the Great Commission by raising up a movement of leaders who will strategically invest their LIFE (Labor, Influence, Finances, and Expertise) in the programs and strategies of *NewLife 2000*. This mission connects committed Campus Crusade for Christ donors with CCC ministries needing assistance in developing resources to accomplish their objectives.

After many fruitful years working with Athletes in Action, Dave Hannah now lends his many talents to leading History's Handful. He and his wife, Elaine, have greatly lightened my load with financial resourcing for this expansive ministry.

History's Handful has four key strategies. First, the *Barnabas Group Strategy* prayerfully and sensitively expands the present ministry base of extraordinary involvement by men and women who have the capacity to give $500,000 or more per year. Second, the *Major Donor Strategy* helps increase the level of giving among existing donors who can give up to $500,000 per year. Next, the *New Donor Acquisition Strategy* challenges influential people to strategically invest their LIFE in the *NewLife 2000* program. The final strategy, *Gift and Estate Design*, helps fund the fulfillment of the Great Commission by equipping individuals with sound principles of biblical stewardship and assists them in planning the disposition of their assets.

In addition to these four strategies, Lightstone Productions ministers under the umbrella of the History's Handful ministry. Their vision is to serve the body of Christ by producing and distributing high-quality, motivational discipleship and evangelistic media tools.

Donors who participate are frequently able to become actively involved in ministry—often on site. Ed Sisam from Minnesota traveled to a small village in Ghana, West Africa, where he was the first American the villagers had ever met. He presented the *Four Spiritual Laws* to the chief and his people. The entire tribe received Christ as a result! One young couple with a newborn daughter asked Ed's permission to name her after his youngest daughter, Andrea.

Among the many people who work with Dave Hannah is

one individual who has the ability to read, absorb, and retain volumes of important information like no one I have ever seen. I have looked to El Ridder for many years to help raise urgently needed finances for this worldwide ministry. He and his wife, Debbie, are a constant source of encouragement.

Hollywood Ministry
Founded 1982

A staff member of the Hollywood Ministry recently attended a formal premiere party of a multi-million-dollar, blockbuster film. He socialized with prominent actors and initiated spiritual conversations. This type of opportunity is great but it is not necessarily standard fare for the Hollywood Ministry staff. On average, the "glitz and glamour" of Hollywood engages only five percent of ministry time. The rest is spent doing vintage Campus Crusade evangelism and discipleship—with some unique twists.

Certainly, the Hollywood Ministry represents one of the most difficult ministry territories in our country. Our goal is to help reach the entertainment industry for Christ and encourage its believers in the work of ministry. We target writers, directors, producers, and actors and also work with professionals in the secular music industry. Staff accomplish this through outreach strategies, encouragement and support efforts, small-group discipleship, and through ten-week evangelism and discipleship workshops.

The Hollywood Ministry's objectives are to reach professionals at higher levels of the entertainment industry in all major studios and production companies. Plans include a ministry to people in technical positions such as light, sound, makeup, wardrobe, and administration.

Hollywood professionals respond to one-on-one relationships more than group events such as outreach dinner parties. Consequently, our staff work hard at developing relationships in an industry that is based on mutual distrust. Large-group fellowships, conferences, seminars, and workshops serve to encourage followers of Christ in Hollywood.

Integrated Resources
Founded 1985

As Campus Crusade grew and increased production of ministry materials, it became necessary for someone to help with distribution needs of the staff and individual CCC ministries. Integrated Resources was established to better equip the staff and ministries of CCC through administrative assistance with evangelistic strategies and by developing and distributing tools for evangelism and discipleship.

Integrated Resources has gone through many developmental stages. The years 1986 to 1988 were spent primarily producing videos. In 1988, the staff participated in a national evangelism strategy. After six years of working on specialized projects, Integrated Resources made a major change in 1991 to expand its distribution efforts. Their approach was to become the "Sam's Club" of Campus Crusade by buying in bulk and passing the savings on to the customer. During that first year of expanded operations, the annual workload increased from processing 600 orders to 6,000. The product base increased from around 50 to more than 500.

The next year they began managing Campus Crusade's Follow-Up ministry, which responds to general inquiries from response cards at the back of booklets, personal referrals, or attendance at a conference.

In 1993, Integrated Resources helped launch the JESUS Video Project by providing distribution services for nearly 400,000 videos. That same year, the Campus Ministry introduced the Inter-Acta Bible study series, a fifty-title series designed for "Generation X." Promptly responding to a last-minute request for a Promise Keepers Conference in 1994, Campus Crusade Direct was born. It is Integrated Resources' marketing effort to the general public. Recent expansion of their services include the tape sales at CCC national conferences. Integrated Resources expanded beyond Campus Cruade in 1997 with a distribution partnership with Mission America. A co-sponsor of the Fasting and Prayer Conferences, Mission America also gives leadership to a national evangelistic effort called "Celebrate Jesus 2000."

InterCultural Resources, U.S.
Founded 1974

The mission of InterCultural Resources (ICR) is to be a catalyst to help reach, disciple, and mobilize ethnic minorities in the community for the cause of Christ. They seek to influence Campus Crusade staff who desire to effectively connect with the ethnic communities of our country to engage them with the truth of the gospel.

Through a network of conference alumni (Impact), ICR disciples people and develops leaders for the Great Commission task. In turn, they help reach other American ethnic communities, thus impacting our nation and the world at large.

Working closely with the ICR Campus staff, the ICR staff organize the Impact Conference, a semi-annual event for African Americans during the Christmas holidays. Over the years this special event has grown from 550 attendees in 1991, to 1,100 in 1994, to 2,450 in 1998. An outgrowth of these conferences is "Impact Career," a major strategy developed to broaden the base of interest in adult-oriented ministries. The vision for this part of our ICR mission includes ministry to men, women, and couples, and a stewardship ministry.

Over the years, ICR has ministered to ethnic staff through conferences and retreats. Staff also sponsored recruiting conferences (Vision '77) and developed inner-city summer projects in Washington, D.C., and Philadelphia. Their ministry's publications include the books *Wild Thing, The Man Behind the X,* and *Fight Like a Man.*

ICR was instrumental in the development of a fund known

as the Ethnic Minority Assistance Fund (EMAF), which is designed to help recruit and maintain ethnic minorities on the staff of Campus Crusade for Christ.

International Leadership Academies
Founded 1993

International Leadership Academies was born out of the need to accelerate Christian leadership preparation worldwide. Pastors and Christian leaders from North America teach courses in two-week intervals. Academy and Campus Crusade staff then train the students in hands-on ministry. The project's long-term vision is to help launch fifty academies in areas of great spiritual harvest.

When the Soviet Union collapsed, the door for sharing the gospel burst open. But it was apparent that even if many new churches were started, trained leaders were not available to meet this need because of the lack of an existing evangelical church base. This became the clarion call to launch the first leadership academies in Minsk, Belarus, and Moscow in 1993. Through accelerated training in Bible and theology, character and leadership, ministry practice and church multiplication methods, academy students are prepared to initiate ministries and multiply their impact by mentoring others. Continuing education refines their knowledge and skills.

As of 1998, 91 graduates of the academies have become church planters and 56 are pastors. Twenty-five others are involved in community ministry, twenty joined Campus Crusade staff, and thirteen pursued further education. The Belarusian academy is now directed and staffed by nationals. The network of academies has since expanded to Costa Rica and Nicaragua.

International School of Theology
Founded 1978

From its inception, Campus Crusade for Christ has had a deep interest in education. As you recall, our ministry began in an environment of higher education—on the campus of UCLA, emphasizing practical training. This emphasis led to the founding of the International School of Theology, whose vision is to educate and train leaders to become effective developers of people who are committed to Christ, the Church, and the Great Commission.

International (as the school prefers to be called) has accredited graduate programs offering M.A. and M. Div. degrees. The distinctives include a field ministry program offering approved Campus Crusade for Christ training, a Partners In Ministry certificate program offering training for spouses of Christian leaders, and sister schools in Manila, Nairobi, and Singapore.

The "Schools Without Walls" (SWW) project is an ambitious plan to offer theological education and training to qualified applicants anywhere in the world. The SWW project will deliver theological education on two levels: the accredited graduate level and the enrichment/continuing education level. This will be accomplished through a combination of resident campuses, extensions, and electronically assisted distance education.

Over the years, many students have gone into ministry through the theology school's training. International in California has over 450 graduates, with over 250 graduates abroad.

In addition to International's academic emphasis, the faculty and students are actively involved in diverse ministry opportunities. One example is Dieter Zander, who is fast becoming one of the most sought-after experts on the "Busters" generation (the 38 million Americans born between 1965 and 1980). While a student at International in California in 1988, he started a church called New Song. By 1994, New Song had an attendance of 1,200 with an average age of 26. That year, Dieter left New Song in the hands of the church staff and leaders and accepted a position as teaching pastor for Willow Creek

Community Church in Illinois, a congregation of 15,000.

The International faculty are also involved in ministry. For example, Dr. Ray Albrektson, along with other faculty members, played a major role in writing the curriculum on ethics and morality which is being used in the former Soviet Union along with the JESUS Project. When Campus Crusade decided to develop a multi-media presentation to reach the Soviet Union, Dr. Albrektson wrote a fifty-five minute script that became *The Scarlet Thread*, a presentation in the Russian language to illustrate redemption in Old Testament history. Pictures portraying Old Testament scenes were primarily from Russian art museums and Russian symphonic music was used on the soundtrack.

On Easter Sunday, 1994, *The Scarlet Thread* premiered in Moscow, a week before the Orthodox Easter. Ray had his first opportunity to see the presentation that summer when he was the main speaker at a convocation of 150 educators in Russia. When the lights came on after the showing, the audience clapped and cheered for five minutes.

JESUS Video Project
Founded 1993

Seventeen new people are attending the Colfax Christian Church in Colfax, Indiana, as a result of the JESUS Video Project. The majority of them are new Christians. How did this happen? Through door-to-door distribution of the *JESUS* video. Thirty-seven teams of two from the church, as well as two teams from the Wesleyan Church, passed out 225 videos to the 324 households in Colfax.

The goal of the JESUS Video Project is to help fulfill the Great Commission by offering a *JESUS* video to every home in the United States. The plan is simple. Churches choose 500 to 1,000 homes around their church for this evangelistic outing. Church members pray for the residents of the homes as they take them the *JESUS* video in a gift bag. The volunteers can choose to knock on the doors and speak with people or just hang the bag on the door handle. Each gift bag also contains a letter from the pastor and a response card that can be returned if the viewer wants more information about the church or how to have a relationship with God.

As of November 1998, 4.4 million *JESUS* videos have gone into homes across the United States, resulting in 2.2 million decisions for Christ. On average (determined through various surveys and tests), for every two *JESUS* videos distributed, one person prayed the salvation prayer at the end of the video. In many areas of the United States, there is an average of one salvation per each video.

The JESUS Video Project enables the local church, whatever its size, to move out of its building and to make friends with the neighbors. When a video with the simple gospel message is placed in private homes, it may be viewed numerous times. This strategy has proven very effective in every area of the country.

Justice LINC
Founded 1974

Despite efforts initiated by numerous government-sponsored programs, evidence reveals that agencies are powerless to affect lasting change. The power of the Holy Spirit is the only answer to changing lives engulfed by crime and sin. Justice LINC's goal is to reach not only incarcerated individuals, but also their families and their communities.

To accomplish this goal, the ministry's role is to effect a systemic change in the criminal sub-culture through a changed-life alternative and to provide resources to facilitate the fulfillment of the Great Commission in this needy area. Its strategy is to establish regional ministry in major population areas and to effectively use volunteer staff in their own communities.

Initially, CCC staff developed a para-chaplain ministry, known as the Prison Ministry, counseling and sharing the gospel with inmates. Today, Justice LINC's training emphasizes the value of each person connected with the prison system—inmates, victims, families, gang members, or law-enforcement personnel—as someone of infinite worth to God.

Committed to helping change the home environment of the ex-offender and to assisting those with criminal potential to change their ways, Justice LINC often partners with other prison ministries. We also use the resources of other Campus Crusade ministries, including projects such as City Focus, Family Life, and Here's Life Inner City.

Following a series of intense disturbances in the federal system which resulted in a nationwide "lock down," Justice LINC sponsored a concert at the Atlanta Federal Prison Camp. About two hundred inmates attended and heard a clear gospel presentation. The chaplain, Bruce Cook, said that the concert really made a difference in the prison atmosphere.

The Legal Ministry International
Founded 1992

The purpose of the Legal Ministry is to assist in the organization and strengthening of Christian legal groups worldwide dedicated to the evangelism of those in the legal profession. To accomplish this goal, the ministry has formed a partnership with the Christian Legal Fellowship in the U.S. and Canada, as well as similar organizations.

The staff implement evangelistic outreach programs. For example, in cooperation with the Executive Ministry, an outreach dinner was held in Miami, Florida. "Ethics, the Universal Bond of the Legal Profession" was the main topic. This cooperation with other ministries is the heart of the Legal Ministry's strategy. They help identify Christian students entering law school, then encourage them to join the national and local Christian Legal Society Law School chapters, and to participate in annual mentoring conferences.

Another project is to help establish a worldwide network

of Christian legal professionals with an international directory. The Legal Ministry also provides speakers, instructors, and workshop directors for retreats and training sessions. The topics include Universal Legal Ethics, Evangelism, the Role of the Christian Lawyer in the Legal Profession, and Reconciliation.

Life Builders
Founded 1998

Using basic Campus Crusade materials that I primarily developed some 40 years ago, a former pastor and his wife launched a new ministry in Dallas, Texas. Their goal as Life Builders is to train the general population of Christian adults to become Great Commission-minded people.

Initially, Ron and Della Proctor met individually with people who showed an interest in learning how to live by faith and reach out to others. After three years of effective mentoring and training of multiplying disciples, we asked them to assume leadership of similar full-time staff ministries in eleven other cities.

Even among professing Christians, 92 percent say they never share their faith and 35 percent say they have never found the meaning of life. Life Builders are equipped to help believers follow God's blueprint found in Scripture. After finding hearts open to the gospel, believers are challenged to get involved in the local church or in follow-up studies. Building on this foundation, the ministry uses a 24-lesson blueprint for Christian living.

The Macedonian Project
Founded 1996

A rectangular-shaped "window" extends from West Africa to East Asia, from 10 degrees north to 40 degrees north of the equator. This region is known as the 10/40 Window. It includes 61 countries, two-thirds of the world's population, 97 percent of the least evangelized people of the world, and 82 percent of the poorest of the poor. Many of the countries within this area are not open to Christian evangelism. The Macedonian Project exists to help equip and send men and women to go and help take the gospel of Jesus Christ into this area.

Acts 16:9,10 says, "During the night Paul had a vision of a man of Macedonia standing and begging him, 'Come over to Macedonia and help us.'" But how will men and women of faith go into areas in which the gospel message is not welcome? The objective of the Macedonian Project is to provide Christians with a hands-on, two-week or more missions experience in unreached areas through "ordinary" tourist trips to unreached lands. These Christians pray for the target area, plan a trip to the country, make contacts with the nationals, and sensitively share the gospel with them using tools like the *JESUS* film. They also help with debriefing and follow-up strategies.

For example, laypeople from a small church with limited international travel experience adopted a major city in a closed country. God opened doors to allow them to get into the provincial government and to see God provide for their language needs, resulting in twenty people hearing about Jesus. Now they plan to return to build on their previous trip.

MarketPlace CrossTalk and Educator's CrossTalk
Founded 1983

The purpose of the CrossTalk ministry is to help the Christian business and professional person address the issues and challenges faced throughout the work week. "CrossTalk" is an interactive Bible discussion oriented toward the marketplace, and helps attendees view their work week as a place of ministry, not as just a place to survive. Training and vision is given for how to reach out to others as a normal part of the work experience. Nearly three years of curriculum are available with a discussion sheet for each session. Normally groups meet weekly in a neutral environment such as a restaurant, board room, classroom, or lunch room. Meetings last 45–60 minutes, with the "leader" simply facilitating the discussion of all those present. The result is a greatly enhanced application of the Scripture to one's personal life.

The Educator application, begun in 1998, uses the same curriculum as the Marketplace application but meets on a public school campus, usually before school. Attendees are teachers, classified staff, and administration from that school. The only thing necessary for involvement in either group is a pad of the curriculum and a Bible.

The curriculum and the businessperson application were developed by David Sunde and Bob Horner, with assistance by Ron Ralston. The Educator application, gaining rapidly in popularity among teachers and classified staff, was developed by Bob M. Caddel.

The Medical Strategic Network
Founded 1985

Millions of people visit health-care providers every year. Yet a credible witness for Jesus Christ is often missing in a place where life and death issues are common.

As an undergraduate student, Dr. Yang Chen was discipled by a CCC staff member, J. Kent Hutcheson, at the University of the Philippines College of Medicine. "When I began to practice medicine," he notes, "it was considered inappropriate for doctors to raise spiritual issues with patients. Yet I knew that God had put me in practice to be an ambassador for Him." Response was minimal at first, but Dr. Chen refined his evangelism approach to gain and hold his colleagues' attention and The Medical Strategic Network was born.

Today, talking with patients about Christ, he finds most people appreciate his concern for their overall well-being. "In recent years, numerous peer-reviewed studies have confirmed the value of spiritual intervention in medicine."

The Medical Strategic Network offers specialized training

to help health professionals integrate their faith and practice. Training is provided through the Medical Evangelism Training and Strategies (METS) conferences. Participants earn 31 hours of CME/CEU credits. Participants learn how to take a spiritual history, master a gospel presentation appropriate for clinical environments, and participate in a spiritual care practicum at a local hospital. Select sites offer sessions for medical spouses. Dr. Chen's wife, Alice, says, "Medical marriages face tremendous challenges. Yet when couples work together as partners in medical ministry, there is fulfillment and cohesiveness of purpose."

The Network also reaches medical, dental, nursing, and allied health students for Christ. Dr. Harvey Elder, Network faculty member, says, "If we can reach and train them as students, they won't know how to practice medicine any other way."

Mission Media
Founded 1991
Mission Media brings Christian churches together around the goal of using the secular media to communicate the gospel. The mission statement is "to unify the body of Christ and use the secular media to communicate God's heart to nonbelievers."

A recent survey showed that 88 percent of Americans do not even know what the gospel message is! But they do know the slogans of top advertisers like Nike and American Express. The power of media is obvious, but the expense of a high-quality, highly visible media campaign requires a cooperative effort. Mission Media acts as a catalyst, challenging churches within television market areas, as well as individuals and businesses, to make monthly financial contributions. These donations enable staff to produce and place all types of media, including billboards, newspapers, television, and radio.

Mission Media ads have won local and national secular awards. One award-winning billboard featured a beautiful photo of the Rocky Mountains. The tallest peak had a picture frame around it and the copy read, "Meet the Artist at a Christian church near you!" Another billboard pictured a young man with a quizzical expression and the copy simply read, "Going to heaven? Find out. Call 1-800-HOW-TO-GO." More than 400 phone calls came in the first month this ad appeared!

Another facet of the ministry is encouraging churches to work together in city-wide outreaches. In one area, churches hosted marriage seminars featuring Gary Smalley. Area businesses, including the local NBC affiliate, co-sponsored the event and the results were tremendous! Thousands of couples attended. One church had 55 couples attend their follow-up sessions and dozens came to Christ and joined that church.

New*Life* Publications
Founded 1991

Developing materials that help Christians introduce others to Jesus Christ and train them to grow in Christ and become witnessing disciples is one of Campus Crusade's main missions. Over the years, we have seen the increasing effectiveness of basic Campus Crusade for Christ materials. For example, the *Four Spiritual Laws*, which has sold more than 2.5 billion copies, has now been translated into more than 200 languages. Recently, we have released specially designed versions for women, children, professionals, and African-Americans. *Ten Basic Steps Toward Christian Maturity* continues to meet a need for discipling believers.

Several years ago, I also envisioned a plan for increasing the production of more books and videos that would meet the needs of today's world. Yet, without a good publishing and marketing strategy, I realized that the best materials we could develop would languish on the warehouse shelves and storerooms. Since these materials were developed to be used in the workplace, home, church, and on the campus, we continue to find better ways to get them into the hands of ministering Christians. *NewLife* Publications was developed as an answer to these needs.

The mission of *NewLife* Publications is to produce, market, and distribute books, booklets, tracts, study guides, audio cassettes, and videos that promote and teach evangelism, discipleship, missions, fasting and prayer, and revival. Recently, I have felt the need to enhance our teaching and training materials by producing 13-session videos featuring teaching, vignettes, drama, and inspiration. Each video series will be accompanied by a video guide for group or family study, a major book, audiocassettes, CDs, booklets, memory cards, and other ancillary products. Titles of such recently completed projects include *Red Sky in the Morning: How You Can Help Prevent America's Gathering Storms* and *GOD: Discover His Character* (the attributes of God).

New Life Resources
Founded 1989

A carpenter cannot build a house without specific tools that enable him to pour a foundation, put up the walls, and finish the cabinetry. As Christians, we can find the right "tools" for our ministry to enable us to be more effective. If you are a church leader or a Christian who wants to be more effective in your ministry, how will you find the best materials available to meet the needs of your congregation or yourself for evangelism, discipleship, and other ministry? How can you keep abreast of the newest materials available in the Christian market?

For almost fifty years, Campus Crusade for Christ has been on the cutting edge of discipleship and evangelism. We are dedicated to sharing with others, especially the local church, everything that we have proven successful to help fulfill the Great Commission.

New Life Resources' goal is to help ministering Christians succeed by providing quality ministry resources to fill their "tool box." New Life Resources staff provide resources to help train, equip, and mobilize churches and individuals to be more effective messengers of the gospel. New Life Resources also serves other Campus Crusade ministries with warehousing, distribution, and marketing assistance. The ministry provides "one-stop shopping" for the numerous resources developed by Campus Crusade over its forty-five years of ministry.

New Life Resources has seen the impact of these materials on churches and individuals. One church ordered an evangelism training package called *Reaching Your World*, a six-hour video package to help leaders train their congregation in simple evangelism. After using the video series, the church saw their small outreach program expand to involve 150 people! New Life Resources also serves as the nationwide distribution center for *NewLife* Publications and the *JESUS* video.

The Orlando Institute
Founded 1991

Located at the Lake Hart campus, the Institute offers Bible and Ministry training programs for laypeople and three graduate degrees: Master of Christian Ministry; Master of Leadership in Ministry; and Master of Divinity. The school uses a mentoring model for education similar to the adult educational methods Jesus used in training His disciples.

The goal of the Institute is to help meet the global need for trained Christian leadership by helping to establish 10,000 sites worldwide and using modern technology with correspondence classes. The school helps fulfill the Great Commission through providing accessible evangelical theological education to developing Christian leaders. The Institute is accredited by the State of Florida Department of Independent Colleges and Universities and is a member of the Consortium of International Schools of Theology. Students are educated for ministry through active, supervised involvement in personal evangelism and discipleship in a church or missions setting.

In 1998, students led more than 400 people to Christ. The

student body includes people from the U.S., Korea, Taiwan, Trinidad, and Latin America. Students and adjunct faculty are located in Chicago, Los Angeles, Seattle, and Orlando.

Passionate Hearts
Founded 1995

We repeatedly see the power of God displayed as just one woman makes the initial contact for a Passionate Hearts conference or retreat that leads to bringing down spiritual barriers in the entire church or community. From the beginnings of humility and brokenness, God brings revival first to the women personally, and then to their families and churches.

In the course of a Passionate Hearts weekend, women enter at the gate of the tabernacle and proceed all the way into the Holy of Holies. Each part of the tabernacle is a picture of Jesus Christ, helping participants understand this blueprint for walking in intimacy with Him minute by minute.

At these conferences, an average of 20 percent receive Jesus Christ as their Lord and Savior, 60 percent commit to the Holy Spirit's control and to incorporating fasting into their prayer life, and 70 percent commit to pray weekly with two other women in a "triplet."

What happened in one church in March 1997 is not an uncommon experience. Several weeks following the conference, the entire church began to experience revival and awakening. Both men and women confessed sins of bitterness, strife, and disobedience; men began to take more responsibility for their homes; divorced couples reconciled; forgiveness was extended; and new ministries sprang up in the church. The church doors were even open at 5:00 a.m. for people to gather for prayer on their way to work!

The People Builders
Founded 1980

Finding and retaining quality people for key positions within any organization is a pressing need. At the same time, Campus Crusade staff and prospective staff are interested in finding the best place to invest their lives. The People Builders help staff with career assessment, job assessment, job match, and leadership assistance.

The goal of The People Builders is to help fulfill the Great Commission by helping Campus Crusade's senior level people and their leaders assess and understand their God-given gifts and demonstrate responsible stewardship through making career and personal decisions in alignment with their God-given bent. The strategy is to do career assessment and identify the critical requirements of a specific job. This empowers senior staff to combine their own wisdom with the latest human resource assessment tools and consulting insights so they can make intelligent decisions.

Pinnacle Forum
Founded 1996

Pinnacle Forum's mission is to help change our nation's culture by inspiring and equipping influential disciples of our Lord Jesus Christ to encourage other Americans and world leaders on their spiritual journey. The Pinnacle Forum seeks to formulate spiritual answers to questions that are being raised by leaders in various facets of society. The staff desire to bring a message of hope and purpose to the most successful men and women in each community who in turn have the greatest impact on our culture—leaders in business, art, government, sports, military, education, media, entertainment, medicine, and law.

Pinnacle Forum seeks to reach the cultural "gatekeepers" —those who lead the leaders for Jesus Christ. Two things tend to be true of these individuals: 1) They often feel that they have done very little of true significance and they are quietly hurting in the midst of their isolation and loneliness even though they may often be heralded as great successes; and 2)

They already know that power, fame, and money do not provide fulfillment. But they do not know what to do or where to turn. Pinnacle Forum seeks to create opportunities for these individuals to begin to move from success to significance in the context of safe and pure relationships. The staff seek to equip them to walk with God and to effectively utilize their God-given platform to bring about positive change within our culture in the person of our Lord Jesus Christ.

Prayerworks
Founded 1972

In 1972, Vonette founded the Great Commission Prayer Crusade to help meet the spiritual needs of our ever-growing ministry and staff. Another goal was to equip and mobilize communities to pray. A decade later, the Great Commission Prayer Crusade expanded to form two branches: the U.S. Prayer Ministry and the International Prayer Ministry.

In 1992, the name of the U.S. Prayer Ministry was changed to Prayerworks. It expanded from encouraging whole communities to help fulfill the Great Commission through prayer to include focus on individual churches and their prayer goals. Today, Prayerworks serves the Body of Christ as a resource and catalyst for national spiritual renewal and revival through awakening, equipping, and mobilizing Christians, churches, and communities through prayer.

Prayerworks offers two main programs designed to encourage Christians to go beyond their homes to affect their churches and communities: Prayer Awakenings encourages churches to come together and seek God and His will; and Citizens Who Care encourages citizens to pray for law enforcement officers in their community.

President's Office
Founded 1951

No organization can exist without a center of operations. In

Campus Crusade, this center is the President's Office, which includes the executive offices. It was just the two of us back in the "I Like Ike" days of the early '50s. New to marriage, Vonette and I were also new to running a ministry to college students from our home in Westwood, California, Campus Crusade's first "headquarters." Today, our dining room table office has been replaced with computers, fax machines, and administrative assistants. If you could walk into our new executive offices at Lake Hart, you would be amazed at how far we have come since those early days.

The Executive Offices of Campus Crusade for Christ exist to assist, support, and serve the leadership of the ministry. This area includes my offices, Vonette's office, the office of Executive Vice President Steve Douglass, the office of Vice President for Administration Ken Heckmann, and my Chief of Staff, Sid Wright. The executive-level load of this ministry is enormous. With the rapid growth and expansion of this ministry, I need special help, and God sent Sid and Ann Wright to my rescue. Sid was a captain in the Navy and spent several years in the Pentagon in charge of public relations. Assisting Sid and the other executive leadership is a faithful staff who coordinate the travel, appointment and meeting schedules, and process correspondence, mailings, and special projects.

As part of the President's Office, the Office of Communications spreads the news worldwide about how God continues to bless the ministries of Campus Crusade. This administrative staff team assists Campus Crusade ministries with public relations and in-house communication. The staff write news releases, develop PR campaigns, and manage media relations between the ministry and the public.

World Changers Radio is an effort by Steve Douglass and myself to help awaken believers to get ready for the coming national and world revival. This 15-minute daily broadcast motivates and trains Christians to share their faith in Christ and help fulfill the Great Commission in this generation. Using the latest technology, staff members research, write, record, produce, and edit programs. Vonette also has a daily one-minute radio program airing on 320 stations.

Other ministries coming directly under the President's Office include the Fasting and Prayer Office, *NewLife* Publications, and Arrowhead Productions.

Priority Associates
Founded 1995

Priority Associates (PA) was born out of a need to reach the young business and professional person—the emerging leader of tomorrow—for Christ. Our vision is to equip the next generation of leaders with opportunities and tools to be Christ-centered, value-driven leaders, possessing a desire to make a difference in their world. The goal is to win people to Christ, build them in their faith, and send them into their workplace to reach others for Christ.

PA staff desire to take the initiative to present Christ to their target group of 25- to 45-year-old business people and professionals of all ethnic backgrounds and develop them into spiritual leaders by building movements of spiritual multiplication. PA's strategy is twofold: develop principle-centered (rather than program-oriented) discipleship with more creative and effective methods of sharing Christ with our target audience; and form partnerships with like-minded groups and churches that share a common mission.

Greg, a business owner in Raleigh, North Carolina, is an example of spiritual multiplication. As a result of attending a Priority Associates outreach and participating in a follow-up series, he came to know Christ personally. At the next outreach, he sponsored a table, filling it with his peers, including his business partner, Robert. They both joined a weekly discipleship group and are growing in a relationship with God, impacting their entire company.

The School Board Strategy
Founded 1990

The purpose of The School Board Strategy is to encourage a school board's policy to embrace biblical truth as it relates to abstinence-based sex education and to expose school board members to the gospel. This is being accomplished through the efforts of Christian parents and a training program offered by The School Board Strategy.

To begin the process, a parent orders a packet of material that will help train a local committee how to influence school board members. The committee orders the material and meets to practice what they will say. Then they select a spokesperson to represent them at a board meeting. Each part of the presentation is planned and practiced.

The Strategy's video and audio tapes and other materials teach parents how to give a twelve-minute presentation to the school board in the presence of a significant number of voters. After the presentation, each board member is given a copy of Josh McDowell's book, *The Myths of Sex Education*. The committee members ask the school board to appoint a task force to recommend policies on sex-ed. Later, members of The School Board Strategy committee follow up by calling board members and asking if they have read the book and sharing their faith with the board members.

Single Life Resources
Founded 1989

Single adults today are a strategic, yet often overlooked, segment of our society, composing over 40 percent of adults in the United States. Often they deeply desire significant relationships, but feel left out of mainstream Christianity. Single Life Resources was founded by Dick Purnell to meet the unique needs of single adults. Regardless of the reason they are unmarried, singles are looking for significant relationships and purpose.

Purnell speaks to audiences throughout the United States and other countries. His presentations, books, discussion guides, tapes, and web site (www.slr.org) address the dynamic issues that single people face and motivate them to total commitment to Christ. The ultimate goal is to provide practical biblical tools to maximize their lives and reach other people for Christ.

Conferences are the main strategy of Single Life Resources. The most popular are: "Becoming a Friend and Lover," "Understanding the Opposite Sex," "Maximizing Your Life," and "Standing Strong in Today's Culture." These are designed to provide single adults with the biblical principles to develop godly relationships with the opposite sex and to bring them to Christ.

As new materials are being developed, the Internet "Single Life Bookstore" is fast becoming a popular online site for single adults. Partnerships with churches and other Christian organizations enable us to impact an ever-increasing number of single adults.

Singles Offering Life to Others
Founded 1995

Singles Offering Life to Others (SOLO) was originally established in 1988 to help reach one of the largest segments of society today—those who are single and single again. SOLO is a community-based ministry staffed by volunteers and field staff of Campus Crusade for Christ. In 1991, SOLO began a ministry partnership with Campus Crusade for Christ and officially became a ministry of Campus Crusade in 1995.

Over the years, the ministry has used a variety of outreach initiatives: large-group Bible studies with contemporary music, service projects, socials, small groups, and one-on-one evangelism and discipleship. Ministry leaders are dedicated to leadership development and prayer initiatives. The staff and volunteers also minister to newcomers in the community and to unchurched singles. SOLO staff also assist small- and mid-sized churches in building a quality singles ministry.

To help build momentum and broaden impact in the community, SOLO works in partnership with area singles groups, churches, and the YMCA. The staff have seen singles participate who would "never darken the door of a church." As a result, outreach is more effective. Many are hearing the life-changing truth of Jesus Christ for the first time in a clear and understandable way. In the new millennium, SOLO will continue to serve in mobilizing single adults through strategic initiatives that take the love of Christ to where the people are, while partnering with churches and Christian ministries.

Women Today International
Founded 1993

To further the Campus Crusade foundation of ministry to women, Vonette founded Women Today International in 1993. Women Today provides intellectual and spiritual resources to help women become effective ambassadors for Christ in their community and workplace.

One of the strategies we use to accomplish this goal is a nationwide one-minute (formerly five-minute) daily radio program called *Women Today With Vonette Bright.* The program offers inspiration and encouragement, as well as ideas and training in evangelism and discipleship. Another strategy is to partner with other women's organizations, like the Women of Faith conferences. More than a half million women attended these conferences in the first three years. Women Today provides conference follow-up by offering materials for growth for the new believer as well as a resource table with materials for personal ministry.

In addition, Women Today offers two seminars providing training in ministry skills. "Conversations That Count" teaches how to have a spiritual conversation with someone, tell your own personal faith story, and lead another person to

Christ. The other seminar teaches women how to host or speak at Christmas Gathering evangelistic home parties.

Through an Internet home page, Women Today also provides information for ministry how-to's. The *Communiqué*, a bimonthly newsletter, offers ideas and instructions for the woman who wants to take the next step of faith in her walk with God.

WorldLINC Ministry
Founded 1987

We found ourselves facing a dilemma as a ministry as God began to lay on our hearts more target audiences and needs. How could we reach so many different kinds of people in so many places with so few staff? We came to realize that laypeople could have a more direct role in ministry. The problem was how to help them begin and lead ministries in areas that were not near a Campus Crusade staff center. This is why World-LINC (Leaders In New Community) was formed.

WorldLINC's main purpose is to more effectively and efficiently enable volunteers worldwide to begin and accelerate Campus Crusade for Christ ministries to their own target audiences by using long-distance teleconsulting and thus more quickly reach the world for Christ. This strategy includes using mail services, facsimile, telephone, and the Internet. WorldLINC functions in a consulting role to other LINC-related ministries within our organization: Student LINC (Campus Ministry), VITAL LINC (Student Venture), Executive LINC (Executive Ministry), Military LINC (Military Ministry), The Athlete's LINC (Athletes in Action), Justice LINC (the former Prison Ministry), JVP LINC (JESUS Video Project), and countries that have LINC ministries such as Canada, Brazil, Argentina, Germany, Great Britain, France, Philippines, Japan, and Taiwan.

The LINC concept multiplies Crusade staff effectiveness anywhere from ten to forty-five times. The staff encourage rapid growth of all current LINC ministries in partnership with other expansion efforts in the United States and internationally. People who are interested in starting a Campus ministry on a local university in their area, for example, may call a toll-free number where Campus Crusade staff coach them and help them obtain the best materials.

The success of the LINC strategy has been phenomenal. In one example, a member of Jack Hayford's "Church on the Way" heard a radio promotion by Josh McDowell about VITAL LINC. The listener called the VITAL LINC office of Student Venture and said, "We need your help. We have twenty high schools in our area, and no ministry from our church on any of these campuses."

Student Venture is currently equipping key laypeople in the congregation in a step-by-step procedure to start ministries on these campuses. This is one more way that Campus Crusade is using technology to be more effective in bringing God's good news to large numbers of people.

Worldwide Challenge Magazine
Founded 1974

In the early days of Campus Crusade's growth and development, the leadership became convinced that mass media plays a vital role in reaching unbelievers and training and informing Christians. Consequently, the *Collegiate Challenge* magazine was launched in 1967. With its colorful layout and relevant themes, the *Collegiate Challenge* took the lead in the 1960s magazine boom. In 1974, its name was changed to *Worldwide Impact*, and in 1975, it was renamed *Worldwide Challenge*.

Worldwide Challenge has won awards from both Christian and secular media organizations, including the Evangelical Press Association, the National Press Photographers Association, the Florida Magazine Association, and the Society of Publication Design. But the goal of the magazine is not to win awards. Its vision is to communicate how God is directing the hearts and hands of Campus Crusade for Christ staff members around the world. Since 97 percent of the readership are ministry partners, the magazine challenges readers to join us in making Christ known to others. *Worldwide Challenge* is committed to using excellent writing, quality photography, and good design to illustrate how God is working in the lives of others.

Worldwide Challenge staff have produced three special issues to serve as evangelistic tools: *The Challenge of Success* in 1989, *A Separate Peace* in 1991, and *LifeSkills* in 1995. These editions help readers become more effective in their evangelism and follow-up. *Worldwide Challenge* also serves the essential role as the chronicler for the history of our movement. Periodically special issues are dedicated to organization benchmarks, such as the 1991 anniversary issue for the 40th year of our ministry.

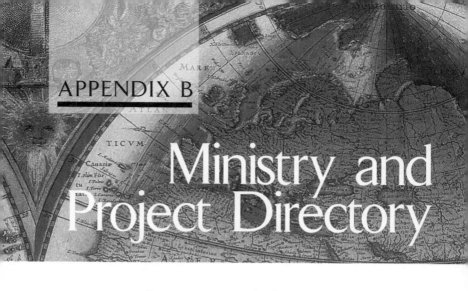

Ministry and Project Directory

Campus Crusade for Christ
100 Lake Hart Drive, Orlando, FL 32832-0100
407-826-2000
www.ccci.org

To read a profile of these ministries and projects, see Appendix A or the chapter indicated in parentheses. Contact any of the following ministries directly, or for more information about Campus Crusade for Christ, you may call the above number or see our web page.

Agape International Training—cross-cultural internship for those desiring to serve overseas.
> Don Urquhart – Director   805-861-1043
> www.aitusa.org   E-mail: info@aitusa.org

Alumni Relations—ministering to the network of former staff and keeping them informed of the broader Campus Crusade ministry.
> Marlyse Milburn – Director/Seminar Staff Director
> 800-456-ALUM (3586)   E-mail: ccci.alum@aol.com

Andre Kole—communicating the gospel as one of the world's foremost illusionists. *(Chapter 9)*

Andre Kole – Illusionist   602-968-8625
E-mail: ak@andrekole.org   www.andrekole.org

Arrowhead Conferences and Events—providing full-service meeting planning.
Enoch Williams – President   800-723-2222
www.arrowheadconferences.org

Arrowhead Productions International—documenting ministries on-location with state-of-the-art video equipment.
Paul Read – Managing Director
www.ccci.org/api   407-826-2350

Arrowhead Springs Conference Center—Christian conference center.
James Pompoco – Director of Guest Services
www.arrowhead-springs.org   800-723-2222
E-mail: info@arrowhead-springs.org

Athletes in Action—using the platform of sports to proclaim Christ. *(Chapter 15)*
Wendel Deyo – President   513-933-2421
E-mail: aiacom@aol.com   www.aisports.org/aia

Award Recognition—expressing appreciation to full-time supported and paid Campus Crusade staff for their years of service.
Marlyse Milburn – Director/Seminar Staff Director
E-mail: ccci.award@aol.com   909-881-7704

Campus Ministry—turning lost students into Christ-centered laborers. *(Chapter 15)*
Steve Sellers – National Director   407-826-2500
www.uscm.org

Children of the World/North American School Project—developing materials for the teaching and training of children.
Vernie Schorr – Director   800-366-4020
E-mail: cotw@character.com   www.character.com

Christian Embassy—reaching government, military, and diplomatic leaders with the gospel.

    Don Hayes – Director, D.C. office

    www.ccci.org/embassy

    United Nations, New York Office 212-759-4039

    Washington, D.C. Office   703-525-1770

Christian Leadership Ministries—dedicated to serving Christian faculty and administration as they fulfill their unique leadership role on their campus.

    Mike Duggins – Director   800-989-7130

    www.leaderu.com   E-mail: clm@clm.org

Christmas Gatherings—informal evangelistic parties for friends and neighbors.

    Joyce Bademan   612-469-4793

Church Dynamics International—serving pastors and church leaders locationally to help develop healthy and dynamic churches.

    Al Broom – President   760-726-9700

    E-mail: chuckflood@juno.com

ChurchLIFE—helping church leaders develop their churchwide plan for prayer, evangelism, and discipleship.

    Howard Ball – National Director 800-873-5222

    E-mail: churchlife@ccci.org   www.churchlife.org

City Focus—seeking to coordinate the activities of all the Campus Crusade ministries in a city as well as bringing together Christian groups and denominations working in that city.

    904-448-0737

Communication Center—helping Christians become skilled and confident communicators of biblical truth.

    Dan Brenton   919-469-2400

    E-mail: office@comctr.org   www.comctr.org

Disciplemakers International—producing practical discipleship and leadership training materials.

Chris Adsit – Executive Director   541-345-3458
www.ccci.org/disciplemakers
E-mail: disciplemakers@compuserve.com

Executive Ministries—reaching the executive community for Jesus Christ.

Tom Preston – National Director 864-370-3115
E-mail: execmin@execmin.org   www.execmin.org

FamilyLife—motivating and equipping families and individuals to leave a legacy of changed lives. *(Chapter 15)*

Dennis Rainey – Executive Director
www.familylife.com   800-358-6329

Global Resources—providing short-term community teams to the world.

Alan Nagel – Director   www.globalresources.org
E-mail: info@globalresources.org

Grad Resources—addressing the personal and spiritual needs of graduate students in the United States.

Nick Repak – Director   972-867-0188

Great Commission Prayer Movement—assisting prayer saturation of territorial, ministry, and administrative goals of Campus Crusade for Christ.

Dan Peterson – Director   407-826-2800

Here's Life Inner City—enabling the urban church to meet physical and spiritual needs in the inner city.

Ted Gandy – National Director
www.ccci.org/hlic   E-mail: hlic@ccci.org

The Hispanic Ministry—committed to acknowledging the varied cultural aspects of Hispanics through a threefold strategy.

Rolando Justiniano – Director
www.cruzada.org   E-mail: lleiva@ccci.org

History's Handful—a movement of leaders committed to a special strategy to provide resources for the fulfillment of the Great Commission.

> Dave Hannah – Vice President   800-705-7834
> E-mail: jheld@ccci.org

Hollywood Ministry—assisting media and entertainment professionals to understand the claims of Christ.

> Mike Chapman – National Director   818-558-4025

Integrated Resources (Campus Crusade Direct)—equipping CCC staff and ministries through administrative assistance with evangelistic strategies and developing and distributing tools for evangelism and discipleship.

> Paul Konstanski – Director   800-729-4351
> www.ccdirect.org

InterCultural Resources/USCM—connecting with the ethnic communities of our country to engage them with the truth of the gospel.

> Thomas Fritz – U.S. Ministries Branch Director
> Charles Gilmer – Campus Ministry Branch Director
> E-mail: 103134.133@compuserve.com

International Leadership Academies—worldwide Christian leadership preparation in Bible and theology, character and leadership, ministry practice and church multiplication methods.

> Carl Combs – Director
> E-mail: ila@compuserve.com

International Leadership University—educating and equipping college students from America and around the world to reach their countries with the gospel. *(Chapter 14)*

> J. Stanley Oakes – President
> www.ilu.edu   E-mail: information@tkc.edu
> Friedhelm K. Radandt – President, The King's College
> www.tkc.edu   E-mail: information@tkc.edu

International Ministries—encompasses all Campus Crusade ministries outside of North America. *(Chapter 17)*
> Bailey Marks – Executive Vice President
> www.ccci.org/international   407-826-2800

International School of Theology—educating and training potential leaders to become highly effective as developers of people who are committed to Christ.
> Don Weaver – President   800-727-ISOT
> E-mail: admissions@isot.org   www.leaderu.com/isot

International Student Resource—providing materials and resources in support of international ministries.
> Randy Harrell – Director of Student Resources
> 800-727-ISOT

JESUS Film Project—seeking to give everyone in the world a chance to hear the gospel in their own language through the *JESUS* film. *(Chapter 13)*
> Paul Eshleman – Director   800-432-1997
> www.jesusfilm.org   E-mail: jfp@ccci.org

JESUS Video Project—renewing America one neighborhood at a time.
> Donna Wright – Interim Executive Director
> 800-29JESUS   www.jesusvideo.org
> E-mail: info@jesusvideo.org

Josh McDowell Ministry—telling the world the truth through lectures, campaigns, and written resources. *(Chapter 15)*
> Josh McDowell – Director   972-907-1000
> E-mail: jmcdowell@mdalink.com   www.ccci.org/josh

JusticeLINC—providing resources and training to chaplains, inmates, and other prison ministries.
> Ron Dooley – Field Director   800-405-LINC (5462)
> www.ccci.org/worldlinc/justice.html
> E-mail: 105521.1040@compuserve.com

Keynote Communications—combining music and multimedia with the life-changing message of Jesus Christ. *(Chapter 9)*
    Randy Ray – Executive Director   800-352-8273
    E-mail: mail@keynote.org   www.keynote.org

Legal Ministry—evangelizing and discipling those who work within the legal realm.
    William P. Bennett, Esquire – Director
    www.grandparentsrights.com
    E-mail: legallinc@juno.com   877-744-3152

Life Builders—training the general population of Christian adults to become Great Commission–minded people.
    513-336-7227

LINC-Net—Campus Crusade's coordination group for internet strategy, philosophy, resources, web page creation, and development of the headquarters' Internet server site.
    Allan Beeber – Director
    www.ccci.org/lincnet.html   E-mail: linc-net@ccci.org

Macedonian Project—providing ordinary Christians with short-term mission experience in what is known as the 10/40 Window countries.
    Paul McKean – Director   888-257-7885
    E-mail: macprojectus@ccci.org www.macproject.com

MarketPlace CrossTalk and Educator's CrossTalk—helping the Christian businessman, professional person, and educator address the issues and challenges faced throughout the work week in an interactive Bible discussion oriented toward the marketplace and educators.
    David Sunde – Curriculum Developer   303-604-1031
    Bob Horner – Curriculum Developer   303-516-1374

Medical Ministry—communicating the gospel message to and through medical professionals.
    Dr. Yang Chen – Director
    www.GOMETS.org   E-mail: fireseeds@GoMETS.org

Military Ministry—communicating the gospel message to and through military personnel. *(Chapter 9)*

Dick Abel – Executive Director   800-444-6006

E-mail: milmin@aol.com   www.ccci.org/milmin

Mission Media—bringing Christian churches together around the goal of using the secular media to communicate the gospel.

Michael Boerner – Executive Director

208-322-9090

www.missionmedia.com   E-mail: missionmed@aol.com

NewLife **Publications**—producing and promoting print media tools for ministering Christians, churches, and Crusade staff.

Joe Kilpatrick – Executive Director   800-235-7255

E-mail: newlifepubs@ccci.org   www.newlifepubs.com

New Life Resources—serving believers by providing affordable resources for evangelism and discipleship.

Pat Pearce – National Director   800-827-2788

www.campuscrusade.com

E-mail: CCCemail@campuscrusade.com

The Orlando Institute—providing accessible evangelical, theological education to developing Christian leaders.

Steve Clinton – President   407-826-2070

www.ccci.org/theorlandoinstitute

E-mail: sclinton@toi.edu

Passionate Hearts—offering conferences and retreats for women and/or teens who want to learn how to walk in intimacy with God.

Laurie Killingsworth   407-826-2075

E-mail: lkil@ccci.org

People Builders—helping staff with career assessment, job assessment, job match, and leadership assistance.

Wendell Lillestrand – Senior Career Consultant

909-785-5720

Pinnacle Forum—inspiring and equipping influential disciples of our Lord Jesus Christ to encourage other Americans and world leaders on their spiritual journey.
> Brad Bright – Director   407-826-2192

Prayerworks—serving the larger Body of Christ as a resource and catalyst for national spiritual renewal and revival.
> Earl Pickard – National Director
> www.ccci.org/prayerworks
> E-mail: CCCPraywks@aol.com

President's Office—assisting and supporting the leadership of the worldwide CCC ministry.
> Sid Wright – Chief of Staff   407-826-2100

Priority Associates—developing multiplying ministries of evangelism and discipleship in the marketplace of America.
> Jack McGill – National Director   407-843-3294
> www.priorityassociates.org
> E-mail: mail@priorityassociates.org

The School Board Strategy—offering how-to training to change a school board's policy, if needed, to abstinence-based sex education and to expose school board members to the gospel.
> Robert Caddell – Director   909-881-7706

Single Life Resources—meeting the unique needs of single adults through conferences and media.
> Dick Purnell – Director/Traveling Speaker
> www.slr.org   888-758-6329

Singles Offering Life to Others (SOLO, Inc.)—mobilizing single adults through strategic initiatives that take the love of Jesus Christ to where the people are, while partnering with churches and Christian ministries.
> Craig Seibert – Director   704-358-0421
> E-mail: singlesofferinglife@juno.com   www.ccci.org/solo

Student LINC—providing resources to volunteers on college campuses that do not have Campus Crusade staff members.
www.studentlinc.com   800-678-LINC (5462)

Student Venture—reaching out to high school students with the claims of Christ. *(Chapter 15)*
Chuck Klein – National Director 800-789-LINC (5462)
www.svlinc.com   E-mail: svlinc@ccci.org

U.S. Ministries—encompasses all of the ministries of Campus Crusade within the U.S. *(Chapter 15)*
Steve Douglass – U.S. National Director   407-826-2450

Women Today International—reaching out to women with the claims of Christ.
407-826-2600
www.womentoday.org   E-mail: women@ccci.org

World Changers Radio—training Christians to share their faith through the medium of radio. *(Chapter 14)*
Bill Freeman – Director   www.worldchangers.net
E-mail: worldchangers@ccci.org   800-745-7600

World Headquarters (Campus Crusade for Christ Lake Hart Campus)—devoting professional skills to help the worldwide ministry function at maximum effectiveness. *(Chapter 14)*
Ken Heckmann – Vice President for Administration
407-826-2000   www.ccci.org/headquarters

WorldLINC—enabling volunteers worldwide to begin and accelerate Campus Crusade for Christ ministries to their target audiences by using long-distance tele-consulting.
407-826-2798   www.ccci.org/worldlinc

Worldwide Challenge—communicating how God is directing the hearts and hands of Campus Crusade for Christ staff members around the world.
Judy Nelson – Director   800-688-4992
www.ccci.org/WWC   E-mail: wchallenge@ccci.org

Worldwide Student Network—offering a network of resources and manpower to reach students and expose every person on our planet to the love of Christ. *(Chapter 15)*

Greg & Charmaine Lillestrand – Director
E-mail: wsn@uscm.org   877-WSNROAD

Campus Crusade for Christ, Canada
20385 64th Avenue, Langley, BC V2Y 1N5
604-514-2000
Mail: P.O. Box 529, Sumas, WA 98295
www.crusade.org

Athletes in Action—winning athletes to Christ, discipling them, and sending them to share their faith with teammates, the media, and fans.

Brent Dolfo – National Director   800-563-1106
E-mail: aia@ccc-van.crusade.org
aia@athletesinaction.com   www.athletesinaction.com

Campus Ministries—taking the gospel to college and university campuses through debates, lectures, and one-to-one evangelism.

Jeff Groenewald – National Director   905-813-6252
E-mail: campusmin@ontarioccc.org

Christian Embassy, Canada—bringing the good news to leaders in the political and diplomatic community.

Jerry Sherman   613-233-1025

FamilyLife—helping people build godly homes by teaching God's blueprint for marriage and family.

Ev Baerg – National Director   800-563-1106
E-mail: familylife@ccc-van.crusade.org

Global Aid Network (GAIN)—committed to helping meet practical needs around the world through strategic relief projects and to spreading the gospel.

Norm Schulz – Director   800-563-1106

E-mail: kevinm@ccc-van.crusade.org

Headquarters Ministry—staff providing Campus Crusade's ministries with the administrative support they need to be effective.

Dennis Fierbach – Vice President of Administration
E-mail: support@ccc-van.crusade.org   800-563-1106

International Ministries—reaching thousands of people worldwide through the *JESUS* film.

Norm Schulz – Director   800-563-1106
E-mail: susanm@ccc-van.crusade.org

Internet Ministries—our websites are reaching people worldwide for Christ and teaching them to walk by faith.

Katherine Kehler – Director   800-563-1106
E-mail: women@mkehler.com

JESUS Film Project—translating the *JESUS* film so that people worldwide can hear the salvation story in their own language.

Brian Vaughan – Director   800-563-1106
E-mail: brianv@ccc-van.crusade.org

KidStreet Urban Children's Ministry—seeking to expose inner-city kids to the gospel before they are pulled into a life of crime, substance abuse, and gang violence.

Hans Tokke – Director   800-563-1106
E-mail: kstreet@infoserve.net

Leadership Ministries—presenting the life-changing message of Christ to leaders in the business and corporate world through evangelistic dinners and one-to-one sharing.

Barry Bowater – Vice President   800-563-1106
E-mail: shirleyl@ccc-van.crusade.org

Michael Horner Speaks Out—Philosopher Michael Horner promotes and defends Christianity on university campuses across North America through lectures and debates.

Michael Horner – Director   800-563-1106

E-mail: michaelh@ccc-van.crusade.org

Mothers Who Care—Christian mothers praying weekly for their children and the schools they attend.
>   Barbara Epp – National Director   800-563-1106
>   E-mail: rosea@ccc-van.crusade.org

NewLife Resources—meeting the needs of the individual, the church, the community, and the world through evangelism, discipleship, and family resources.
>   Paul Paterson – Manager   800-667-0558
>   E-mail: orders@ccc-van.crusade.org

New Scholars Society—challenging Christian professors to use their academic platform to spread the gospel.
>   Kirk Durston – Director   905-813-6252
>   E-mail: durston@ibm.net

Women Today—encouraging and teaching Christian women to make a difference for Christ in their area of influence.
>   Janet Fierbach – Director   800-563-1106
>   E-mail: marilynr@ccc-van.crusade.org

(Note: Any omissions or corrections of the above information should be forwarded to NewLife Publications.)

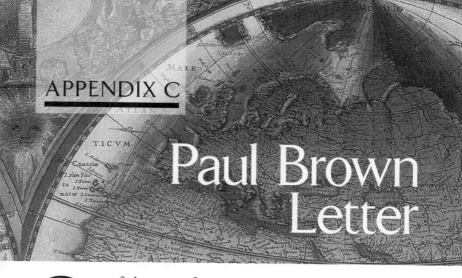

Paul Brown Letter

One of the most frequent questions people ask me is how to determine God's will for their life. This letter, written to a fictitious Paul Brown, contains the basic counsel that I give to students and adults about how to know God's will for their life according to the Sound Mind Principle of Scripture.

Dear Paul,

Thank you for your recent letter sharing some of the exciting experiences you are having in your new adventure with Christ.

When I read the part of your letter in which you expressed the desire to invest your life fully for Christ, I paused to give thanks to the Lord, first, for His great love and faithful direction in the lives of all who will trust Him, and second, for your response to His love and your willingness to trust Him with every detail of your life.

It is at this crucial point that many Christians deprive themselves of the full, abundant, and purposeful life that the Lord Jesus promised in John 10:10. Failing to comprehend the true character of God—His absolute love, grace, wisdom, power, and holiness—many Christians foolishly choose to live according to their own plans rather than do the will of God. Some have such a distorted view of God that they think of

Him as a tyrant one must either appease or experience His wrath. Since they are afraid of Him, they cannot love and trust Him. This is sometimes true of individuals who have transferred to God their fear of an earthly father who may have been overly strict, unduly demanding, or even tyrannical.

Many sincere Christians want to do the will of God but do not know how to go about discovering His will for their lives. A choice young college graduate came recently for counsel. "How can I know what God wants me to do?" he asked. Briefly, I explained the safest approach to knowing the will of God: to follow what I call the Sound Mind Principle of Scripture. In less than an hour, by following the suggestions contained in this letter, this young man discovered what he had been seeking for years. He knew not only the work God wanted him to do, but also the very organization with which he was to be affiliated.

Now you may ask, "What is the Sound Mind Principle of Scripture?" Second Timothy 1:7 says, "God has not given us the spirit of fear, but of power, and of love and of a sound mind" (KJV). The sound mind referred to in this verse means a well-balanced mind, a mind that is under the control of the Holy Spirit, "remade" according to Romans 12:1,2: "Therefore, my brothers, I implore you by God's mercies to offer your very selves to Him, a living sacrifice, dedicated and fit for His acceptance, the worship offered by mind and heart. Adapt yourselves no longer to the pattern of the present world, but let your minds be remade and your whole nature thus transformed. Then you will be able to discern the will of God and to know it is good, acceptable, and perfect" (NEB).

There is a vast difference between the inclination of the natural or carnal man to use "common sense" and that of the spiritual man to follow the Sound Mind Principle. The first man, for example, depends on the wisdom of man without benefit of God's wisdom and power; the second man, having the mind of Christ, receives wisdom and guidance from God moment by moment through faith.

Are your decisions as a Christian based on unpredictable emotions and chance circumstances—the common sense of the natural man? Or do you make your decisions according to the Sound Mind Principle of Scripture?

Through the years as I have counseled with many Christians, the question I hear most frequently is, "How can I know the will of God for my life?" Inevitably, the majority of Christians who come for counsel are looking for some dramatic or cataclysmic revelation from God by which they will know God's plan. Without minimizing the importance of feelings, which Jesus promised in John 14:21 will follow as a result of obedience, more emphasis needs to be placed on the importance of the sound mind that God has given us. Multitudes of sincere Christians are wasting their lives, immobile and impotent, as they wait for some unusual or dramatic word from God.

The Scripture assures us that "God has not given us a spirit of fear, but of power, and love, and of a sound mind." Thus, a Christian who has yielded his life fully to Christ can be assured of sanctified reasoning and a balanced, disciplined mind. Also, according to James 1:5,6, God has promised to give His children wisdom. Further, we can know with absolute assurance that when we pray according to God's will, He will always hear and grant our petitions (1 John 5:14,15). Since the Christian is to live by faith, and faith comes through an understanding of the Word of God, it is impossible to over-emphasize the importance of Scripture in the lives of those who would know and do the will of God.

If you would like to know the will of God for your life according to the Sound Mind Principle of Scripture, may I suggest that you follow this bit of logic. Consider these questions: First, "Why did Jesus come?" He came "to seek and save the lost" (Luke 19:10). Then, "What is the greatest experience of your life?" If you are a Christian, your answer quite obviously will be, "Coming to know Christ personally as my Savior and Lord." Finally, "What is the greatest thing that you can do to help others?" The answer again is obvious, "Introduce them to Christ."

Every Christian is under divine orders to be a faithful witness for Christ. Jesus said, "By this My Father is glorified, that you bear much fruit; so you will be My disciples" (John 15:8, NKJ). The most important thing I can possibly do as a Christian is to allow the Lord Jesus Christ in all of His resurrection power to have complete, unhindered control of my life. Otherwise He cannot continue seeking and saving the lost through me.

Thus, every sincere Christian will want to make his God-given time, talents, and treasure available to Christ so that his fullest potential will be realized for Him. For one Christian, this God-given talent may be preaching, evangelism, or teaching; for another, it may be business; for another, the ministry or missions; for another, homemaking, as described in Romans 12:5; 1 Corinthians 12; 1 Corinthians 14; Ephesians 4; and other Scriptures.

As you evaluate the talents that God has given you in relation to your training, personality, and other qualities, may I suggest that you take a sheet of paper and make a list of the most logical ways through which your life can be used to accomplish the most for the glory of God. With the desire to put His will above all else, list the pros and cons of each opportunity.

Campus Crusade		Teaching		Church Ministry		Business or Profession	
Pro	Con	Pro	Con	Pro	Con	Pro	Con

Where or how, according to the Sound Mind Principle, can the Lord Jesus Christ through your yielded life accomplish the most in continuing His great ministry of "seeking and saving the lost"? Like my young friend, this procedure will inevitably result in positive actions leading to God's perfect will for your life. But note a word of caution—the Sound Mind Principle is not valid unless certain factors exist:

First, there must be no unconfessed sin in your life. Obeying 1 John 1:9 takes care of that: "If we confess our sins, [God] is faithful and just and will forgive us our sins and purify us from all unrighteousness."

Second, your life must be fully dedicated to Christ according to Romans 12:1,2, and you must be filled with the Holy Spirit in obedience to the command of Ephesians 5:18. We are filled and controlled by the Spirit through faith.

Third, to know the will of God, you must walk in the Spirit (abide in Christ) moment by moment. You place your faith in the trustworthiness of God with the confidence that the Lord is directing and will continue to direct your life according to His promise that the "steps of a good man are ordered by the Lord" (Psalm 37:23, NKJ). For, "as you have therefore received Christ Jesus the Lord, so walk in Him" (Colossians 2:6, NKJ). How? By faith, place your complete trust in Him. Now you must go on walking by faith. Remember, "everything that does not come from faith is sin" (Romans 14:23); "the righteous will live by faith" (Romans 1:17); and "without faith it is impossible to please God" (Hebrews 11:6). Faith is the catalyst for all our Christian relationships.

Prayerfully consider the counsel of others, especially that of mature, dedicated Christians who know the Word of God and can relate the proper use of Scripture to your need. However, care should be taken not to make the counsel of others a crutch. Although God often speaks to us through other Christians, we are admonished to place our trust in Him. Psalm 37 tells us to delight ourselves in the Lord and He will give us the desires of our hearts, to commit our ways to the Lord, to trust Him, and He will bring it to pass. Also, Proverbs 3 says, "Trust in the Lord with all your heart and lean not on your own understanding; in all your ways acknowledge Him, and He will make your paths straight" (Proverbs 3:5,6).

God never contradicts Himself. He never leads us to do anything contrary to the commands of His Word. According to Philippians 2:13, "It is God who is at work within you, giving you the will and the power to achieve His purpose" (Phillips).

Through the centuries, sincere religious men have suggested spiritual formulas for discovering the will of God. Some are valid; others are unscriptural and misleading. For example, a young seminary graduate came to see me. He was investigating various possibilities of Christian service and had come to discuss the ministry of Campus Crusade for Christ. Applying the Sound Mind Principle approach to his quest, I asked him, "In what way do you expect God to reveal His place of service for you?"

He replied, "I am following the 'closed door' policy. A few months ago I began to investigate several opportunities for Christian service. The Lord has now closed the door on all but two, one of which is Campus Crusade for Christ. If the door to accept a call to a particular church closes, I shall know that God wants me in Campus Crusade."

Many sincere Christians follow this illogical and unscriptural method, often with most unsatisfactory and frustrating consequences. Don't misunderstand. God may and often does close doors in the life of an active, Holy Spirit–controlled Christian. This was true in the experience of the apostle Paul. In Acts 16:6–10, he was forbidden by the Spirit to go into Bithynia because God wanted him in Macedonia. My reference to "closed door" policies does not preclude such experiences, but refers to a careless hit-or-miss attitude without the careful evaluation of the issues.

This approach is illogical because it allows elements of chance to influence a decision rather than a careful, intelligent evaluation of all the factors involved. It is unscriptural because it fails to employ the God-given faculties of reason that are controlled by the Holy Spirit.

Further, the closed-door policy is in error because it seeks God's will through the process of elimination rather than seeking God's best first. It should be understood that true faith is established on fact. Therefore, vital faith in God is emphasized rather than minimized through Spirit-controlled reason. In making decisions, some sincere Christians rely almost entirely on impressions, or hunches, fearful that if they use their mental faculties they will not exercise adequate faith and thus will grieve the Holy Spirit.

Others assume that a door has been closed simply because of difficulties that have been encountered. Yet, experience has taught and Scripture confirms that God's richest blessings often follow periods of greatest testing. This might include financial needs, loss of health, objection of loved ones, or criticism of fellow Christians. God's blessing is promised, however, only to those who are obedient, who keep on trying, who demonstrate their faith in God's faithfulness. For example, the apparent defeat of the cross was followed by the victory of the resurrection.

An acceptable consideration for discussing God's will contains four basic factors somewhat similar to the Sound Mind Principle. God's will is revealed in: 1) the authority of Scripture; 2) providential circumstances; 3) conviction based upon reason; and 4) impressions of the Holy Spirit upon our minds. Such an appraisal is safer with a mature Christian than with a new or worldly Christian, and there is always danger of misunderstanding impressions.

You must know the source of leading before responding to it. To the inexperienced, what appears to be the leading of God may not be from Him at all, but from "the rulers of darkness of this world" (Ephesians 6:12, KJV). Satan and his helpers often disguise themselves as angels of light by performing miracles and signs, by foretelling events, etc. The enemy of our souls is a master counterfeiter.

Remember, just as the turning of the steering wheel of an automobile does not alter its direction unless it is moving, so God cannot direct our lives unless we are moving for Him. I challenge you to begin employing the Sound Mind Principle today in all your relationships. Apply it to the investment of your time, talents, and treasure, for this principle applies to everything you do in life. Every Christian should take spiritual inventory regularly by asking himself these questions: Is my time being invested in such a way that the greatest possible number of people are being introduced to Christ? Are my talents being fully invested so that the greatest possible number of people are being introduced to Christ? Is my money, my treasure, being invested in such a way as to introduce the greatest number of people to Christ?

Every Christian is admonished to be a good steward of his God-given time, talents, and treasure; therefore, these investments must not be dictated by tradition, habit, or emotions. Every investment of time, talent, and treasure, unless otherwise directed by the Holy Spirit, should be determined by the Sound Mind Principle of Scripture according to 2 Timothy 1:7.

Each Christian must be a witness for Christ. This is simply an act of obedience for which one need not possess the gift of evangelism. If normal day-to-day contacts do not provide opportunities to witness for Christ, an obedient Christian will make opportunities through personal contacts, church calling, letter writing, etc. Two of the most radiant, effective, and fruitful Christians I have known were bedridden invalids who, though in constant pain, bore a powerful witness for Christ to all—stranger and friend alike.

Second, a careful evaluation should be given to determine

if God may not have a better position for you. Again, the Sound Mind Principle applies. Be very careful, however, not to run from what appears to be a difficult assignment. A careful appraisal of your present responsibilities, with this new understanding of God's leading, may reveal a great potential for Christ.

One further work of explanation must be given. It is true that God still reveals His will to some men and women in dramatic ways, but this is the exception rather than the rule. God still leads men today as He has through the centuries. Philip, the deacon, was holding a successful campaign in Samaria. The Sound Mind Principle would have directed him to continue his campaign. However, God overruled by a special revelation, and Philip was led by the Holy Spirit to share the gospel with the Ethiopian eunuch. According to tradition, God used the Ethiopian eunuch to communicate the message of our living Lord to his own country.

Living according to the Sound Mind Principle allows for such dramatic leadings of God, but we are not to wait for such revelations before we start moving for Christ. Faith must have an object. A Christian's faith is built on the authority of God's Word supported by historical fact and not on any shallow emotional experience. However, a Christian's trust in God's will as revealed in His Word will result in the decisions which are made by following the Sound Mind Principle. The confirmation may come in various ways according to many factors, including the personality of the individual involved. Usually, the confirmation is a quiet, peaceful assurance that you are doing what God wants you to do, with expectancy that God will use you to bear "much fruit."

When any sincere Christian gives himself to a diligent study of the Scripture and allows a loving, all-wise, sovereign God and Father to control his life, feelings will inevitably result. Thus, the end result of a life that is lived according to the Sound Mind Principle is the most joyful, abundant, and fruitful life of all. Expect the Lord Jesus Christ to draw men to Himself through you. As you begin each day, acknowledge the fact that you belong to Him. Thank Him for the fact that He lives within you. Invite Him to use your mind to think His thoughts, your heart to express His love, your lips to speak His truth. Ask Jesus to be at home in your life and to walk around in your body that He may continue seeking and saving souls through you.

It is my sincere prayer, Paul, that you may know this kind of life and that you may fully appropriate all that God has given to you as your rightful heritage in Christ. I look forward to hearing more from you concerning your personal application of the Sound Mind Principle.

Warmly in Christ,

Bill Bright

Resources

Other Resources by Bill Bright

Resources for Fasting and Prayer

The Coming Revival: America's Call to Fast, Pray, and "Seek God's Face." This inspiring yet honest book explains how the power of fasting and prayer by millions of God's people can usher in a mighty spiritual revival and lift His judgment on America. *The Coming Revival* can equip Christians, their churches, and our nation for the greatest spiritual awakening since the first century.

7 Basic Steps to Successful Fasting and Prayer. This handy booklet gives practical steps to undertaking and completing a fast, suggests a plan for prayer, and offers an easy-to-follow daily nutritional schedule.

Preparing for the Coming Revival: How to Lead a Successful Fasting and Prayer Gathering. This easy-to-use handbook presents step-by-step instructions on how to plan and conduct a fasting and prayer gathering in your church or community. The book also contains creative ideas for teaching group prayer and can be used for a small group or large gatherings.

The Transforming Power of Fasting and Prayer. This follow-up book to *The Coming Revival* includes stirring accounts of Christians who have participated in the fasting and prayer movement that is erupting across the country.

Five Steps to Fasting and Prayer. The need for Christians who can lead our nation out of its moral morass is desperate. Fasting and prayer can be the answer for those who desire a deeper walk with God—and to influence our society for Christ. This five-part study teaches you how to tap into the power of fasting and prayer.

Resources for Group and Individual Study

Five Steps of Christian Growth. This five-lesson Bible study will help group members be sure that they are a Christian, learn what it means to grow as a Christian, experience the joy of God's love and forgiveness, and discover how to be filled with the Holy Spirit. Leader's and Study Guides are available.

Five Steps to Sharing Your Faith. This Bible study is designed to help Christians develop a lifestyle of introducing others to Jesus Christ. With these step-by-step lessons, believers can learn how to share their faith with confidence through the power of the Holy Spirit. Leader's and Study Guides are available.

Five Steps to Knowing God's Will. This five-week Bible study includes detailed information on applying the Sound Mind Principle to discover God's will. Both new and more mature Christians will find clear instructions useful for every aspect of decision-making. Leader's and Study Guides are available.

Five Steps to Making Disciples. This effective Bible study can be used for one-on-one discipleship, leadership evangelism training in your church, or a neighborhood Bible study group. Participants will learn how to begin a Bible study to disciple new believers as well as more mature Christians. Leader's and Study Guides are available.

Ten Basic Steps Toward Christian Maturity. These time-tested Bible studies offer a simple way to understand the basics of the Christian faith and provide believers with a solid foundation for growth. The product of many years of extensive development, the studies have been used by thousands. Leader's and Study Guides are available.

Introduction: The Uniqueness of Jesus
Step 1: The Christian Adventure
Step 2: The Christian and the Abundant Life

Step 3: The Christian and the Holy Spirit
Step 4: The Christian and Prayer
Step 5: The Christian and the Bible
Step 6: The Christian and Obedience
Step 7: The Christian and Witnessing
Step 8: The Christian and Giving
Step 9: Exploring the Old Testament
Step 10: Exploring the New Testament

A Handbook for Christian Maturity. This book combines the *Ten Basic Steps* Study Guides in one handy volume. The lessons can be used for daily devotions or with groups of all sizes.

Ten Basic Steps Leader's Guide. This book contains teacher's helps for the entire *Ten Basic Steps* Bible Study series. The lessons include opening and closing prayers, objectives, discussion starters, and suggested answers to the questions.

Resources for Christian Growth

Transferable Concepts. This series of time-tested messages teaches the principles of abundant Christian life and ministry. These "back-to-the-basics" resources help Christians grow toward greater spiritual maturity and fulfillment and live victorious Christian lives. These messages, available in book format and on video or audio cassette, include:

How You Can Be Sure You Are a Christian
How You Can Experience God's Love and Forgiveness
How You Can Be Filled With the Spirit
How You Can Walk in the Spirit
How You Can Be a Fruitful Witness
How You Can Introduce Others to Christ
How You Can Help Fulfill the Great Commission
How You Can Love By Faith
How You Can Pray With Confidence
How You Can Experience the Adventure of Giving
How You Can Study the Bible Effectively

A Man Without Equal. This book explores the unique birth, life, teachings, death, and resurrection of Jesus Christ and shows how He continues to change the way we live and think today. Available in book and video formats.

Life Without Equal. This inspiring book shows how Christians can experience pardon, purpose, peace, and power for living the Christian life. The book also explains how to release Christ's resurrection power to help change the world.

Have You Made the Wonderful Discovery of the Spirit-Filled Life? This booklet shows how you can discover the reality of the Spirit-filled life and live in moment-by-moment dependence on God.

The Holy Spirit: Key to Supernatural Living. This booklet helps you enter into the Spirit-filled life and explains how you can experience power and victory.

Promises: A Daily Guide to Supernatural Living. These 365 devotionals will help you remain focused on God's great love and faithfulness by reading and meditating on His promises each day. You will find your faith growing as you get to know our God and Savior better.

GOD: Discover His Character. Everything about our lives is determined and influenced by our view of God. Through these pages Dr. Bright will equip you with the biblical truths that will energize your walk with God. So when you're confused, you can experience His truth. When you're frightened, you can know His peace. When you're sad, you can live in His joy.

GOD: Discover His Character Video Series. In these 13 sessions, Dr. Bright's clear teaching is illustrated by fascinating dramas that bring home the truth of God's attributes in everyday life. This video series, with the accompanying leader's guide, is ideal for youth, college, and adult Sunday school classes or study groups.

Our Great Creator (Vol. I). Dr. Bright explores God as all-powerful, ever-present, all-knowing, and sovereign—and how those attributes can give you hope and courage in life.

Our Perfect Judge (Vol. II). God your perfect Judge, is holy, true, righteous, and just, and Dr. Bright explains how those characteristics help you to live a righteous life.

Our Gracious Savior (Vol. III). Dr. Bright introduces you to the God who is loving, merciful, faithful, and unchangeable, and shows how you can experience those awesome attributes every day.

Resources for Evangelism

Witnessing Without Fear. This best-selling, Gold Medallion book offers simple hands-on, step-by-step coaching on how to share your faith with confidence. The chapters give specific answers to questions people most often encounter in witnessing and provide a proven method for sharing your faith.

Reaching Your World Through Witnessing Without Fear. This six-session video provides the resources needed to sensitively share the gospel effectively. Each session begins with a captivating dramatic vignette to help viewers apply the training. Available in individual study and group packages.

Have You Heard of the Four Spiritual Laws? This booklet is one of the most effective evangelistic tools ever developed. It presents a clear explanation of the gospel of Jesus Christ, which helps you open a conversation easily and share your faith with confidence.

Would You Like to Know God Personally? Based on the *Four Spiritual Laws*, this booklet uses a friendly, conversational format to present four principles for establishing a personal relationship with God.

Jesus and the Intellectual. Drawing from the works of notable scholars who affirm their faith in Jesus Christ, this booklet shows that Christianity is based on irrefutable historical facts. Good for sharing with unbelievers and new Christians.

A Great Adventure. Written as from one friend to another, this booklet explains how to know God personally and experience peace, joy, meaning, and fulfillment in life.

Sharing Christ Using the Four Spiritual Laws (audio cassette). Imagine being personally trained by Bill Bright to use the remarkable *Four Spiritual Laws* booklet. Through a five-part teaching series on WorldChangers Radio, this cassette will increase your confidence level and desire to share the good news with those you know.

Would You Like to Belong to God's Family? Designed for elementary-age young people, this booklet gives the simple message of salvation and includes the first steps for starting their new life in Christ. (Based on the *Four Spiritual Laws*.)

Resources by Vonette Bright

The Joy of Hospitality: Fun Ideas for Evangelistic Entertaining. Co-written with Barbara Ball, this practical book tells how to share your faith through hosting barbecues, coffees, holiday parties, and other events in your home.

The Joy of Hospitality Cookbook. Filled with uplifting Scriptures and quotations, this cookbook contains hundreds of delicious recipes, hospitality tips, sample menus, and family traditions that are sure to make your entertaining a memorable and eternal success. Co-written with Barbara Ball.

Beginning Your Journey of Joy. This adaptation of the *Four Spiritual Laws* speaks in the language of today's women and offers a slightly feminine approach to sharing God's love with your neighbors, friends, and family members.

Response Form

☐ I have received Jesus Christ as my Savior and Lord as a result of reading this book.

☐ With God's help, I will faithfully pray for revival, the harvest, laborers, and donors.

☐ I want to be one of the two million people who will join Dr. Bright in forty days of prayer and fasting for revival for America, the world, and the fulfillment of the Great Commission.

☐ Please send me *free* information on ☐ full-time staff, ☐ mid-career change, ☐ associate, ☐ volunteer, ☐ short-term trips, or ☐ summer intern opportunities with Campus Crusade for Christ International.

☐ Please send me *free* information about the other books, booklets, audio cassettes, and videos by Bill and Vonette Bright.

NAME (please print)

ADDRESS

CITY   STATE   ZIP

COUNTRY   E-MAIL

Please check the appropriate box(es), clip, and mail this form to:

Dr. Bill Bright
Campus Crusade for Christ
P.O. Box 620877
Orlando, FL 32862-0877 U.S.A.

You may also fax your response to (407) 826-2149, or send E-mail to newlifepubs@ccci.org. Visit our website at www.newlifepubs.com, www.discovergod.org, and www.rsm.org.

This and other fine products from *NewLife* Publications are available from your favorite bookseller or by calling **(800) 235-7255** (within U.S.) or **(407) 826-2145** (outside U.S.).